THE IDEA OF KURDISTAN

The Modern History of Kurdistan through
the Life of Mullah Mustafa Barzani

Davan Yahya Khalil

Davan Yahya Khalil

UK

Copyright © 2014 by Davan Yahya Khalil

All rights reserved. No part of this publication may be reproduced, stored in a retrieval system, or transmitted in any form or by any means, electronic, mechanical, photocopying, recording or otherwise, without prior permission of the author.

First Edition (Paperback) 2014

ISBN: 978-1500996932

Manufactured in the UK

Cover concept: Simon Avery www.idobookcovers.com
Cover illustration: Lucie Russell www.lucierussell.co.uk
Cover design: Paul Couling www.cultzeros.co.uk
Interior design/typesetting: Bek Pickard www.zebedeedesign.co.uk
Author photo by: Irena Gorniak

Contents

Chapter One: Introduction	7
Chapter Two: Birth and Childhood	26
Chapter Three: Growth to Revolution	45
Chapter Four: Revolution	70
Chapter Five: Republic of Mahabad	91
Chapter Six: The Soviet Union	113
Chapter Seven: Return to Kurdistan – The 1960s	132
Chapter Eight: Revolution in the 1970s	151
Chapter Nine: Kurdistan in the 1980s and 1990s	174
Chapter Ten: Family and Kurdistan	193
Chapter Eleven: The Idea of Kurdistan	212
Chapter Twelve: The Wider World	230
Chapter Thirteen: Kurdish Democracy	244
Chapter Fourteen: The Future	264
Chapter Fifteen: Conclusion	283
Bibliography/Further Reading	300
Glossary	302
Key Dates	307

I would like to thank my sister, Shirin Yahya Khalil, and the Varsan Group Company for their very generous sponsorship.

I would also like to thank Shaheen H Mirkhan, Safar Yousef Jajoki and Kovan Rashid Sherwani.

Last, but by no means least, I thank Samya Karim Sherwani.

Chapter One: Introduction

There are few, if any, names that mean as much in Kurdistan as that of Mullah Mustafa Barzani. For decades, his name has been inextricably bound up with the idea of Kurdish independence, with Kurdish nationalism, and simply with the idea of Kurdistan itself. His life and death have become in many ways a symbol of the region, a rallying point even for Kurds who might not have agreed directly with his politics. Certainly, when Kurdistan has his son as its president, his political party as one of the key components of its democracy, and his ideas as essential elements of political debate, understanding the life of Mullah Mustafa Barzani is crucial to understanding the region.

More than that, understanding the life of Mullah Mustafa Barzani is crucial to understanding the idea of Kurdishness. Peoples and countries are defined by their histories, by the stories they tell about themselves and by the values that they hold. Mullah Mustafa Barzani affects all three of these areas. He is a key figure in modern Kurdish history, if not *the* key figure. His actions crucially affected the course of Kurdish history on several occasions, and he played key roles in some of the most memorable events in Kurdistan's recent past. His historical legacy is an important one, and one that is likely to

The Idea of Kurdistan

continue to have an effect long into Kurdistan's future.

He is also central, in many ways, to Kurdistan's national story; its explanation of where it comes from and why it exists. Yes, there are other figures in the more distant past. Yes, many elements have combined to bring Kurdistan to where it is today. Yet, in a country where much history beyond the recent past has been damaged or destroyed, Mullah Mustafa Barzani has come to be almost as much a symbolic figure as a purely historical one. His story has come to stand in so many ways for Kurdistan's story, and while this may not be a story that takes in every facet of Kurdistan, it is certainly one that does more to symbolise Kurdistan than almost any other life story in the recent past.

Finally, Mullah Mustafa Barzani helped to shape the values that have become important in Kurdistan, whether the values in question are a particularly Kurdish mixture of self-sufficiency and engagement with the outside world, the nature of its relationship with its neighbours, or even the general shape of the political debates within the country. As a relatively new political unit, Kurdistan has needed to learn quickly from experience. On so many occasions, it seems that the experiences that have been learned from have been those of Mullah Mustafa Barzani's life. Or perhaps it is more accurate to say simply that his role in Kurdistan's history means that he was present in those moments that Kurdistan has looked to learn from.

Either way, it seems impossible to look at Kurdistan without at least trying to understand the man who was one of its most complex figures. Who tried to give the region the status its people desired, and whose journeys took him across half the world, through both the Soviet Union and the United States of America. Who was part of movements standing up to several different governments, yet whose structures and symbolism have been crucial in crafting Kurdistan's current governmental systems. A man whose attempts to change Kurdistan directly did not quite reach fruition in his lifetime, but who dreamed dreams big enough to eventually sweep along the whole region with them.

Theoretical Issues

How can we start to produce a biography of a man of such importance to the history of a people? How can we produce a biography of any man? Both of those questions are valid ones, because there are theoretical and technical issues that touch all biography, but also other issues that have to be addressed specifically when writing about someone held in great esteem by his people. Some of these are general theoretical or philosophical points relating to the nature of writing history, some are specific technical issues regarding the nature of the available evidence, while others relate specifically to the concepts and approaches needed to write about Mullah Mustafa Barzani.

While discussing these issues may seem a little dry in comparison to exploring his life, understanding them is important. Not only do they give us a sound technical basis on which to proceed, they also help to uncover at least once facet which is key to this biography.

The Problem of Heroes

One such point is the issue of 'ownership' of a public figure's image and story. Important public figures are likely to be debated extensively while they are alive. They are discussed by the media, by their friends, by their opponents, by ordinary people and more. Different versions of the same individual seem to appear depending on whom one talks to.

For figures who achieve a heroic status, this is the case to an even greater extent. They can find their lives debated and pored over, key actions assessed and reassessed in a dozen different ways. Each version of a story is an act in a debate, attempting to add force to a position by aligning the meaning of their life

The Idea of Kurdistan

with that position. Living figures can attempt to affect the way they are perceived, but even for them, attempts to manage their image are not always successful.

For figures from the past, even the recent past, the issue is an even more pointed one. The years after a public figure's death often represent a kind of battle of biography, as different groups attempt to control the ways in which they will be perceived for years to come. Recollections of them will be shaped consciously or unconsciously with the aim of presenting them in the way that fits with the image of the subject that those recalling the memories wish to present.

This is not to suggest that there is anything nefarious about this process. Most of the time, the individuals taking part in it are not deliberately attempting to reshape people's opinions. They may even be providing the most accurate representation of that person that they can provide. It is simply that it *is* a representation, and that is inevitably shaped by the needs, beliefs and views of those doing the describing.

What does that mean for this piece? Since this is at least partly another attempt to represent the life of Kurdistan's most famous figure, it cannot be exempt from the same kind of elements. Simply by writing this, I am taking part in the amorphous tug of war over the meaning of Mullah Mustafa Barzani's life. I cannot avoid that. Nor can I avoid my views being shaped by facts such as being one of the Barzani, by being Kurdish, or by having lived most of my early life in Kurdistan. I will not write the same book on Mullah Mustafa Barzani that someone on the other side of the world might write, and I should not try to.

What I can do is to go further. I want to understand Mullah Mustafa Barzani's life in this book, but I also want to understand what he meant to people. Since the lives of important figures are so readily argued over and adapted, I want to understand the ways in which his image and meaning have been used both

Introduction

in his lifetime and in the wake of his death. As well as taking part in the debate, I want to show it to you, because I believe that it says at least as much about Mullah Mustafa Barzani as the raw facts of his life do.

The 'Story' of a Life

Kierkegaard famously told us that that life can only be understood backwards, but must be lived forwards. It is an important point regarding finding meaning in a life, and is particularly relevant to the process of biography. Does biography impose meaning on a life? More importantly, how exactly do we understand a life?

It's a fundamental question, and one that relates closely to quite a lot of general historical theory. It may seem like an obvious point, but biography attempts to allow the reader to understand a life by telling us the 'story' of it. It provides things with a logical order, emphasises what seem like the key points of that life, and tells us the meaning of it that the biographer feels is important through emphasis and analysis.

This emphasis on meaning and order is at odds with some postmodernist approaches to history. Many theorists have pointed out that the historian or biographer's job inevitably involves an imposition of meaning on the past, rather than finding it 'naturally'. Writers such as Karl Ankerschmidt have argued that historical research's role as an essentially narrative form means that it may not be able to fully represent the past. That people do not live in the stories we tell about them, but in something much messier and more complicated, without the clear narrative threads that a biographer might impose on them.

If this is true, what use is biography? How can we represent the story of a life without it veering off into essentially unworkable territory? Can we ever present the truth of the past? There are probably those who say that we cannot. That a narrative form doesn't connect well enough with lived

The Idea of Kurdistan

experience to be workable. I would argue against that. Not because narrative is somehow an accurate representation of the past, but because it is a form that people are used to using to understand things. As humans, stories are fundamental to our existence. Indeed, an acceptance of that can help to put notions of meaning back into history largely stripped of it by postmodernist historiography, because it allows history the freedom to do all the things that stories do. To entertain and educate, to give meaning to complex situations, and possibly even to show us things about our relation to the past that a simple list of historical facts with no interpretation couldn't.

Of course, we're back to the idea that the story of Mullah Mustafa Barzani's life has been told in many different ways. That the meaning of his life to different groups in Kurdistan and beyond is in many ways at least as important as the simple facts of that life. If we see a life as being like a rock hitting a pool of water, then it is not enough for a biography to look just at that rock, or at the moment of impact, or even at the forces throwing it. It must also try to examine the spreading ripples in the water, and to see the reflections of others trying to do the same thing.

Individuality

Just how many ripples can one man set in motion? In the case of Mullah Mustafa Barzani, the temptation is to say a great many and leave it there. It is easy to see his role within so many events of key importance to Kurdistan, and to see his influence on many more, directly or indirectly.

Yet this is one of the classic questions of any kind of historical biography. To what extent is it possible for a single individual to influence great historical events? Do we side with the Victorian historians who felt that real history consisted of a small number of great men and their actions? Do we go to the

Introduction

opposite extreme and ascribe everything to relentless historical forces and pressures that would have achieved the same effects regardless of who was there? Or can we find a position somewhere in between that better reflects the balance between individual action and the events around it?

In the case of this biography, it is a question that must have a central role, not least because it is crucial to understanding some of the different ways in which Mullah Mustafa Barzani has been seen since his death. At least some of the arguments over his legacy have been over how crucial he was to that legacy, and whether it is indeed possible for a single individual to have affected modern history to the extent that he seems to have.

So, can an individual affect history to a meaningful degree? Since I am writing a biography of arguably Kurdistan's most important figure, it is probably natural that I would argue that they can. Yet it is also important to take into account the situations individuals found themselves in, and the circumstances that dictated many of the consequences of their choices. The precise degree to which Mullah Mustafa Barzani's actions changed the historical landscape is a question that I will need to ask throughout this work, and one that is crucial to understanding his importance to Kurdistan.

Inevitability

So far, we have discussed issues of representation in history and biography, the potential for arguments over the meaning of an individual's achievements, and how much those achievements can be seen as coming from the circumstances around them. There is a final theoretical issue which is crucial to biography, and that is the idea of inevitability.

To some extent, issues of inevitability are one of the consequences of the narrative form of biography. If we tell the story of a life, then we naturally make it appear that there

The Idea of Kurdistan

is a single narrative thread running through it. Every action is seen as leading towards the place they ended up. From a public figure's earliest childhood, we are looking, not for the normal experiences of childhood, but for those experiences that helped to shape them into the people they later came to be. We present it in a clear line of consequences to try to understand the elements of the past that helped to shape the future individual.

The danger is that in presenting such a clear step-by-step progression, we make it seem inevitable that things ended up as they did. We can potentially create the impression that no other outcome was possible, and that the subjects of biography were always heading for greatness. In the world of sporting biography, the Australian writer Gideon Haigh has talked about the tendency of biographers to look for early successes at school level as 'proof' that their subjects were always destined for greatness, conveniently ignoring all those similar children who succeeded at the same level but went on to achieve little.

The same tendency potentially applies here, and while I can understand the temptation to provide the impression of a smooth rise towards greatness, I also suspect it potentially does the subject of a biography a disservice. By suggesting that what happened is the only thing that could have happened, a biographer makes it harder for his readers to understand the difficulty of the decisions their subject took, or the consequences they avoided through their actions. I would like to suggest that it is only when you understand the many ways that things could have gone wrong for someone like Mullah Mustafa Barzani, the ways in which the things he did were *not* inevitable, that it becomes possible to see the importance of the things he did achieve.

Introduction

Structure of this Work

You can see that there are more than a few theoretical issues that touch any attempt at biography. They range from issues over the means of doing it to ones over assessing any individual's impact on the world around them. In the case of Mullah Mustafa Barzani, we also have issues that come from his dual role as a historical figure and as a symbol of Kurdishness, whose role within and importance to Kurdistan are the subjects of continued debate.

To address these issues, the structure of this work must reflect them. It will consist of two main strands. First, there is the simple biography of Mullah Mustafa Barzani, trying to present and understand the things he did in his life. No doubt there will be many issues relevant to the later sections, and issues for deeper discussion, but the main focus will be on the historical account. On Mullah Mustafa Barzani the man. The second section is more about the idea of Mullah Mustafa Barzani. It will attempt to assess his impact on Kurdistan, but also his symbolic role and the way he is seen both in Kurdistan and elsewhere.

I believe that it is difficult to discuss one of these strands without the other. It seems clear that we cannot begin to understand Mullah Mustafa Barzani's importance to, and impact on, Kurdistan without understanding the details of his life. Yet it is also true that we cannot begin to truly understand his life without understanding the effects that life had on the world around him, or by understanding the ways in which the rest of the world understands him.

By rights, both elements should be inextricably interwoven with one another. Yet to understand them and present them in a logical way, it is necessary to present them one after the other. Even so, as you read through each section of this work, I urge you not to lose sight of its implications on the other. Mullah Mustafa Barzani's life was a complex one, and both

The Idea of Kurdistan

sides were true at once, man and symbol of rebellion, fighter and representation of what it meant to be Kurdish abroad. Lose track of one element, and you get only half the story.

Life Story

In discussing Mullah Mustafa Barzani's life, I intend to take a broadly chronological approach for the first half of the book. That is probably hardly surprising, for a biography, and represents the best way to understand the often significant events in which Mullah Mustafa Barzani was involved. I intend to begin by exploring his birth and childhood. I will also try to understand the history of Kurdistan as it stood at the time of his birth, because I feel that is important in getting a sense of his life. It is important to understand not just how Mullah Mustafa Barzani grew up, but how Kurdistan grew into a position where he could achieve everything he did.

From there, I intend to discuss his early involvement in the cause of Kurdish independence/democracy, leading up to the revolutions that eventually led to him having to leave for the Mahabad Republic. In these chapters, I want to discuss the elements that drove him into the cause of Kurdish independence, the nature of his involvement in those early revolutions, and their likely impact on his future attitudes.

I then intend to discuss Mullah Mustafa Barzani's role within the Mahabad Republic, since this can be seen as one of the key early attempts at the formation of a Kurdish state. I will look broadly at its foundation and eventual fall, but my focus will be primarily on how Mullah Mustafa Barzani fitted into it and the effects that the experience had on him and his future actions. I will suggest that his experiences at this time were crucial in shaping later aspects of Kurdistan, including its relations with the outside world.

His time in the Soviet Union may also have had an important impact on many issues that followed, including the extent to

Introduction

which Kurdish politicians have been able to work with and trust the Soviet Union's successors. There are several key arguments over elements of Mullah Mustafa Barzani's life in the Soviet Union, and it is important to at least try to disentangle fact from fiction when it comes to these.

After that, I intend to discuss Mullah Mustafa Barzani's return to Kurdistan, his attempts to gain independence for the region through political means and why they failed. I will ask why he chose to return, why what followed was unable to work, and whether any alternative course of action might have changed what followed. The attempted revolution that ensued, and the reasons for its failure, I will discuss immediately afterwards, as the two are inextricably bound up.

Mullah Mustafa Barzani's time outside Kurdistan is just as important as his time in it if we are to truly understand his life. Because of that, I intend to devote the next chapters to the periods that followed, first in Iran, and then in the United States. I will ask to what extent he was able to continue to exert influence over events in Kurdistan from so far away, but also whether this mattered. I will discuss whether his presence in the USA in particular may have in fact helped to do more for Kurdistan than being present there might have. I will also discuss the extent to which these periods of absence from Kurdistan helped to shape the region's current relations with the outside world, in particular allowing it to shape a relationship with the USA separate from the rest of Iraq.

Impact of a Life

The second section of this work is concerned with the ways in which Mullah Mustafa Barzani has been remembered since his death, with his symbolic role in Kurdistan, with the pressures that have shaped and re-shaped his meaning, and with his long term effects on Kurdish politics. In this, I will be concerned to some extent with what many writers would call his political

The Idea of Kurdistan

afterlife, but also with broader elements, such as the construction of an idea of Kurdistan and the continuing debate over its values.

I will begin this second section by looking at some of the most obvious legacies of Mullah Mustafa Barzani, including the continuing role of his family in the region. I will argue that many aspects of Kurdistan's current political climate are influenced indirectly by Mullah Mustafa Barzani's legacy through his family, and that his legacy also had a role to play in determining the shape of Kurdistan as a whole.

More than that, I will go on to examine Mullah Mustafa Barzani's role in helping to construct an *idea* of Kurdistan. I will suggest that, without his role in the movement towards Kurdish independence, there would not be such a strong sense of Kurdistan as a place, or of the Kurdish people as a political, as well as simply an ethnic, group. I will try to demonstrate his key role in helping to craft a sense of Kurdistan as a real, modern entity; in creating a *dream* of Kurdistan. A dream that he did not live to see fulfilled, but which was crucial in providing a shape for the modern region to assume.

After that, I want to discuss the meaning of Mullah Mustafa Barzani. By that, I mean that I want to discuss what he has come to mean to different groups of people within Kurdistan: to his family, his political allies, and the wider populace. I want to discuss how his name and image are used for symbolic value, and the extent to which debates over the meaning of national heroes are usual in other places. I would like to suggest that in Mullah Mustafa Barzani's case, debates over his historical meaning are also frequently debates over the way Kurdistan is perceived, and that he has become so synonymous with it that it is difficult to separate the two.

Of course, the impact of Mullah Mustafa Barzani was not simply limited to Kurdistan. I want to go on to discuss the extent of his impact in the wider world, and also the way he is perceived outside Kurdistan by figures from ordinary people to politicians. I want to show, as inside Kurdistan, how the 'story' of Mullah Mustafa Barzani is also often the teller's story about Kurdistan.

Finally, I want to discuss the future, which is not always usual in a historical biography. Yet in Mullah Mustafa Barzani's case, it is relevant, because I intend to discuss the ways in which his legacy is likely to continue to evolve over time, as well as the ways in which his memory is likely to continue to be viewed by people both within Kurdistan and elsewhere. In concluding this work, I will argue that fully understanding Mullah Mustafa Barzani involves both an understanding of his life, and a continuing understanding of the way Kurdistan has been affected by his memory.

Sources

The sources available to a biographer vary greatly according to the subject. For some, there are letters and personal journals, their words and the words of those around them. For others, buried deep in the past, there are no more than fragments to be pieced together, a small collection of facts and half facts from which to start crafting some semblance of reality. Important leaders and nationally important figures tend to be the focus of more material, but even for them, it varies. For Mullah Mustafa Barzani, several factors apply when it comes to the sources of information we have about him. Some of them improve the amount of material available, but others reduce it.

On the positive side of the balance we have the fact that he was seen as an important figure in his lifetime. That means that people tended to write about him while he was alive, that those who met him tended to remember the occasion, and that there was a general awareness that what he said and did might need to be preserved for posterity. Even when it comes to sources such as photographs of him, there is a sense that several of

The Idea of Kurdistan

these photographs were of Mullah Mustafa Barzani rather than of someone else simply because the photographer knew who he was. More than that, this information is often publicly available, since he was a public figure.

This is in complete contrast to the situation that sometimes presents itself when the importance of a historical figure is only understood long after their death. In that situation, we can find that their letters, thoughts and other potential sources of evidence are long gone, destroyed because no one thought that they would be of use.

We also have the fact that Mullah Mustafa Barzani is a relatively recent historical figure, rather than one from the distant past. That is important on two levels. First, there is the simple fact that the modern world produces far more information about people than older societies used to. Modern individuals produce letters and records, written information and ephemera on a scale that would have been inconceivable even a few hundred years ago. Where the problem for the historian of the distant past is one of finding information, for the biographer of the more modern figure, the issue is more one of working out what is relevant.

There is also the point that Mullah Mustafa Barzani lived sufficiently recently that people who met or worked with him are still alive. There is a level of direct access to memories about him that is simply impossible with more distant figures. Such oral sources can potentially provide us with a wealth of information, and certainly a level of feeling, that is impossible to get in other ways. Indeed, one of the reasons why it is important to write this book now is to capture some of those reactions to his life before they are gone forever.

Of course, there are things to bear in mind with those sorts of recent memories. There is a potential for accidental distortion either by the feelings of the person being interviewed or by the interviewer's choice of questions. There is a potential for

Introduction

forgetfulness, or for not stating a case as clearly as people generally do in writing. Even so, I feel like the memories of those who knew Mullah Mustafa Barzani are useful. Indeed, given that I want to explore the relationship between his memory and the modern Kurdistan, they are essential.

One useful point for our sources is that Mullah Mustafa Barzani was a figure at the heart of important historical events. Although this can have the disadvantage that sources mentioning him are more focused on those events, it is primarily an advantage. It means that writers on those events tend to give us at least some information about his role, and it also means that to a great extent, the history of his life is the history of those events. Understanding them helps us to understand his life better, and so even quite general sources about the events in which Mullah Mustafa Barzani was involved are of use here.

There is also the point that Mullah Mustafa Barzani was to some extent an international figure. By that I mean both that he spent time in a number of countries, and that the media of a number of countries talked about him. While those are sources that probably don't give us much in the way of extra depth when it comes to his life, they do give us some clue as to the breadth of opinion about his life, which is especially useful when it comes to understanding the ways in which he has been perceived around the world.

Of course, there are also limits to the sources available. Kurdistan has long been a region troubled by warfare and violence, neither of which made it easy to keep large bodies of records for Mullah Mustafa Barzani's lifetime. The Iraqi regime attacked the Kurds on several occasions, and was also concerned with damaging notions of Kurdishness during at least one period in Mullah Mustafa Barzani's life. As such, there has been damage to at least some of the potential historical sources for the region.

Then there is the fact that for at least some periods of his life, Mullah Mustafa Barzani was forced to operate in relative secrecy. During the uprisings he was involved in, for example, his concern would have been to avoid information about his whereabouts and actions escaping, because either could have been used by his enemies. The relatively irregular structure of the Kurdish *peshmerga* fighters, meanwhile, meant that it they did not generate the level of record keeping that a more regular army might have. Both limit the availability of written sources for those periods. The extent to which Mullah Mustafa Barzani had to move around during his lifetime may also have limited the availability of records, or at least scattered them across the collections of several different countries.

Yet I feel that in general, the advantages that Mullah Mustafa Barzani brings to the question of the sources about his life outweigh the potential disadvantages. Although there is the potential for gaps in his story to appear, in general, his is a life about which we have the potential to know more than that of almost any other Kurdish man of his generation. Even more importantly, he was a public figure of sufficient importance that information about his impact on Kurdistan is still being generated. People are still forming opinions about him, still reacting to what he did in his life. All of these things give us a great opportunity, not only to understand his life, but also to understand the way he relates to the modern Kurdistan.

Key Questions

In order to understand both those aspects, we need to ask questions. Without questions we end up simply telling the story of a life in chronological order, with no opportunity to provide any deeper understanding. Which questions though? That is one of the choices that can fundamentally shape the direction a work like this takes, which is why I want to set out some of the questions I want to answer here. I hope that by doing so, you will understand some of my reasoning in going in one direction rather than another in the rest of the text.

Introduction

So, what questions am I trying to answer here? The overarching one is the question of Mullah Mustafa Barzani's impact on Kurdistan as it stands today. I want to try to understand his life, but there have been other biographies of it, and that alone would not be enough to justify another. I am more concerned with understanding how much that life has helped to shape modern Kurdistan, because I do feel that Mullah Mustafa Barzani had a crucial impact on it. That main question has a number of other questions embedded within it, each of which brings something slightly different to the issue. Those questions include the following:

- How important was Mullah Mustafa Barzani to the formation of modern Kurdistan? Clearly, he did not live to see the birth of a modern region that seems to be moving slowly towards independence, but can any of its foundation be seen as a consequence of his actions in earlier decades? To what extent did Mullah Mustafa Barzani's uprisings and political work help to create the conditions necessary for the creation of Kurdistan as it currently exists? Were the connections he made, the structures he helped to create, or the symbols he helped to produce crucial in bringing about the existence of Kurdistan?
- How much did Mullah Mustafa Barzani's life help to shape the current form of Kurdistan, geographically, politically and socially? Whatever his impact on the formation of the budding near-state, did his life help to shape Kurdistan's political structures or the ways in which its military runs? Does the memory of him have a significant impact on social forms and structures? Did the events of his life or the connections he made outside Kurdistan help to determine either Kurdistan's geographical limits or its political scope in the region?

- How much did Mullah Mustafa Barzani help to shape ideas of Kurdistan and Kurdishness, both in Kurdistan and outside it? Did Mullah Mustafa Barzani serve as a kind of archetype of Kurdishness, either for my people or for the world? Did his life help to shape people's opinions of my people and their cause? Is there any sense in which it can be said that people, either of his lifetime or beyond, learned to understand Kurdistan through the prism of Mullah Mustafa Barzani's actions?
- How is Mullah Mustafa Barzani perceived in Kurdistan and the wider world? How is his life seen and how is his memory preserved? How much does he still matter to the average inhabitant of Kurdistan? How well known is he outside of Kurdistan? How is he viewed by different groups within society, and by foreign sources? Do the ways in which he is perceived have any knock-on effects for Kurdistan?

As a follow on from that last question, I want also to try to take a more general look at the way figures with key roles in their country's formation are seen at home and abroad, and to try to contrast that experience with the ways in which Mullah Mustafa Barzani is remembered. Are figures in similar positions to him historically treated in similar ways the world over? To what extent *is* Mullah Mustafa Barzani comparable to similar figures from other regions?

A Life – A Symbol

By answering these questions, it is my hope that you will leave this book understanding not just more about the life of Mullah Mustafa Barzani, but also more about Kurdistan. By showing Kurdistan through the lens of Mullah Mustafa Barzani's life, I believe that there is an opportunity, not just to see it in a new way, but also to understand many of the reasons why it sees

Introduction

itself in the ways that it does. More than that, there is an opportunity to understand something about the relationship between important figures and the ways in which they are represented by the groups around them. The ways, if you like, that they slowly transform from people into symbols.

My aim in this book is to help you to understand both of those facets of Mullah Mustafa Barzani: the man and the symbol. By commenting on both, it is my hope that you will come to see something about the ways in which Kurdistan's place in the world was built, about the factors that have helped to make it the place it is today, and about the elements that are likely to influence its future for years to come. Certainly for as long as Mullah Mustafa Barzani's life continues to be seen as such a crucial emblem of the region's history, and such a crucial element in defining what it means to be Kurdish.

Chapter Two: Birth and Childhood

Every story must have a starting point, and for the biographer, it is usually with the subject's birth. The same is true here, but it is also true that Mullah Mustafa Barzani's story only makes sense if it is seen in its proper context, against the backdrop of the times in which he was born.

To understand the life of Mullah Mustafa Barzani, we need to understand the situation in which Kurdistan found itself in 1903, the year of his birth. In fact, we need to understand something about the situation of the world as a whole, because most of Mullah Mustafa Barzani's efforts towards an independent Kurdistan only truly make sense when viewed in the context of the wider international circumstances. More than that, we need to understand something of the deeper history of Kurdistan and my people, the Kurds, if we are to understand the issues behind the life he chose for himself.

Kurdistan and its History

Kurdistan's deeper history runs at least as far back as that of any other civilisation. Indeed, Erbil has a claim to being one of the oldest continuously inhabited cities in the world, while it was an area that adopted agriculture earlier than many human civilisations. Our earliest written sources for Kurdistan came

Birth and Childhood

when Ancient Greek writers referred to fighters who were probably Kurdish fighting against Alexander the Great's forces for the ancient Persian Empire, but archaeological sources suggest that Kurdistan was occupied well before that.

The whole region seems to have been one that was attractive to empires. From the early Mesopotamian empires of Babylon, Assyria and Sumeria, parts of Kurdistan have been frequent targets for conquest or absorption by powerful rulers. In those early days, when Kurdistan was probably composed of numerous relatively separate communities and nomadic tribes, it is doubtful how much difference the 'ownership' of their land by a particular empire really made in a lot of cases. Large settlements (by the standards of the time at least) would have been important centres in their own right, and notions of empire probably came down to the spread of a particular culture as much as to formal control.

Another kind of empire came to Kurdistan in the seventh century, with the arrival of Islam in the hands of Arab settlers and conquerors. Although there were much broader empires around Kurdistan though, this was a phase when a number of Kurdish princes held their own territories, and at least one (Saladin) became a crucial figure for the wider world, ruling much of the surrounding area and defeating invading forces in the twelfth to thirteenth centuries.

Following him, the region seems to have been divided into a number of independent principalities again, in a pattern of repeated coalescences and fractures that mirrored the level of power of the Persian Empire to which it nominally still belonged.

From about the year 1500, things began to change, albeit slowly. The growing Ottoman Empire began to target some of the Kurdish principalities as a part of its broader process of expansion, gradually taking them into itself either through force or negotiation. This was a slow process, and probably not a comprehensively planned one, given the piecemeal way in which it happened. Rather than a plan to absorb all of Kurdistan, this was more about a series of individual moments, each of which led to the incorporation of a particular area into the empire. In this, the Ottoman Empire was no different to any of the other big empires growing around the world in the period, picking up pieces of territory as opportunities presented themselves, holding onto them jealously, but also functioning by trying to make its new acquisitions a genuine part of something larger. In the case of the Kurdish principalities, for example, the Ottomans generally used them as buffer zones to guard the borders of their empire.

This process of slow acquisition lasted for more than 400 years, finally being complete in the mid-nineteenth century, taking advantage of famine and plague within Kurdistan to draw it in entirely. This period in Kurdistan's history was also characterised by a substantial refocusing of Kurdish life away from its towns and cities, towards a more fully nomadic life.

Kurdistan in 1903

By 1903, Kurdistan was in some ways a very different place both to the one it had been in the deeper past and to the region it is today. It was less focused around its cities than it had been, thanks to the impact of public health disasters in the nineteenth century. It also had very different borders to today, as it had not yet been carved up by colonial powers trying to create a balance of power between the surrounding Arab and Turkish states.

The extent of the interaction between cities was probably also a little different in an era when rapid transport and mass communications were only just starting to filter into the wider region. It seems likely that each area within Kurdistan, and each tribe, was relatively independent simply because of the difficulties that would have existed in exercising tighter control. Not that this always stopped the Ottoman Empire from attempting to

Birth and Childhood

do so. Indeed, that empire's reflexive need to tighten its grasp in order to show that it was not completely weakened may have been behind some of the events of 1908.

Aside from the differences in its borders, it seems likely that there would have been relatively few geographical differences between the Kurdistan of 1903 and the Kurdistan of today. The same geographical factors that influence things today – the presence of the mountains, the fertile but not always predictable growing plains in between – would have had roughly the same effects even then.

Perhaps one of the most important differences is an obvious geological/industrial one. Kurdistan was not then the major producer of oil that it is today, both because it had not been discovered there at that point, and because the world market for oil and petroleum had not yet taken off with the rise of the motor car. In that sense, the attention of the world was not on it in the same way as it is today as a source of vital resources. It might have been important to the world's various empires as a potential acquisition, but it was not one that seemed to come with the kind of prizes that resulted from, for example, diamond rich African countries.

Socially and politically, Kurdistan would have been a very different place in 1903. The whole world was. Remember that countries like the UK would not give women the vote for another fifteen years, that the United States did not oppose racial segregation until the 1960s, and that the Communist/Western tensions that would dominate much of international politics through the twentieth century had yet to come about, since the Russian revolution was another fourteen years away.

Today, Kurdistan is one of the most progressive regions in the Middle East. Its politicians will still admit that it is not yet a perfect democracy, and that there is still work to do, but in general, it is a far more open and democratic society than most of those that surround it. Women have a much bigger role to

The Idea of Kurdistan

play in public life, and if there are occasionally still accusations of corruption or nepotism, or disputes between its political parties, then at least it is a society where those accusations and disputes can take place safely and freely.

In 1903, it was, entirely understandably, a more conservative society. Indeed, several of the tensions between it and the Ottoman Empire that sought to rule it came because the modernising tendencies within Turkey at the time disagreed with the stances of leaders within Kurdistan. At that stage, Kurdistan was still highly tribal, which was really the only effective way to rule an essentially nomadic population. An emphasis on affiliation and family is still a crucial one even today as a way of finding people to work with who can be trusted. It was probably also more religious than the increasingly secular Turkish state of the time, although in a region that was home to a wide variety of religious beliefs including the almost uniquely Kurdish one of Yedizism, it seems likely that there was still a greater degree of toleration than in many other societies in the region.

The World in 1903

What can we say about the wider world in 1903? It was not the world of just over a decade later, plunged into a global conflict that brought to an end many old ideas about warfare while killing on a scale that had been inconceivable before. Perhaps it was to some extent building up towards the events of the First World War, with relatively newly unified countries like Germany and Italy striving to make their marks on a world stage, yet perhaps that perception is merely one provided by hindsight. I have already highlighted the dangers of assuming the inevitability of events.

At the time, 1903 must have seemed like both a period of endings and of beginnings, the way the start of centuries so often do. The British Empire had lost its most prominent ruler,

Birth and Childhood

Queen Victoria, just two years before, was embroiled in the violence of colonial wars against the Boer people of South Africa and an expansion into Tibet. Serbia suffered a *coup d'état*. Panama obtained independence from Columbia, and Macedonia rose up against Turkey, yet the French were still expanding their empire, annexing Benin in that year even though French Equatorial Africa found itself split into three new countries later in the year.

It was a period of bright new discoveries and grand events too. The Wright brothers had their first powered flights in the year of Mullah Mustafa Barzani's birth, while Ford sold his first model A car. Thomas Edison electrocuted an elephant to make a point over electrical current, Norway gave women the vote, and the first Tour de France cycle race took place. It had still been only seven years since the first modern Olympics, too. It was as if people wanted to push on in the otherwise fading days of the grand empires, trying to create something new and spectacular to try to outdo what had gone before. Perhaps all this technological advancement and these grand events were symptoms of a kind of optimism that only fled under the shadow of world war. If some aspects of the old ages were starting to draw to a close, people truly believed that they could make whatever followed better.

Closer to Kurdistan, this complex mixture of feelings seems to have been just as present. 1903 was the year in which agreement over building the Berlin–Baghdad railway was finally reached. In some quarters, it was spoken against as presenting a strategic disadvantage, allowing Germany to move troops too easily, and it was only finished in 1940, yet it represented a concerted desire to connect what was not yet Iraq to the rest of the world and allow for easy transport. It represented a threat to Russian, Ottoman and British interests, but it also represented the kind of major public works project in the region that helped it to be so important later on.

The Idea of Kurdistan

The Ottoman Empire

One of the most important wider considerations for Kurdistan in 1903 was the state of the Ottoman Empire, of which it was still a part. Powerful for a number of centuries previously, the Ottoman Empire had gone into decline during the nineteenth century, in spite of an extensive programme of modernisation. Perhaps because of it, ultimately, as that programme only served to alienate those areas of its empire that did not share its aims and views.

It had moved in the direction of a more secular, open state, but had done so only when forced to do so by internal pressures. This did little to alleviate those pressures, and also created divisions within the empire which eventually led to the formation of Ataturk's government in the twentieth century.

Crucially, those divisions also created an impression of weakness that the other great powers of the time sought to exploit. In the same way that the Ottoman Empire had added territories piecemeal as it grew, in the nineteenth century rebellions and conquests picked off those territories again. From the Crimean War and the Russo-Turkish war to the British seizure of Egypt on the pretext of helping the Ottoman Empire to put down rebellion there, every conflict seemed to leach away more of its strength and possessions.

By the late nineteenth century, this had reduced it to a mere shadow of its former self, but had also encouraged it to take brutal measures against any resistance to its rule. The mass murder of hundreds of thousands of Armenians in the events known as the Hamidian Massacres was just the most extreme example of this attitude.

What did this mean for Kurdistan? It had been a fringe territory of the empire, kept as a part of it largely through the degree of autonomy it had, and because it offered the Ottomans a way to protect their borders. By the late nineteenth century, it had seen other such territories leave the empire, either falling

Birth and Childhood

to other great powers or breaking free completely. Many elements in Kurdistan at the time also disagreed with the forcible modernising tendencies coming from within Turkey. These elements, as we will see, made for an explosive combination.

Kurdish Identity in the Past

Because I want to suggest that Mullah Mustafa Barzani had a profound influence on Kurdish identity and its perception, both at home and abroad, it is important to take a look at the ways in which that identity has been envisaged historically.

One important component of that historical identity seems to have been a warlike nature. Quil Lawrence has noted that the very word 'Kurd' isn't that far from several ancient words for 'warlike' or 'strong'. If other writers have sought to counter that by suggesting that 'Kurd' was originally a word just for nomadic herders, that fails to take account of the number of other references to war or warriors in Kurdistan's history. Even the Ancient Greek description that may be our first mention of my people is in reference to them as particularly effective warriors in the Persian Emperor's army.

Later references reinforce that image. Kurdistan's most famous historical figure, Saladin, gives us an image that is founded on his success in war. Surrounding countries warned travellers of the dangers of brigandage. Even the way some of the Kurdish princes held out against the Ottoman Turks until the nineteenth century adds to an essentially military image.

In some ways, that image may be seen as a positive one. It suggested to outsiders that Kurdistan and its people were strong and willing to defend themselves. Yet in other contexts, it could be problematic. As we will see elsewhere, the Treaty of Sèvres in 1920 required that the Kurds should show that they were 'ready' to govern themselves before the foundation of the independent Kurdistan it promised. The same warlike image that could seem so beneficial on some occasions also brought with it patronising assumptions about my people's ability to behave in a 'civilised' way when seen through the eyes of the early twentieth century's colonial powers.

Even the Ottomans probably held the same sorts of views, despite being in considerably closer contact with the Kurds than the British or French were at the time. They were perfectly willing to use the Kurdish tribes of the time for war, including employing them against their own citizens in other regions where required, but the Kurds were never seen as fully a part of the empire. They were seen by Istanbul as a fringe part of their holdings, and were typically treated as secondary within their plans. To some extent, that is one of the inevitabilities of a large empire – a centre talking down to everyone further away – yet a good part of it must have come from a sense by the Ottoman Turks of the Kurds as being somehow inferior, less civilised. Warlike and useful, but not like them.

If that was one key element of the perception of Kurdish identity in 1903, there were certainly others. One was as quite conservative and old fashioned, clinging on to old ways of life in the form of a nomadic, tribal existence, resistant to change or reform. In some respects, we can see that elements of this may have been true. Sheikh Abdul Salam's seven demands to the Ottoman Turks, which we will discuss towards the end of this chapter, were frequently quite conservative in tone, although there were other elements of them, such as the attempt to stop forced marriages, which were far more progressive for the time. My people *were* still governed through tribal mechanisms, and had little time for the reforms of Turkey's modernist, secularist state at the time.

In other ways, that perception wasn't so justified. In the early years of the twentieth century, my people's reliance on a less urban existence was not an attempt to cling to the past, but an attempt to adapt to the rigours of famine and disease that had made large scale city living untenable. Tribal governance

Birth and Childhood

was at least partly a rejection of large scale government from outside the region. Conservatism probably only seemed so in comparison to what must have appeared to be an aggressive modernising tendency imposed from outside.

Yet ultimately, if we are talking about Kurdish identity, the perception may have been more important than the reality. It was that which shaped Kurdistan's interactions with the world, after all, and that perception that would have long term consequences throughout Mullah Mustafa Barzani's life.

To what extent was there a single Kurdish identity in 1903? That is a complex question, and one that has often become bound up in the politics of independence, since it has always been in the interests of those seeking independence to show the Kurds as one people, striving for their own nation. That is probably even an accurate portrayal, for the modern world. Yet for 1903?

In 1903, the picture was a complex one, and understandably so. No individual has a single identity. Instead, their identities are multi-layered things, connecting on a number of different levels. It is obvious for example that Mullah Mustafa Barzani identified himself both as Kurdish and as Barzani, the ethnic and tribal identities interacting in sometimes unusual ways.

The same was true for the majority of Kurds in 1903. Did they have a sense of being Kurdish? Yes. Was there a sense of an overarching Kurdish identity? Yes, up to a point. Even the generalisations made by outsiders show that there was an awareness of my people as an ethnic group, as well as the connection of that group to a specific territory (Kurdistan). Yet in spite of the attempts of figures such as Abdul Salam to bring together multiple tribes, we can probably say that at that point, tribal identity was still crucial to my people. Maybe even more so than an identity built on ethnicity or regional identity. Not by much, perhaps. After all, just a couple of decades later, Kurdistan was willing to fight for independence on the strength of a shared sense of Kurdishness, but in 1903 there was still work to be done in strengthening that sense of collective identity.

Family and Birth

If Kurdistan can only be understood in terms of its history, then Mullah Mustafa Barzani must be understood at least partly in terms of both his family and the place he was born. Both are important to understanding his story, but how important? To what extent were Mullah Mustafa Barzani's achievements a consequence of his family history and circumstances? To understand that, we need to understand both the place of his birth and the family around him.

Barzan

Mullah Mustafa Barzani was born in the village of Barzan on 14th March 1903. The village sits approximately 95 miles to the north of Erbil, and is the main administrative centre for its sub-district. Certainly in 1903, it would have been the principal village for many miles around, and an important fixed point for a still semi-nomadic people.

Today, Barzan is the name of both the village and the area around it. It is one of Kurdistan's most mountainous regions, largely cut off from the outside world by the peaks that surround it, far from the plains that characterise some other areas in Kurdistan. If Kurdistan is a region defined by its mountains, then Barzan and its surrounds represent the essence of it.

The mountains probably explain some of the importance of the village. They represent a natural defence against attackers, allowing for the kind of hit and run tactics and sudden ambushes that have characterised Kurdish warfare down the centuries. They make a natural safe haven for those who fear that a far off authority might not like their politics, and certainly did so in 1903.

Birth and Childhood

More than that, the village was at what might be considered the optimum distance from the city of Erbil. Close enough that it could be reached relatively quickly, certainly with the improvements in transportation that were starting to filter into the region in that period, yet still far enough to allow for a warning should troops arrive. Far enough too to be largely free from any governmental control directed through the city. Life in the mountains might have been tough, certainly tougher than in Kurdistan's flatter and more fertile areas, but that toughness probably only helped to sharpen the fighters who came from there.

That combination of factors made Barzan and the surrounding area a natural home for those who were dissatisfied with the Ottoman Empire's rule. Yet those geographical elements are not uncommon in Kurdistan. Why did this particular village produce a leader like Mullah Mustafa Barzani, and not some other? What was it about this place that made it different to the surrounding villages?

The Barzani

Part of the answer to that is the Barzani tribe. Claiming descent from Imadia princes, the Barzani have long had strong leaders, able to command respect within the surrounding tribes. If Barzan's geography helped to create the conditions and people to stand up to repressive authorities, then that connection helped it to stand out from the surrounding villages by providing it with leaders who could speak with authority at more than just a tribal level.

That was crucial for the region, allowing leaders such as Abdul Salam to gel together disparate tribes and speak with the voice of Kurdistan rather than just their own voice. For Mullah Mustafa Barzani to be born into this particular tribe and family provided him with opportunities and examples that few other people had.

The Idea of Kurdistan

It provided him with the example of leadership. With the opportunity to be around people who were expected to be leaders, so that he could learn what it meant to be a leader from them. As he grew, it would provide him with opportunities to exercise that leadership, being given positions of command on the strength of his family's authority that he would later prove more than worthy of.

It also provided him with a name already associated with authority on more than the level of a single tribe. Looking back from the vantage point of history, it is perhaps hard to believe that Mullah Mustafa Barzani would need such advantages. We know what he was able to achieve, and so it is perhaps easy to forget that there was a time when he was an unproven young man, in need of opportunities to demonstrate what he could do and experience in leading men. Had he been born into another family, in another village, he might not have had those opportunities in the same way, if at all.

The crucial element here is not just the tribal identity, although that was certainly important in 1903. In the mountainous conditions, far enough from Erbil that it was not possible to simply head down there for food and shelter, relying on other members of the tribe was vital for survival. That tribal identity certainly built an important level of trust. Yet what really provided an advantage for Mullah Mustafa Barzani was that succession of ancestors reaching back into the past, each with a history of achievement and authority.

Mullah Mustafa Barzani's Family

Who were Mullah Mustafa Barzani's family? As suggested above, his family were the main family of the Barzani tribe, able to trace their ancestry back through tribal leaders to princes. When it came to day-to-day life in Kurdistan, that might not have made a huge difference in 1903, because the mountains and the elements were no respecters of authority. Yet when it came

Birth and Childhood

to anything involving tribal life, politics or defence, the Barzani name represented a significant advantage.

Sheikh Abdul Salam was his grandfather, and he made significant contributions to bringing the surrounding tribes together. He also began the process of crafting a shared sense of Kurdish identity working towards independence. His father Mohammad Barzani took over leadership of the Barzani area and succeeded in administering it well, even though he did not live to see his son grow up, dying in 1903.

Mullah Mustafa Barzani also had brothers, Sheikh Abdul Salam, Sheikh Ahmad and Mohammed Siddique. Each of them achieved a great deal in his own right, and yet it is Mullah Mustafa Barzani we remember, and who achieved the greatest amount. This serves to remind us that his life wasn't just down to the circumstances in which he happened to be born.

What elements account for the differences? A lot of it is about personal attributes. Some of it is about the particular circumstances each brother faced. As the youngest brother, Mullah Mustafa Barzani found himself born at just the right time to be involved in many of the most important events for Kurdistan. He also had the opportunity to be involved for a long time. Yet so much more of his life must be put down to his own work, insight and choices. Family was crucial for Mullah Mustafa Barzani, and it played an important role throughout his life, but his life was about so much more than that.

Imprisonment

In 1907 Sheikh Abdul Salam, a leader of the Barzani and respected by many of the surrounding tribes, wrote a telegram to the Ottoman controlled government in Istanbul. In it, he made seven demands relating to various aspects of Kurdish life. These included the use of Kurdish in all schools and in public life, the banning of forced marriages, and the adoption of Islamic jurisprudence. Although the letter may originally have been intended to be private, it was quickly made public, turning into an open set of demands of an Ottoman government that was not willing to renegotiate the positions of its empire's territories.

Sheikh Abdul Salam must have known that the Ottomans would not ignore such demands. At best, they represented an attempt to build up a sense of Kurdish identity that would eventually have threatened the Ottomans' control. At worst, they may have represented a deliberate attempt to provoke a response by the Ottomans, in the expectation that they were weak enough that a mass uprising could defeat them.

If provoking a response *was* Sheikh Abdul Salam's intention, it certainly worked. The Ottomans sent soldiers in force, and the Barzani, angered by their position within the violent and frequently corrupt Ottoman Empire, and perhaps sensing that it had been weakened by previous struggles, rose up against their rulers. They sought, as Kurdish rebellions before and since have generally sought, to obtain freedom from an outside authority, attempting to rule them from afar. It was part of a general pattern of rebellions that is sometimes seen as characterising my people.

While that is not an assessment I can agree with – it overlooks too many of Kurdistan's other achievements – it is possible to see the almost unbroken chain of attempts of self-rule stretching back into the past and on into Mullah Mustafa Barzani's lifetime. Whatever their profession, sons also took up the cause of independence from their fathers, nephews from uncles. Each successive generation seemed to bring a new wave of young men – and women, because they have often been just as closely involved in the cause of Kurdish independence – eager to try once more for the country that they felt they should have.

Perhaps that explains some of the Ottoman response to the rebellion. Perhaps a fear that young men would be the next generation of rebels was behind the decision. Perhaps it should

Birth and Childhood

also be seen in the context of wider problems within the empire, where the Turks in particular were attempting to forge a cultural identity distinct from that of their Ottoman rulers around that time. Perhaps the Ottomans, knowing that they had all but lost Turkey, feared that the same was likely in Kurdistan if they did not respond harshly.

Perhaps their next decision can even be seen as a normal one for the times. After all, at the start of the twentieth century, the world had not yet seen the horrors of Nazi Germany's concentration camps, and the large scale internment of rebels and their families was a widespread practice for empires dealing with uprisings. In the Second Boer War in South Africa, just a year before Mullah Mustafa Barzani was born, more than 26,000 women and children were confined to internment camps, while a similar number of men were taken from their families and imprisoned overseas. By our modern standards, it is abhorrent, yet it was clearly a key tool for empire rulers the world over.

Whatever the reasoning behind it, in the wake of the 1907 demands, the decision was taken to imprison all the Barzani males who could be found, of whatever age, along with many of their women and children. That included Mullah Mustafa Barzani, then only five years old, along with his uncles, cousins and more distant relatives. Would he have known what was happening at that point? My own experience of imprisonment as a child under Saddam's regime suggests that children understand both more and less than adults think. The general situation cannot be hidden from them. It is impossible to pretend to a child that he is not in a prison camp. Yet at the same time, there is something about the situation that almost becomes normal after a while. They still find ways to play and be children. It is all they have ever known, after all.

Yet almost normal is not the same thing as normal, and it is in his childhood that we find some of the experiences that must have shaped Mullah Mustafa Barzani for much of his life. We

The Idea of Kurdistan

have, for example, the deaths of so many of his immediate male relatives. His father died in 1903, the year of his birth. He lost uncles and his grandfather to execution, either for their part in the resistance to the Ottoman incursion or for their parts in other uprisings. These things cannot have failed to have had an influence on his life.

Yet this uprising was one that ended relatively successfully. In 1908, Kurdish forces were able to ambush the Ottomans' army, inflicting significant losses. At a time when the world was teetering on the edge of war, the Ottoman Empire realised that it could not afford a protracted conflict against an enemy capable of inflicting significant losses against them. It had relied on Kurdistan to protect the fringes of its empire, and so could not countenance any kind of lengthy campaign to bring it into line. By that point, with the loss of other territories, it probably wasn't even sure that such a campaign would succeed.

That left the Ottoman Empire with one choice: to negotiate. As a part of those negotiations, Kurdistan stayed as a part of the empire, but the Ottoman Turks agreed to make reparations, and prisoners, including Mullah Mustafa Barzani, were freed. That moment may have been a defining one for both Kurdistan and Mullah Mustafa Barzani. On a personal level, it must have been important to know that something as terrible as imprisonment could happen but that he would still be freed. That even as a small child he could survive the consequences of a failed insurrection, and that he could come through it. For Kurdistan, this first attempt to assert its status was not a claim to full independence, but it must have started many people thinking about it. If they could fight the Turks and win concessions, they must have thought, then why should they stop there?

Mullah Mustafa Barzani: The Child and the Man

There is only so much it is possible to write about Mullah Mustafa Barzani's childhood. The evidence for the events

Birth and Childhood

around him, and for the actions of his family, is much better in that period than the direct evidence about him. In that respect, it is about what we would expect for a small child in an area where there were few formal records.

Indeed, the lack of information can itself tell us a lot. The areas where we have information about Mullah Mustafa Barzani as a child – his imprisonment, his place in the Barzani tribe's most important family – are all instances where things were far from normal. They were elements of the exceptional and they stood out because of that.

In turn this suggests that for a lot of the time, in spite of everything that was happening around him, Mullah Mustafa Barzani's childhood was a normal one. With the exception of the period when he was imprisoned in Mosul, he would have grown up the way so many children in Kurdistan did, learning and playing, living as so many of his peers did. He would have learned about the mountains and the land around him, which would have proved crucial in his later life, and he would have learned to fight, but again, this is no more than would have been normal for any other child born where and when he was.

To what extent then can we say that Mullah Mustafa Barzani's childhood helped to prepare him for the role he was eventually to play? I have discussed the idea that his family background lent him authority above. The period that he spent imprisoned may well have helped him accept the possibility of it later in life, and to be prepared so that he and his followers could avoid it. The events of Sheikh Abdul Salam's insurrection and its success may also have persuaded him that standing up to authority with military force was an option that worked better than merely asking for what his people wanted.

The loss of his father and other male relatives in childhood may also have helped to shape his future. At the very least, such losses are likely to have shaped his attitudes, both by making him aware of the dangers that came with being in such

The Idea of Kurdistan

a prominent position, and also by forcing him to grow up faster than many other children have to.

I mentioned in the introduction though that there is a problem in much biography with a sense of inevitability. There is always a part of us that wants to look back and say that of course our subject was always heading for greatness. Yet can we look back at Mullah Mustafa Barzani's childhood and say that? Would his contemporaries have assumed that, or would they have thought something else?

He was from an important family, certainly. He was born at a time when the Kurdish people were starting to show that they could stand up to outside authorities trying to control them. Yet he was the youngest son of that important family. The one who was too young at the time of the uprising against the Ottomans to take part. It seems unlikely that, when he was a child, there would have been any expectation that Mullah Mustafa Barzani would grow to become a man who would play a crucial role in Kurdistan's independence movement.

He did though, so what changed? How did the child who was merely a victim of Ottoman aggression turn into a man who would attempt to lead a revolution? Understanding that also helps us to understand something about the way Kurdistan changed, and so it is a crucial question to explore.

Chapter Three: Growth to Revolution

World War One

By the time World War One broke out, the relationship between my people and the Ottoman Empire had been established as an antagonistic one. The Ottomans had ruled over Kurdistan for a long time, but the Barzani rebellions of the early twentieth century made it clear that they were not prepared to stay within a political system that involved them being ruled from afar.

Despite that, many Kurds served within the armed forces of the Ottoman Empire during the war. Indeed, the majority of the Ottomans' Ninth Army was made up of Kurdish forces. We also know that while portions of the Kurdish population helped to shield Armenian residents from the massacres of 1915 in which the Ottomans sought to take revenge for their uprisings, many more took part in them.

Why? Why did my people not take what may have seemed like an obvious opportunity to rise up against those who ruled over them? Why did they take part in a bloody war on the side of those many of them had fought against so soon before?

There are several answers here. One is the length of time the Ottomans had ruled over Kurdistan, so that even when nationalists might look for an independent nation, many ordinary people felt that the Ottomans had a right to expect

The Idea of Kurdistan

their military service. It must also be noted that my people had been used in an essentially military role by the Turks for centuries, as guardians of their distant borders.

Then there was the nature of the military threat. World War One was a war between Great Powers, with vast empires on both sides. It was a *world* war, where local conflicts over regional freedom probably seemed less important than they had been before it. It may well have seemed that the choice was not between being ruled and being free, but simply over the identities of Kurdistan's foreign rulers. Certainly, we know that is how things ended up.

Then there is the element of coercion. On numerous occasions in the preceding decades, the Ottoman Empire had made it clear that it was prepared to use force against any large scale rebellion, and to respond brutally to any such 'betrayal'. Even those massacres some Kurdish forces were made to participate in served as much as an example to them of the measures the Ottomans were prepared to countenance for disobedience as they did as an action against groups such as the Armenians or Cossacks.

Then, of course, there is the most important point, which is that not all Kurds fought on behalf of the Ottoman Empire. The Barzani tribe, and Mullah Mustafa, did not. Many others did not. There were those among my people who sought to protect those the Ottomans would have killed. There were those who actively fought against them, perhaps not as part of the main war efforts, but certainly on a local level. In the Kurdish areas of what is now Turkey, an uprising of 1916 against the Ottomans led to the mass deportation of Kurds and an attempt to re-settle the area with Turks.

We also know that in 1913–14 the Ottomans managed to arrange the capture and execution of Sheikh Abdul Salam. That action suggests that even as the First World War was taking shape, the Ottomans still had to worry about resistance from

Growth to Revolution

the Kurds on a local level. Indeed, such a move immediately before a war that everyone could see coming suggests just how worried the Ottomans were by the potential for Kurdish uprising. It seems reasonable to argue that the main reason Kurdistan was not able to rise up against its Ottoman rulers at that point was because the Ottomans had done so much damage in removing potential leaders.

Perhaps this explains why the main Kurdish uprising of the war occurred in Turkey, rather than at the heart of Kurdistan. Instead of taking advantage of the opportunity offered by the war, the Kurds in the region were forced into a process of consolidation. We know, for example, that many fighters pulled back towards the village of Barzan to protect it and the surrounding region, thus stopping them from engaging in a more active campaign. Sheikh Ahmad, who took over the leadership of the Barzani following his brother's death, was also just eighteen at the time. In the shock of events following the death of his brother, and with major world events playing out all around, it may have seemed like the wisest course for my people simply to defend the territory they held and see how things turned out.

Indeed, there is a case for saying that World War One brought a curious kind peace to Barzan and the surrounding area. Not because it was somehow insulated from the war, or because its fighters did nothing. But the war provided what must have seemed almost a respite when the Ottomans could not pursue a more serious campaign against my people, because they were too busy with the larger scope of international events.

World War One is another period where there is little if any direct evidence for Mullah Mustafa Barzani's activities. Again, he was still too young at this point to play a major part, or even to truly fight. Yet he would have been learning to do so in this period, knowing that the war could bring violence sweeping through the region at any moment. Even if we do not know the details of Mullah Mustafa Barzani's life at this point with any certainty, it seems likely that this would have been a formative period within it. Certainly, children who grow up in times of war are often forced to grow up faster than those elsewhere, and often find themselves exposed to experiences that even many adults prefer to avoid.

Yet we can see that this early exposure to the realities of warfare may have served Mullah Mustafa well. It meant that he would have already been used to what warfare meant when the later rebellions and attempts at revolution came. It meant that he understood the need to protect those around him and do what was necessary for his people. As terrible as the First World War was, it may also have had the effect of hardening a young man like Mullah Mustafa Barzani in the same way that a flame can harden metal. Without the experience of a world at war in his youth, who is to say that he would have turned out to be the same man as he grew older?

The Aftermath

In many ways, the immediate aftermath of World War One matters more to the story of Kurdistan than the war itself did. In the war, Kurdistan can be seen as largely peripheral when compared to Europe's Western Front. It was a place to be fought over, certainly, and the very nature of the war dragged it into the fighting as one of the Ottoman Empire's possessions, yet the long term effects of the fighting on the country were far less than the long term effects of the peace. The same is true of their effects on Mullah Mustafa Barzani.

In Kurdistan, the date of the 10th of August 1920 is a well-known one. The Treaty of Sèvres, bringing about peace with the Ottoman Empire, is generally taken as the key moment when Kurdistan could have achieved nationhood peacefully and without further argument, backed by the weight of the international community. The promise was there, enshrined in articles 62–64 of the treaty, that Kurdistan would be granted independence after a referendum if the international community felt it was ready. To those who were aware of the treaty's text at the time it must have seemed an almost magical moment for Kurdistan, even if what was being offered was quite limited. After all, the Kurdistan the treaty envisaged was quite a small country contained within mostly Turkish territory, while making it contingent on the international community feeling that Kurdistan was ready suggests quite a lot about the way the region and its people were perceived at the time.

Yet we know that ultimately, this proposal did not come to pass. The Treaty of Lausanne in 1923, designed to bring about peace with Ataturk's still belligerent Turkey, superseded the first treaty. It made no mention of a homeland for my people, and instead sought to divide the greater region of Kurdistan up between four countries in the form of Turkey, Syria, Iran and Iraq. Writers on Kurdistan have frequently traced this as the moment when the Kurdish independence movement really gained traction, but they have less frequently explored the reasons why it came about.

Why? Why did the Allies of the First World War backtrack on what seemed to be a firm commitment for autonomy for the region? To understand that, we must see the two more famous treaties as a part of a sequence of treaties and agreements dating back at least to the Treaty of London in 1915, which was designed to persuade Italy to join the fight against Germany and its allies.

That treaty did not mention Kurdistan or any territory relating to it, yet it did involve making agreements for portions of territory belonging to the German and Ottoman empires in the wake of the war. Italy, as a relatively new country, was eager to expand its foreign possessions and join the top table of colonial powers. It was a treaty about giving the Western participants in the war more territory, not about providing

The Idea of Kurdistan

settled, independent states. This is true of the majority of other treaties around the time. In that sense, the Treaty of Sèvres was the anomaly in proposing anything more equitable for the populations of the region.

The reason it did so seems to have been the desire to prevent further war. At the end of the First World War, most of the Great Powers had lost their appetite for further conflict. Measures like the establishment of the League of Nations were meant to limit the potential for another round of slaughter on that scale ever occurring again. In that sense, it may have been significant that at the time of the Treaty of Sèvres, Kurdistan was in revolt against the British occupation. Mahmud Barzani's rebellion created a threat of further instability in the region, and the potential for an extension of the conflict.

That explains some of why the Treaty of Sèvres' terms were contingent upon both a referendum and the League of Nations agreeing that Kurdistan was 'ready'. The referendum was to provide proof that the uprising represented the popular will, while the condition of Kurdistan can be seen as a thinly veiled condition that the Kurds stop their uprising and cooperate. It was the act of a parent promising a child a reward if they behaved.

So what changed? Why did the Great Powers not follow through with the terms outlined in the Treaty of Sèvres? Why did they make another in the form of the Treaty of Lausanne? Again, part of the answer lies in seeing both Sèvres and Lausanne as part of a broader sequence of territorial treaties dating back to 1915. The Great Powers had drafted and redrafted these treaties, with the most famous ones such as Versailles being only the most prominent points of an extended process of negotiation between those powers. It would have seemed natural to them that they could have renegotiated, even if doing so was a betrayal of Kurdistan's interests.

That it was a negotiation purely between those powers would

have seemed natural to them as well. Remember that the Treaty of Versailles was imposed on Germany four years previously, and that was with a power the likes of Britain and France had regarded as their equal. By those standards, Kurdistan, as a part of a defeated Ottoman Empire, could expect no say in what happened to it next.

In that sense, it seems almost predictable that the Great Powers would want to carve up the region and claim it as their own. Treaties such as Versailles make it clear that countries such as France, Britain, Italy and even the United States were eager to gain as much as possible. There were voices calling for long-term peace, but they were often drowned out by those who said that in the wake of a war that had left perhaps thirty-seven million soldiers and civilians dead, the winners deserved to take something of value, if only to show that it wasn't completely in vain. Kurdistan's oil resources made it, in an era when motorised transportation was coming into its own, too valuable to let go. In recent years, oil has provided Kurdistan with the revenue for major building works and a good standard of living compared to the rest of Iraq, but it may well be that it would have been independent many decades ago had those resources not existed.

Yet the presence of oil doesn't explain everything. It doesn't explain, for example, why the Treaty of Sèvres would make an offer of independence in the first place, or what changed over the course of three years for it to be withdrawn. For that, I think we need to look more at the nature of the proposed Kurdistan, and at the nature of the Treaty of Lausanne.

While the modern Kurdistan lies within Iraq, we know from the text of the Treaty of Sèvres that the version of Kurdistan it was proposing was much more focused on territory in what is now Turkey. We also know that the Treaty of Lausanne was aimed at bringing about peace with the emerging country of Turkey. Turkey was, quite simply, not prepared to accept a big bite out of its newly claimed territory, and the Allies placed the idea of bringing about peace with Turkey ahead of the peace they already had with my people.

That is not the only reason, of course. The evidence suggests that at least part of the reason my people found their region split between multiple powers had as much to do with the politics of race as with anything else. The Great Powers didn't want a single large Arab state, on a scale to become a power of its own. As such, they parcelled out land into what would become Iraq and Iran, not caring if they split my people between them in the process. There is even some suggestion that they may have seen the Kurds as a balancing force, creating enough conflict with the Arab rulers to prevent the kind of large scale joining together they feared at the time. Yet the demands of Turkey were there, and it was those that the Great Powers listened to.

Iraq

Whatever the reason, the result of the wrangling by the Allies was the creation of an entirely new state in the form of Iraq. A state that the Kurdish population of the region suddenly found themselves a part of, despite the assurances that they would have their own country.

It is tempting to see this as the cause of much of the violence in the period, sparking uprisings by those such as Sheikh Mahmud and Sheikh Ahmad. Yet the timeline here suggests that the creation of Iraq caused at best a continuation of the violence in the longer term, rather than the start of the rebellion. The uprising had started well before the final decision on the country had been made. Certainly before the Treaty of Lausanne.

Indeed, the uprising began as early as 1919, in response to efforts by the British occupying forces to impose their governmental structures on the region. With the benefit of hindsight, it is probable that the forces in question were merely repeating the patterns they had applied in so many other places. With early twentieth century Western attitudes, they saw what they perceived as a 'lawless' and essentially chaotic place. They could not understand a society in transition at its own pace, and so attempted to impose elements of their brand of local government such as police stations and central taxation on the region.

The attempted revolt did not last long. Sheikh Mahmud was injured and captured shortly after the revolt began. Sheikh Ahmad attempted to keep it going, succeeding in killing the British commissioner in Mosul and one of their district governors (Colonel Bill and Captain Scott) and taking the treasury at Aqra, but in the absence of the revolt's original leader, and with alternative leaders such as Saiyid Taha attempting to set themselves up as replacements in other parts of the country, it was hard for the revolt to maintain momentum.

Instead, faced with increasing divisions between the different tribal forces under his command, Sheikh Ahmad found himself placed in a position where the best course of action was a withdrawal back to the villages by all those involved in the revolt. This withdrawal may also have been influenced by a desire to wait and see if the Great Powers of the time would make good on the promises they had made in the Treaty of Sèvres.

It says something about the complex nature of events in this period, and indeed throughout much of Kurdistan's modern history, that this did not exactly end the revolt. Instead, it merely drove it underground, marking the beginning of an ongoing period of guerrilla warfare where the Kurdish tribes sought to strike when targets of opportunity presented themselves, but mostly sought to defend their villages and autonomy.

The Treaty of Lausanne marked an upsurge in the violence, with small revolts taking place across a number of areas. The

The Idea of Kurdistan

difficulty lay in creating the kind of conditions needed for any kind of general revolt, rather than a series of smaller ones. Several writers have remarked that there does not seem to have been the general Sèvreswill for revolution at the time. I would put it a little differently.

It seems likely that the majority of Kurds were upset by the British occupation. It seems likely, from reactions afterwards, that the majority would have wanted the independent Kurdish state they had been promised in . Yet there is a difference between wanting something and being prepared to take on an occupying military force en masse to achieve it. There is a difference between wanting it and agreeing on the details of how it should be implemented, too.

Put simply, while some groups such as the Barzani were prepared to rebel where they could, the majority of people in Kurdistan had just seen Britain and the other Great Powers crush much more powerful foes. To ordinary people, revolt must have seemed like an unwinnable proposition in 1919, one that might have actively made their lives worse by attracting the attention of authorities that were currently too caught up in their own international games to bother about the details of governance on the ground that much.

More than that, Kurdistan was still relatively splintered in 1919. It is possible to make a case for the importance of Sheikh Mahmud's revolt, but it is as a precursor to everything that followed, not as an indication of the general will of the people of Kurdistan. Later revolts were general Kurdish ones, but this was still more tribal in nature. The people of Kurdistan might have wanted rulers other than the British, but in 1919 at least, there was not yet a consensus over who represented the best alternative. Those who presented themselves as potential leaders of a revolution were also by implication presenting themselves as potential rulers afterwards. Even Sheikh Mahmud, on release from imprisonment, wasn't able to gather the general support to achieve that. My people were more united in what they *didn't* want than in what they did.

So, while revolts were able to spring up in the 1920s, they were rarely strong enough to trouble the British. Indeed, how could they be? In 1925, the RAF bombed Sulaymaniyah. It was just one of the highlights of a campaign focused on the use of the newly developed air power against civilian targets. The Kurdish fighters of the time had no answer to that superior level of force. The best they could hope for was a continuing level of opposition and guerrilla warfare, rather than the open conquest of territory.

Which meant that slowly, Iraq slid into being. King Faisal found himself appointed by the British to take over when their mandate ended. Referendums were arranged, but the local level results ignored. Steps such as the guaranteeing of Kurdish language teaching in Kurdistan were taken to assuage public opinion in the region, while never addressing the core problem of my people not wishing to be ruled from Baghdad.

Perhaps this is because Baghdad had made it clear that it wished to continue ruling Kurdistan. King Faisal, in particular, seems to have been keen to retain control of the region. In part, that was simply a function of being a king. No ruler wishes to simply give away territory, however he has gained it, and however tenuous his grip on it. As king of a newly created country, moreover, he must have been aware that the unity of the new Iraq was still a fragile thing, not backed by any sense of shared history or the symbolic value of a pre-existing border. If one part of the new country had been allowed to break away, there is a case for saying that Iraq would have disintegrated completely at that time.

There is also some suggestion that King Faisal was against the idea of Kurdistan as an independent nation for other reasons. It seems that he may have felt that Kurdistan and the other 'older' nations such as Turkey, Persia/Iran and Syria might well have combined to put pressure on his country in the event of Kurdistan's freedom. He also seems to have had religious grounds for his position, believing that keeping Kurdistan's largely Sunni population as a part of Iraq provided an advantage in maintaining a Shiite majority over them.

In 1926, Iraq was given formal entry into the League of Nations, but the British mandate there lasted until the formal handover of power in the 1930s. Even then, it seems likely that considerable British influence remained. At the very least, the governmental structures had been designed on British lines, the civil servants and police were trained with British ideas in mind, and British ideas had taken root in many areas of authority. More direct influence may also have remained through British–Iraqi diplomacy of the time.

The Lessons of the 1920s

Why focus on a period where Mullah Mustafa Barzani had yet to come to real prominence like this? Partly, it is so that we understand the issues and conflicts that played out throughout his lifetime and beyond. Mostly, however, it is because in this period, Mullah Mustafa was old enough to start commanding men, and to play a full part in what took place.

It was not yet a leading part. We do not have full accounts of what he did during these early revolts, any more than we have full accounts of what most other individual peshmerga did. He was not yet the Barzanis' leader, still less the leader of the whole of the Kurdish cause. He was in many ways still learning the role that he would come to occupy in future decades. Yet that is important in itself, because these early revolts must have served to teach him much of what he later believed about the nature of revolt.

Those glimpses that we get of him in the historical record certainly suggest a learning experience. Sheikh Ahmad put him in charge of men for the first time that we know of, for example,

Growth to Revolution

sending him to aid Sheikh Mahmud. That he was not able to get there in time must have taught him something about the precarious nature of small scale, asymmetrical warfare, while the simple experience of commanding peshmerga must have taught him many lessons that would come in useful later as combat became a reality.

I think though that many of the lessons Mullah Mustafa drew from the rebellions of the 1920s will have been political. Its difficulties must have served as lessons to him, showing him the importance of building genuine mass support over time, and the importance of preserving visible leaders. It must have taught him something about the divisive and difficult nature of internal politics even at times when it seemed like they ought to be set aside, and about the lengths to which rulers were prepared to go to hang on to what they had decided was theirs.

More than that, I would guess that this early situation represented the best examples Mullah Mustafa had been given so far in his life of two ideas that would crop up repeatedly later on. The first was the importance of long-term thinking. The revolt did not achieve its aims in one attempt, or even at all. Yet it was able to do something to preserve the Kurdish way of life a little longer by forcing small concessions out of the new Iraqi government. Secondly, it probably taught him the importance of the interconnected nature of warfare and politics, especially when dealing with the kind of stop-start guerrilla warfare that would characterise relations between Kurdistan and Baghdad for at least another seventy years.

The combined lesson of the 1919 revolution must have been this for Mullah Mustafa: that against superior forces, such revolts don't succeed all at once, but by managing to maintain yourself and your people, it is possible to create political pressure in the long term. It is a lesson that we see again and again throughout his life.

Rebellion

The rebellions of the 1930s represented something different for Mullah Mustafa, but in some ways they were also just the continuation of struggles that had been going on in the background in the ten years previously. Yes, there was a handover from British to Iraqi authorities within Iraq, but that did nothing to change the tensions between my people and the central authorities in Baghdad. If anything, it seems to have exacerbated them.

There is a story of how Mullah Mustafa Barzani requested from the Governor of Mosul in 1929–30 that the British forces in Kurdistan be replaced by Iraqi ones. The story says that the governor agreed, but that he told Mullah Mustafa that he would soon see what happened next. Some sources have taken this as evidence of British plotting, yet actually, it seems more likely that the governor was simply pointing out that, in a country where the Iraqi government was trying to extend its influence, an Iraqi force in the area was much more likely to take hostile action than a British one.

Certainly, they were quick to use the excuse of inter-tribal conflict to try to clamp down on the region, sending forces to villages including Barzan. Some writers have tried to portray this tribal warfare as purely a response to unprovoked aggression, but it seems more realistic to see it either as the kind of conflict that had been considered normal for decades before, or as an attempt by Sheikh Ahmad to improve his power base. When the 1919 revolt failed largely through lack of sustained support, it seems logical that a charismatic leader with dreams of separation from Iraq would have sought to expand his influence before seeking that separation again.

We know that Sheikh Ahmad *did* succeed in building up a great deal of respect within the region. He was able to enforce measures that started to move Kurdistan away from a purely tribal system, that improved the position of women, and that sought to protect the natural resources of the region against overuse. It seems unlikely that he would have been able to begin any of these processes had he not been able to command considerable respect.

Certainly, the aftermath of inter-tribal warfare makes little sense as the main reason for the Iraqi authorities to seek his arrest, as some sources have suggested. That might have been the pretext, but with hindsight, we can see that it probably had more to do with his success in building up power in the region, and with his potential for rebellion. In a context where they had only just been handed official control of the region, and where a figure who had already been involved with one rebellion was starting to build up his power and position, it must have seemed to the Iraqi authorities like they were nipping another potential conflict in the bud by attempting to arrest him.

This must have been especially true in the context of the times. Remember that just the other side of the Turkish border, there was already a conflict going on between my people and a central authority. In 1930–31, the Arrahat Rebellion was in full swing, with the Turkish forces involved using frequently brutal methods to put it down. We know from the records at the time that Sheikh Ahmad was willing to receive those who were driven from their homes by the Turkish attempts to put down that rebellion, and that he was in favour of it in at least general terms.

From the outside, therefore, it must have looked like Sheikh Ahmad was preparing for some kind of general rebellion, possibly joining together with that in Turkey to bring the whole wider Kurdistan region into the conflict. Faced with that apparent possibility, the Iraqi authorities probably felt that they had no choice but to attempt to act against the Kurdish population in general and Sheikh Ahmad more specifically. They probably felt that it would stop the potential for further conflict. In that, they were wrong. Mullah Mustafa Barzani played a key role in stopping the initial assault, while other forces acted against the local government. By 1932, the rebellion had begun in earnest.

The two sides of the conflict paint very different pictures of the rebellion of the early 1930s. For the Iraqi government of the time, it is clear that they saw it as an operation to put down a potential threat in the region. They saw Sheikh Ahmad as attempting to create essentially his own country, striving for control over more tribes and, crucially, refusing to pay taxes to their central administration. Those who have supported the cause of Kurdish Independence over the years have tended to paint the conflict as an essentially defensive one, with the Kurdish forces reacting to aggression from outside.

There is probably some truth in both sides of this. In all honesty, Sheikh Ahmad probably *was* trying to build the power to bring about a truly independent region, working through the military expansion of his authority because the region had yet to embrace the democracy that would come to it later. He certainly wasn't paying taxes to a regime he didn't recognise the legitimacy of. In that sense, he was rebelling on a civil level, refusing to be a part of the new country of Iraq, long before the conflict reached a military level. Yet we can also see that the military aspects of the conflict consisted almost entirely of Iraqi forces coming into the region with the intention of killing or arresting those the central government had decided were rebels, and we can also see that Sheikh Ahmad and the rest of my people did not act against the existing civil government of the region until that attack began. In that sense, it was a purely defensive war, aimed at preserving villages, individual freedoms, and a way of life that was in danger of being lost.

From Follower to Leader

The period of the 1930s rebellion is crucial in the life of Mullah Mustafa Barzani, because it is the phase where we first see him wielding real authority. Yes, he commanded men in the 1919 rebellion, but the evidence seems to be that for the key battle, his force was not in a position to see significant action. Yes, it seems likely that he would have been involved in small scale, running conflicts after that. But it is only in the period around this rebellion that we really start to see signs of him emerging from the role of a follower, into a role of military leader, diplomat and key figure in the fortunes of Kurdistan.

We know, for example, that it was he who delivered the ultimately fateful request to replace the British forces in the region with Iraqi ones, which suggests that he was trusted to negotiate with and persuade key figures in the government of the area. It seems likely that in the inter-tribal battles designed to unify the tribes of the time under Sheikh Ahmad, he commanded forces. We know for certain that he was a part of the forces that defended Sheikh Ahmad and the village of Barzan when the initial attempt to make arrests there was made. We know that when fighting broke out in earnest in 1932, he was given command of one of the three sections of the Barzani forces, while Sheikh Ahmad and Mohammed Siddique Barzani took the other two.

It is at this point that we can see the first attempts to build up the legend of Mullah Mustafa, in the attempts by observers to emphasise the low numbers on the Barzani side in this conflict. Some have emphasised that the Barzani forces could not have numbered more than about a thousand in total, with Mullah Mustafa not commanding more than a third. I am not saying that these numbers are necessarily inaccurate. In truth, it is probably quite difficult to assess the number of fighters on either side accurately, although it seems that the Barzani numbers cannot have been much more than those stated, while the total number of troops available to the Iraqi authorities was probably much greater.

What I am saying is that we must see the numbers involved

The Idea of Kurdistan

more as a reflection of the ways in which Mullah Mustafa was already becoming a symbol for his people than as simply an accurate count. There was an effort made to emphasise the scale of the victory and the odds overcome, because even at that stage, everyone involved knew that the Kurdish side of the conflict was in need of symbols to rally around. The reporting of events in this conflict was the first step in a process that would turn Mullah Mustafa into the symbol Kurdistan needed to rally around later.

Can we unpick the reality and get to the real numbers? We have the government reports suggesting a main force consisting of at least three infantry regiments, a brigade of cavalry and more, but the size and composition of regiments can vary considerably by period and area. The general impression is one of a much larger, better equipped force than the Barzanis had, however. Certainly, the adoption of essentially guerrilla tactics by the Barzani forces suggests that they were not able to meet their opponents head on. However, this may have been at least partly a consequence of RAF support for the Iraqi forces, including large scale bombing. So again, we are forced to ask questions of the exact numbers on the ground. In the Battle of Dola Vazhe, we know that more than 250 of the Iraqi force were killed, with more taken prisoner or wounded. Even if we assume something like twice as many wounded or captured as killed, however, and even if we suggest that some got away, it seems difficult to place the numbers from this force on the ground at much more than those claimed by the Barzani side in total.

Of course, it is worth remembering that Mullah Mustafa was working with probably not much more than three or four hundred of those available, armed with light weaponry and no artillery. In that sense, it *was* an important victory. And a crushing one. In employing tactics that allowed the advancing forces to believe that they had succeeded before moving in to

Growth to Revolution

strike back at them, Mullah Mustafa created a situation that minimised his own losses while maximising those of the enemy. I want to emphasise again that in no way am I attempting to belittle the achievement of this victory. I am simply trying to understand the ways in which Mullah Mustafa the legend/symbol and Mullah Mustafa the man were starting to interact even at this early stage.

The outcome of this battle was to slow the advance of the government's forces, forcing them to rely more on air power. The release of prisoners also seemed to slow the advance, showing a willingness to combine military and political tactics in a way that probably reduced the government's ability to send in another major force immediately. Yet ultimately, it must have been clear that the Barzanis could not win militarily against the full forces the Iraqis and British could potentially bring to bear. Their best hopes lay in a combination of negotiation and preparations to leave Iraq if necessary. Along with other key Kurdish figures, Mullah Mustafa Barzani took his forces to positions from which they could withdraw into the surrounding countries if necessary.

One last attempt was made at negotiation. Could it have succeeded? Writers looking back have stressed that Sheikh Ahmad was prepared to live as a part of Iraq, and was prepared to negotiate with the Iraqi authorities. This is perhaps a little hopeful, when the essence of so many of his actions previously had suggested that his people could not accept this. Yes, Sheikh Ahmad had taken a consistently conciliatory tone that suggests that he personally may have been interested in peace, but when so many of those around him wanted freedom from the laws and taxes imposed from Baghdad, could any peace really have lasted? It seems likely that even if negotiations had taken place, they would have found too little common ground between the two sides to succeed long term.

As it was, the negotiations didn't take place. We're told that

Sheikh Ahmad was worried that the British intended to arrest him if he showed up for the negotiations (which is supported by the later evidence) but the reporting of his reasons also suggests that he was not interested in any continuation of British rule over his people. That left only one option. Mullah Mustafa Barzani was about to experience his first period of exile abroad.

Exile

The first exile of the Kurdish fighters following the 1930s rebellion was not the hurried and badly organised flight to safety that many of us think of when we hear the term. Indeed, it was not an exile as such, in that it was not enforced by government forces. Instead, it was a pre-emptive move made by Sheikh Ahmad and Mullah Mustafa Barzani, along with their most immediate followers. It was an attempt to avoid defeat and punishment at the hands of a more powerful opponent rather than a punishment in itself.

That initial withdrawal into Turkey was carefully planned, backed by negotiations with the Turkish government. It was necessarily small scale, both because the Turks would not have accepted a larger influx of refugees and because Sheikh Ahmad and Mullah Mustafa felt that by leaving, they were taking away the British/Iraqi justification to further harm others. The Turks required that the Barzani not bring weapons with them, but other than that initially seemed willing to accept their presence.

Here we can see that there was little genuine trust on either side. At a time when the Turks had already been fighting against one Kurdish revolt, putting it down through the brutal use of artillery, it is perhaps hardly surprising. The Barzanis' refusal to genuinely hand over their weaponry, instead pulling the classic trick of handing over a few old pieces while hiding the things they really needed, suggests that they may well have suspected they would need to fight the Turks as much as they had the Iraqi government.

Growth to Revolution

The Turkish lack of trust comes across in the way they changed the terms of their deal, turning back the majority of Kurdish families who tried to cross the border, allowing only Sheikh Ahmad, Mullah Mustafa, and a few other members of their family through. They kept them separated and moved them around several cities. From a distance, especially considering its similarity to Iraqi tactics in the next few years, it looks very much like a tactic designed to remove key leaders from the Barzani in the hope that it would pacify the situation in Kurdistan. Why would the Turks do that? Presumably not from any sudden sense of altruism towards the Iraqi government, although there could have been at least an element of bridge building between the two involved.

It seems more likely, however, that Turkey's Kurdish uprisings had something to do with it. That they felt the removal of key Kurdish figures would have an effect on their own situation with still potentially rebellious Kurdish tribes, or that their presence would look like the Turkish government was engaging in dialogue. Certainly, we know that in the later 1930s, after Mullah Mustafa and Sheikh Ahmad had returned to Iraq, the Turkish government began a much more sustained campaign against my people.

Possibly, both of these explanations have something to be said for them. We know from subsequent events that Turkey had no love for my people in that period, and indeed sought to deny their very existence, referring to Kurds as merely a branch of mountain Turks rather than as a distinct ethnic group. We know that they did have problems with rebellions, and that Sheikh Ahmad had expressed his support for the most recent of those rebellions. In that sense, it seems likely that the effective capture of both him and Mullah Mustafa Barzani was designed at least partly to solve Turkey's internal problems.

Yet we also know that Turkey handed Sheikh Ahmad over to the Iraqi authorities in 1933. This seems very much like the move of a regime attempting to buy favour with its neighbours. Indeed, the whole process of separating Sheikh Ahmad from his followers, and the ease with which Turkey acceded to the plan for my people to flee there following the rebellion, suggests that the two countries may have had that in mind from the start.

Negotiation, Arrest, Removal

Whatever the process behind Sheikh Ahmad's arrest and effective extradition, in 1933 Mullah Mustafa Barzani found himself in a difficult situation. He had left Iraq at Sheikh Ahmad's suggestion, backed by promises of safety from the Turkish government, to avoid a situation that could not be won. He could not stay. His brother was no longer there, and it seemed obvious from what had just happened that the Turkish government could not be trusted to look after the interests of his people. He must have even feared that he might have been the next to be handed over. Yet to return home might simply be placing himself and his people back in danger.

Ultimately though, he did return, adopting a curious combination of tactics. On the one hand, he and his forces agreed not to strike at targets for the time being, both to avoid exactly the kind of unwinnable conflict that had driven them to Turkey in the first place and to preserve the safety of his brother. Yet at the same time, they did not return to their villages, in spite of promises of a general amnesty. That move can best be explained in terms of a lack of trust, with Mullah Mustafa unwilling to risk coming out into the open with his brother still in government custody, yet it probably contributed to the tension of the situation. From the point of view of the government, it must have looked like someone who had already rebelled, refusing to give up on the life of banditry in the mountains that had characterised that rebellion.

Ultimately, the government succeeded in luring Mullah

Growth to Revolution

Mustafa to Mosul by using Sheikh Ahmad as bait. They trapped the other Barzani brothers and their families, taking them south as well. The first period of exile from Kurdistan had given way to a second phase, this one enforced by the government.

This idea of an internal exile had been practiced by the Ottomans before, but it continued to say something about the nature of the new Iraq. It emphasised that the new country was not a unified one, and that it was still possible to effectively exile someone even within it.

The next few years saw the government acting step by step against the Barzanis. In 1935, there were trials for many of those who had returned, followed by a number of executions. In 1936, there was an attempt to poison Mullah Mustafa Barzani. Following this, things seem to have grown quieter for several years. Mullah Mustafa found himself and his family moved, first to Baghdad in 1936, and then to Sulaymaniyah in 1939.

This pattern seems to say a lot about the feelings of the Iraqi government through that period. Initially, they seem to have been concerned with punishment for the previous rebellion, with deterrence, threats, and the removal of leaders. They seem to have been concerned to stop any possibility of further rebellion. Yet as time went on, they seem to have been willing to move Mullah Mustafa back to Kurdistan, even if it was to an entirely different area of it.

It looks very much like the government of Iraq was confident that it had succeeded in dealing with the rebellion. Although it maintained a watch on Mullah Mustafa and his family, it became increasingly lax compared to the situation when he was first taken in Mosul. Perhaps they also believed that the Turkish attacks on the Kurds across the border had also discouraged future rebellions. In short, they forgot about Mullah Mustafa, believing that the issue of Kurdish rebellion had been dealt with.

As we will see in coming chapters, it hadn't.

The Lessons of the 1930s

In this chapter, we have seen many of the key phases of Mullah Mustafa Barzani's growth as a leader. We have seen him starting to command troops, acting on behalf of his brother Sheikh Ahmad, leading important segments of the rebellion in the early 1930s, and gradually growing in importance to the point where the Iraqi authorities considered him the second most important target for capture after his brother.

The phase between the end of the First World War and the exiles of the 1930s is crucially important because it is the first time in the historical record that we see Mullah Mustafa Barzani appearing in his own right. Indeed, the story of this period in terms of his life is one of him becoming more and more his own man, taking on greater and greater responsibility within the revolts.

It is also in this period that we start to get a sense of his personality. In particular, it is possible to compare and contrast Mullah Mustafa Barzani in this period with his brother Sheikh Ahmad. Both would lead the Barzani in rebellions at different times, both were brothers, both were in very similar situations. In that much, we can say that the similarities between them were far greater than the differences. Yet if we make an effort, we can see certain distinctions between them in the evidence.

It seems, for example, that Sheikh Ahmad may have taken a more conciliatory approach than his brother. Although he was at the heart of the rebellions of the period, he comes across as in many ways more of a diplomatic figure than a military one. He was willing to pull away after early victories in the rebellions he was involved in, and was willing to put himself in the hands of the authorities in an attempt to resolve the violence. He wasn't prepared to give in, in that the brothers shared a clear sense of resolve, but it seems like Sheikh Ahmad may have been looking for solutions based on talking to a somewhat greater degree than his brother in the period.

Growth to Revolution

Mullah Mustafa Barzani comes across as a much more military figure in the 1920s and 1930s. When we hear about him, it is primarily in a military context, leading groups of peshmerga. Even his capture in Mosul has a military edge to it, obeying an order from his brother to go there, even when he suspected what would happen. This period gives us an opportunity to compare and contrast the two brothers in a way we cannot do with later circumstances.

This period also gives us clues as to Mullah Mustafa Barzani's later history. In many of his later circumstances, we can see an unwillingness to trust authorities offering what appeared to be good deals. That seems like a direct consequence of events in Turkey. We can see a series of escapes to neighbouring countries that mirror the flight to Turkey. We can see tactics and political approaches directly influenced by the events of the 1930s in particular.

By 1939 Mullah Mustafa Barzani was in exile, watched but not entirely imprisoned. He had taken part in two unsuccessful rebellions and had memories of a third. For anyone else, that might have persuaded them to give up. Yet for Mullah Mustafa Barzani, his role was just beginning.

Chapter Four: Revolution

Escape and Return

Mullah Mustafa Barzani remained in Sulaymaniyah until 1943. He was, along with many of his relatives, effectively a prisoner, even though his was a prison constructed out of watchers and limits on his movement rather than bars and stone. He had been moved to at least three different cities in the course of his captivity, and was now at least back in Kurdistan, even if he was still far from Erbil and the heart of his family's influence. Partly, that move back to Kurdistan was a reward for what the authorities saw as good behaviour. In the years preceding 1943, Mullah Mustafa had not sought to escape, nor had he tried to incite rebellion against Baghdad. The authorities there probably thought that after half a dozen years with no attempt to return to revolt, Mullah Mustafa had given up on it. That he had decided his cause was an unwinnable one, or did not want to risk those close to him.

So what changed? Why did Mullah Mustafa choose to escape from his captivity? Why did he return to revolt, when he had shown no sign of doing so for close to a decade? In this, it is easy to make the same mistake that it seems his captors did by assuming that a long period with no signs of imminent revolt meant that Mullah Mustafa had changed his mind. It looks

Revolution

very much like they took elements such as his surrender, the lack of trouble from the tribes, and the failure of Mullah Mustafa to try to contribute to Kurdish revolts elsewhere as evidence that he had no plans to do so in future. Certainly, moving him to Sulaymaniyah from Baghdad seems like a loosening of watchfulness towards him by the Iraqi authorities.

So why not escape in 1939, when he was moved there? Why leave it until 1943? Part of the answer probably lies in a combination of the British putting down revolts in other areas over which they maintained claims and other revolts by my people failing elsewhere. By 1939, revolts in Palestine and Turkey were coming to an end, while the Turks had used particularly brutal tactics against those Kurds in their territory. So soon after other revolts had failed, not only would the authorities probably have been alert to the possibility of revolt, but it must also have seemed unlikely that one could succeed.

What had changed by 1943? The key answer there seems to be the progress of the Second World War. In 1943, the end of the war was still two years away for Britain, and it simply could not afford to commit resources to maintaining its Empire in the face of local uprisings. Committed to fighting Japan across much of East Asia, and German forces through much of the Middle East and Africa, it was simply too distracted for one escape and essentially nationalist uprising to matter very much to it. Combined with Iraqi forces that were already complacent when it came to Mullah Mustafa, it must have seemed like the perfect opportunity for escape. More than that, it must have seemed like the best opportunity to influence Kurdistan's eventual fate. After all, Mullah Mustafa and his brothers had already seen what came of waiting until after a war to try to carve out their people's place in the world.

The influence of the First World War on Mullah Mustafa's reaction to the second probably cannot be overstated here. Remember that it was the aftermath of the First World War that effectively trapped my people in fragments of a number of separate countries. Perhaps Mullah Mustafa believed that another world war could undo what the first had done. Certainly, his experiences as a child during and immediately after the First World War must have taught him that when negotiating with outside powers, it was important to do so from a position where they could not bring their full strength to bear, and to do so before the political realities on the ground changed.

There were other, more immediate reasons, too. Britain had occupied Iraq directly in 1941, rather than relying on the policies of diplomatic intervention that had been their focus there since the start of the 1930s. This seems to have been intended to prevent its occupation by German forces, but must have seemed like a return to the bad old days for Mullah Mustafa and those around him. Wartime conditions also brought with them hyper-inflation and shortages, situations that encouraged dissent within the country. Those may have convinced Mullah Mustafa that the time was ripe for a popular uprising, fuelled by anger at conditions on the ground. The tough economic conditions also had a direct impact on Mullah Mustafa and his family, making it impossible to live on what they had in Sulaymaniyah. In that sense, escape may have been literally the only option for the long term survival of his family.

Whatever Mullah Mustafa's reasoning, in 1943, he escaped from Sulaymaniyah. The exact details of how he did so remain unclear, but it seems likely that his approach simply took advantage of the distractedness of any watchers, moving with speed to safety in the North. This phase of the revolt in the 1940s is interesting, because it involved an initial flight to Iran, where Mullah Mustafa would eventually seek refuge after the failure of the 1970s revolts. He presumably chose Iran because Turkey had already demonstrated its willingness to hand him over to the Iraqi authorities, but it would prove an effective choice as he found both help and shelter there while he prepared for his return.

Revolution

This pattern of leaving Iraq to try to gather support and escape immediate threats represents a continuing theme throughout Mullah Mustafa's life. He had already tried it as an approach with his temporary exile in Turkey, yet this brief foray to Iran in 1943 represented the first time that such an approach proved successful for him. He was not arrested. He was not handed over to Iraq. He was able to prepare in relative safety for what would come next. That combination must have convinced Mullah Mustafa of the effectiveness of the strategy in a way that leaving for Turkey in the early 1930s had not. Indeed, it is possible that if the 1943 escape had gone as badly as the one then, Mullah Mustafa might not have used it as a tactic later on, and might well not have survived all that he did.

Instead of failing though, the escape from Sulaymaniyah to Iran worked perfectly. It allowed Mullah Mustafa to make plans without having to worry about his safety. It allowed him to gather together resources and followers. His stay in Iran was only brief, but it allowed him to prepare for what happened next: a return to Kurdistan.

1943

We know that Mullah Mustafa was warmly received in the Barzan region following his escape. Family and friends were quick to welcome him in this return from exile. Many didn't recognise him after a decade away from the region, but even those who didn't seem to have offered traditionally high levels of hospitality. That lack of recognition seems to have become something of a source of amusement for Mullah Mustafa, who apparently told the story of at least one man talking about the scale of the bounty on his head in front of him, not realising who he was.

It is possible to read quite a bit into these tales of hospitality and non-recognition. They tell us something about the nature

The Idea of Kurdistan

of support in the region at the time and about the growth of Mullah Mustafa's symbolic role even then. That he was given hospitality without being recognised suggests that the hospitality was not itself about the joy with which he was being welcomed back, yet we know that when he was recognised, people generally reacted well to Mullah Mustafa's return.

That they reacted with hospitality, rather than by pointing him in the direction of an army already prepared to rise up, suggests something else. It suggests that if Mullah Mustafa did escape from Sulaymaniyah in the expectation that the time was ripe for a sweeping, popular revolution, he was somewhat mistaken. Although a revolt did happen in time, it happened in stages, essentially as Mullah Mustafa Barzani was able to organise it. People welcomed him home as an exile returning to his homeland more than as a military leader coming to deliver the revolution they had been waiting for.

We can also see something of Mullah Mustafa as a symbol in the stories about people not recognising him. Mullah Mustafa was already, for them, a name with a complex set of connotations, a kind of shorthand for the Kurdish independence movement. They could speak about him, or at least about the idea of him, without having enough information about the real him to recognise him when they saw him. Of course, the same is true for many public figures. I would not want to suggest otherwise. It is entirely the case that with almost any major public figure it might be possible to form an opinion on them without being able to recognise them if they were in the same room. I am suggesting that is the point. By 1943, Mullah Mustafa *was* very definitely a public figure. One for whom the idea behind the man stood for at least as much as the reality.

That symbolic value served to make Mullah Mustafa Barzani's return to his home a major event. If it was met with joy by most of those around him, it was also a cause for concern among those in authority. The Iraqi government (rightly) assumed that any such return would be only the precursor to a wider insurrection, while those surrounding tribes with reasons to hate Barzani and his followers looked for ways that he could be returned to Sulaymaniyah. On a local level at least, and possibly even on a national level, it seemed that there was no one without an opinion on Mullah Mustafa's return.

That return translated into action relatively quickly, but if those around Mullah Mustafa had expected immediate and widespread rebellion, they had to be disappointed by the response. The most optimistic reports on the progress of the rebellion suggest that Mullah Mustafa had around seven hundred fighters within a fortnight, growing to perhaps two thousand within a month. On a scale of local warfare, and even by the standards of previous uprisings, that number probably represented a significant force. By the standards of the forces moving around the region as part of the wider war, however, it was so small as to almost go unnoticed. Even as a percentage of the population of Iraqi Kurdistan, it seems to have been a relatively small number. It certainly wasn't the popular uprising Mullah Mustafa seems to have envisaged.

Instead, probably the best way to characterise the force he managed to raise is as an essentially local one. The numbers involved are consistent with those of previous Barzani forces, and the speed with which he was able to raise them helps to reinforce that idea. This was essentially a force of Barzani peshmerga supplemented by those their allies could spare.

It was not a big enough force to act on a large scale. It could not take on the might of one of the Western powers in open battle, or even a full scale Iraqi army. That necessarily limited both the tactics involved and the scope of the operations Mullah Mustafa had planned. We can see, both from Mullah Mustafa's correspondence and from what happened on the ground, that there was a significant focus on police stations in the early days of the uprising. Mullah Mustafa sought information on how

The Idea of Kurdistan

they were organised and their role in controlling the region. He also organised attacks on a number of them. Although this tactic seems like an unacceptable one to modern eyes, it is worth remembering that these police stations were typically the biggest symbolic step in the extension of Baghdad's reach in the period, that they had been the primary way of extending the central government's power after World War One, and that the police force at the time had a distinct military element to it. Striking against those stations represented the best way of weakening Baghdad's hold on the region at the time.

Significantly, the initial operations against the police stations were relatively bloodless ones. The aim was to capture the existing structures of power within the region rather than to destroy them. The violence only escalated once those initial successes prompted the Baghdad government to try to retaliate. Mullah Mustafa, aware of the relatively small size of his forces, used ambush tactics and well prepared safe points to strike at advancing government forces in battles such as those of Khairzok and Gora Tu. Seventeen police stations were taken in all, leaving government forces in just three areas, while attempts to retaliate against Barzani villages while the peshmerga were occupied failed. The military was brought in to support the police, but for the time being, Mullah Mustafa's forces were able to fight those of the government to a standstill.

This first year of the Kurdish uprising was a success on many levels. It succeeded in taking territory and defeating both police and military forces. It took over key instruments of governmental influence in the region, in the form of the captured police stations. It successfully defended itself against the initial attempts to put it down by striking at the heart of Barzani territory. Those early days were personally successful for Mullah Mustafa as well. He succeeded in forming peshmerga groups with clear command structures and rules of operation. He succeeded in gathering local support for his actions, and in crafting a command structure that led back to him effectively enough to allow him to coordinate the revolt. He was able to avoid being targeted or removed in the ways that had brought down previous insurrections.

And yet we have to say a couple of other things about the revolt in 1943. First, it was relatively small scale. There were battles, but never with more than a hundred or so wounded or killed on either side. The operating size for a peshmerga group was fifteen to thirty men, brought together only for particularly important operations. It was warfare, but it was warfare between a relatively small peshmerga force and governmental forces that had been equally depleted by the requirements of the bigger war around them.

We can also suggest that the popular support for the revolt was probably widespread, but shallow. People did not come out into the streets to support it. They did not join Mullah Mustafa's forces. But nor did they try to turn him in to the authorities or impede him. Indeed, in several cases, the taking of police stations would not have been possible without inside help. Nor would it have been possible to maintain control over the areas the revolt took if the populations had been actively opposed to it. It is probably best to characterise public attitudes in the region, therefore, as broadly supportive, but not actively so.

Finally, I have to say that the 1943 rebellion seems always to have been limited in scope. There was only so much that Mullah Mustafa Barzani could hope to achieve with his forces and only so much time in which to do it. He was only safe while the wider war prevented greater forces from being brought to bear. Mullah Mustafa Barzani must have known this. Therefore, it seems unlikely that the immediate goal of the revolt was to conquer Kurdistan by force. Instead, its goal must have been what eventually happened, which was to force the Iraqi government to the negotiating table.

Talking

Can we, at this distance in history, establish what the different sides hoped to achieve by talking? Inevitably, negotiating parties enter talks with aims in mind: things that they need to achieve, things that they would like to achieve if they can, red lines that they cannot go beyond and things that they wish to stop others achieving. There are reasons that they choose to talk, rather than continuing to fight. What reasons did Mullah Mustafa and the Iraqi government have? What did they want? If we can establish that, then we are in a much better position to explore the extent to which they achieved their aims.

There are difficulties in trying to pinpoint those objectives. Difficulties that other writers on Mullah Mustafa have not always acknowledged. It is easy to impose agendas on the past and say that Mullah Mustafa was already committed to the full cause of Kurdish independence. Or indeed to make generalisations about Iraqi/British intentions that may be true, but may also have more to do with their roles as the 'villains' of Mullah Mustafa's story than with any evidence.

Where can we find the reality of such intentions? Ideally, documents from the time would tell us, but only some of Mullah Mustafa's correspondence has survived and public utterances inevitably owe more to what the speaker was trying to achieve at the time rather than to the reality of their aims. We can look at their overall aims in the long term, but that takes no account of the immediate situation they faced. We can look at what they did, and that is probably the biggest clue, but even that is not perfect.

Some combination of all these things should, however, be able to give us at least an impression of what the different sides were trying to achieve. It is at this point that we should remember that it was not as simple as Mullah Mustafa and the other Barzanis on one side and the Iraqi government on the other. Although those were essentially the sides for the start of the rebellion, by the time negotiations began, there were other pressures to consider. There was the influence of Britain and the needs of the wider World War going on at the same time. There was a broader spectrum of needs brought in by the inhabitants of Kurdistan as the revolt became more general, moving from an essentially Barzani revolt to a Kurdish one.

So what can we say about Mullah Mustafa's aims in the talks? His overarching aims undoubtedly had a free Kurdistan at their heart by this point. All the previous revolts he had been involved with had that as their stated aim, and it continued to be a central plank of his demands in the 1943–45 revolt. Yet while that was certainly one of his long term aims, we can suggest that his immediate ones were probably more limited. The talks were about consolidating the gains made in the initial revolt and protecting them from reprisals. He was undoubtedly aware that there was little or no chance at the time of achieving full independence, and he must have been aware that whichever side eventually came out ahead in the World War, they would have enough strength to put down the revolt if it was still continuing. As such, it seems likely that from Mullah Mustafa's point of view, the talks were about normalising the situation as it stood after the first revolt. About ensuring a level of stability that would make it less likely that the British would want to undo those gains once they were in a position to bring their full strength to bear.

The Iraqi position seems to have been one of clear opposition to Mullah Mustafa Barzani. They saw him as an escaped criminal attacking 'their' territory by taking over their police stations. It was their soldiers and police who had fought against the peshmerga in the revolt's main clashes. Yet at the same time, they had been fought to a standstill, and the Iraqi authorities must have been grateful for the opportunity the talks offered them to avoid further losses.

The intentions of the British were probably heavily influenced by the international situation. They were occupied with the larger threat posed by the Second World War, and so could not afford to commit to a conflict in the region. Yet Kurdistan represented a vital supply route through to the USSR, and so they could not afford to lose it. There was also an issue over the potential for any conflict to cause wider difficulties in the region, as Turkey had yet to commit its troops in 1943. They had to be worried about the potential for revolts to destabilise the region, cutting off access to oil resources needed for the war effort. Stability is probably the key word here. The British needed a stable region to achieve their wider aims, and were prepared to achieve that through concessions if it would work, and superior military force if it would not.

Early Talks

We know that the Iraqi government appointed a number of Kurdish ministers in 1943, and that one of them, Majid Mustafa, was effectively placed in charge of resolving the issue of Kurdistan. In this, it seems that the Iraqi government was starting to understand that the revolt was spreading beyond just a local, tribal issue. If it didn't understand it by the time Majid Mustafa met with Mullah Mustafa Barzani, it certainly began to understand it afterwards. Mullah Mustafa effectively demanded the creation of an independent Kurdish state with only tenuous links to Iraq. Indeed, his demands read almost like a description of the current Kurdistan.

The Iraqi government countered with an offer that amounted to the re-imposition of its authority over Kurdistan, but with the return of Sheikh Ahmad to Kurdistan and a general amnesty for most of those who had been involved in the revolt, excepting any government officials who had joined the revolt. It was in many ways a classic move to put down a revolt, banking on the idea that ordinary people would desert it if given the opportunity to do so safely and return to normal. To reinforce that idea of normalisation, the Iraqi government had food distributed in Kurdistan, allowed Sheikh Ahmad to return, and persuaded Mullah Mustafa to visit Baghdad to discuss the agreement.

What followed was a curious in between time, where it seemed that both sides were hunting for a resolution, but neither was confident that one could be found. It was a time of building support and jockeying for position, while Mullah Mustafa sought to build up his alliances amongst the tribal leaders of Kurdistan, and the Iraqi government sought to sever those ties. Neither was prepared to publicly accept what the other was willing to offer, and there is a sense of both sides trying to build a position of strength from which to negotiate further, while being aware of the potential for more violence.

More than that, there is a sense of both sides attempting to cast the revolt in different lights. Mullah Mustafa, perhaps inspired by the work of the literate and persuasive Hiwa Party, focused increasingly clearly on presenting the revolt as a popular revolution with the aim of full independence for Kurdistan. He tried to emphasise the ways it had gone beyond a simple matter for the Barzanis and become one for all Kurds. The Iraqi government and the British tried to do the opposite and presented the revolt as a small, essentially tribal matter in which the wider people of Kurdistan should not get involved.

The Failure of the Talks

Why did this in between state give way to open conflict again? Why did the talks fail and the violence resume? There have been writers who have laid all the blame for this at the door of the British, saying that they wanted violence all along and were merely waiting for an opportunity to bring their forces to bear. There is perhaps some truth in that, inasmuch as the renewal of the violence coincided with the freeing up of British forces in 1945 as Germany fell.

Yet there were also probably other factors. A crucial one was a lack of understanding between the two sides. The British consistently cast the revolt as no more than a simple tribal matter, and their actions suggest that at least sections of them may have believed it in truth, rather than it just being a convenient position for negotiations. They seemed to be incapable of understanding that this revolt potentially represented something different than those that had gone before. Perhaps that was because earlier revolts had used some of the same language, talking about general Kurdish freedom even while they sought to make essentially local gains.

It also seems that Mullah Mustafa may have underestimated the Iraqi and British sides. Perhaps he had backed himself into a corner by portraying the revolt as a general one, but he consistently refused to settle for anything less than the full implementation of the demands he had made, even though those were not the offer the Iraqi government had countered with. Yes, this was a period of the breakup of Empire, but realistically, neither the British nor the Iraqi governments were going to agree to cede Kurdistan in 1945.

Yet that was a recipe for stalemate, not violence. So what changed? That was simple. Mullah Mustafa Barzani made a bold move that, had it paid off, might have resulted in a free Kurdistan. Instead, it triggered a conflict he could not win. He formed what became known as the Freedom Committee.

1945

The events of 1945 represented a significant return to a rebellion that had in some senses been dying down over the preceding months. The formation of the Freedom Committee was a major step, which in many ways decided the future course of the revolt.

What was the Freedom Committee? At its most basic, we can say that it was an attempt to organise all aspects of the

Revolution

struggle for a free and independent Kurdistan under a single umbrella group. It was an attempt by Mullah Mustafa Barzani to focus the efforts of the disparate groups working with him and to coordinate their actions for maximum effect, as well as ensuring that they did not get in one another's way. It also represented an interesting attempt to put the revolt on a basis that had less to do with tribal affiliations than with general political will.

I believe that was a crucial step along the path that led to the modern Kurdistan, and one that was fundamental to re-shaping the terms of the revolts within Iraq. Previously, there had been attempts by the Hiwa Party to express a political desire for independence, and those attempts were certainly important. They represented a transition from individual tribal revolts to a more widespread sense of Kurdish nationalism. Yet ultimately, the Hiwa Party's members were mostly educated intellectuals, divorced from the day-to-day business of the revolts.

The Freedom Committee's crucial step was in joining together the military actions of the peshmerga rebels with the political statements and will represented by the Hiwa Party. For the first time, it connected together the military force of the revolts with a sense of general Kurdish political will that went beyond simple tribal issues. It sought to make the revolt more than a Barzani one, turning it into a matter for the whole of Kurdistan's people. It both created a general basis for support of the peshmerga and backed up the political desire for an independent nation with the force to be taken seriously.

On an immediate level, it is easy to see that Mullah Mustafa Barzani was concerned to counter the attempts by the Iraqi government to portray his revolt as essentially local and tribal. By crafting the Freedom Committee and seeking links with the Hiwa Party, he sought to emphasise the larger nature of this revolt, and also to avoid the kind of isolation that he knew from previous experience could quickly lead to defeat.

This kind of transition was also crucial in the longer term, however, and was in many ways the most important thing the 1945 revolt achieved. It created a framework for future revolts, showing them how to produce clear lines of communication and command, but it also made them about freedom for the whole of Kurdistan, rather than improved circumstances for a particular tribe or cluster of tribes. It even started to create some elements that would continue even after the creation of the modern Kurdistan, including the strong links between the peshmerga and the civilian government.

Yet we can also see with the benefit of hindsight that the creation of the Freedom Committee was a dangerous move. Precisely because it started to place the revolt on a broader and more interconnected footing, it demonstrated to the Iraqi and British authorities that they were no longer facing a minor tribal revolt that could be ignored. The very fact of its creation demanded action from those authorities if they wanted to keep Kurdistan as a part of Iraq. Creating the Freedom Committee helped to prepare Kurdistan for the struggle that Mullah Mustafa Barzani must have seen coming, and it helped to turn the revolt into something broader than it had been, but it also punctured the fragile peace between the sides. It showed the Iraqis and the British that the issue of Kurdistan was not going to fade away if they left it alone.

Their immediate response to this, and to the seizure of more police stations, was an escalation to what they termed at the time 'military manoeuvres'. The British Ambassador effectively demanded the cessation of the revolt and the acceptance of Iraqi military forces throughout the province, while Mullah Mustafa took the opportunity to reiterate demands for an independent Kurdistan. An attack on Walli Beg by the police brought a further round of demands and counter demands, with the positions the same. The British required the immediate

Revolution

cessation of revolt, while Mullah Mustafa stipulated the freedoms he had demanded in 1943. Each must have known while making their demands that the other would never agree, and yet it seems that both felt it necessary to go through with that formal process before any further violence.

Essentially, the reasons for that seem to come down to the symbolic value of the demands, and to an awareness that the conflict was being watched by the wider world in spite of the continuing war elsewhere. The British ambassador may well have been genuinely attempting to bring a peaceful end to the revolt, although if so, he was naive in misunderstanding the depth of feeling in Kurdistan. His employers, however, must have been aware that they no longer lived in a world where Great Powers could just go to war because they felt like it. They needed the situation to be clear.

Mullah Mustafa probably also needed the situation to be clear, both to a Kurdish population who needed to see him standing up for their interests rather than giving in, and to a wider international audience. We have seen in earlier chapters the way Turkey was able to bring about changes to the promises made to Kurdistan following World War One, simply by continuing to fight until the Allies gave it what it wanted to avoid further war. With World War Two coming to a close, Mullah Mustafa Barzani may well have seen an opportunity to employ the same tactics to redraw the maps back in Kurdistan's favour. Certainly, he tried to create a sense of the rightness of the Kurdish position by demanding that the British implement what they had agreed to in 1943 and give Kurdistan a measure of independence. That they had not actually agreed to this, and had only made a lesser counter offer, did not matter at this point.

The two sides had essentially irreconcilable positions. Iraq wanted Kurdistan to remain within it, and Mullah Mustafa would settle for nothing less than its independence. The period after the 1943 revolt had been one of both sides trying to grind down the other's resolve, but now it seemed that both knew that only military action was likely to resolve the issue.

That was a problem for Mullah Mustafa Barzani, because now, with World War Two coming to an end, the British military was free to act against him.

Success

Perhaps the strangest thing about the resumption of violence in 1945 is just how successful the Kurdish forces were at first. The Iraqi government resolved to occupy the Barzan region, capture Mullah Mustafa and put down the revolt in August 1945, declaring martial law and the advancement of elements of the first and second divisions. On paper, the government made it sound like no more than an easy police action.

Yet it didn't prove to be that way. There were a number of reasons for this. On the Kurdish side, those ranged from the prepared positions of the peshmerga, the advantages of the terrain and the tactical experience of leaders like Mullah Mustafa Barzani and Mohammad Siddique Barzani. On the Iraqi side, there were problems stemming from the World War that included a lack of soldiers and weapons, a reliance on the RAF trying to solve the problem through bombardment, and a lack of support on the ground from the populace for the government's actions. Declaring martial law in the cities of Mosul and Erbil was one thing, but policing it without the support of the inhabitants was quite another.

As with so many occasions in these complex counter insurgency campaigns, it is hard to say with any accuracy how many fighters there were on each side. We know the units that were involved on the Iraqi side, but not what their strength on the ground was, how many men they took in support from the police forces, or the real extent of the air support available to them from the British. On my people's side, the numbers are confused.

Revolution

Reports from 1943 suggested about 3,000 fighters, but we then find numbers such as 5,000 and 10,000 being given for 1945. My guess would be that these numbers are no more than the broadest estimates, designed to suggest generalities about the rebellion. Where the numbers before were kept small to emphasise the heroic nature of the victories when they occurred, these numbers seem to have been produced to suggest the more general nature of the support. Yet when it is possible to suggest that the total forces numbered 5,000 but there were 10,000 in position along one front, it becomes impossible to take those estimates as representing any kind of reality on the ground.

What we can say is that the violence in 1945 was almost certainly on a larger scale than in 1943, since it seems to be generally agreed that both the Iraqi government and Mullah Mustafa Barzani's forces were able to bring more troops to bear.

We know that the Kurdish forces achieved early victories. They were able to drive back early attempts to advance up the slopes of Mount Qalander and Bradost, ambushing government forces as they over-extended on the 5th of September at the gorge known as Maidan Morik. There, according to Mullah Mustafa's account, they managed to inflict hundreds of casualties and capture supplies while suffering relatively few casualties in return.

Indeed, that seems to have been the pattern for the early actions of August and September 1945. Although the government forces sought to engage peshmerga on numerous fronts, the reports were consistently of low casualties for the Kurdish fighters. While we could suggest that those low reported numbers had a lot to do with propaganda and the need to maintain morale, they also say something about the tactics the Kurdish forces tried to employ. They avoided direct conflict where they could, trying to work with ambush tactics and

The Idea of Kurdistan

striking only when they were able to do so with relatively low chances of counter attack. In a period where the Iraqi and British forces had just been a part of the biggest conventional war the world had seen, such unconventional warfare must have come as a shock.

Mullah Mustafa commanded the fighters on the Aqra front himself. His primary tactics, if the events of the 4th and 12th of September are representative, seem to have been to try to use the terrain of the mountains to encircle the advancing Iraqi forces as they sought to take villages in the Nahla valley, only withdrawing when subjected to aerial bombardment. In both cases, the Kurdish forces were successful in capturing supplies from the enemy as well as inflicting losses. Given the nature of the warfare, the acquisition of such supplies was crucial to maintaining any resistance.

Defeat

Why, if Mullah Mustafa Barzani's forces were able to win battles so decisively, was the revolt ultimately unsuccessful? If you were to tell someone about the battles without any of their context, then surely they would believe that the Kurdish forces were on the verge of victory? So why did the revolt end with Barzani and his followers fleeing the country to avoid capture?

There are two elements to this. One is an issue of reporting. Views on the rebellion from 1943–45 have been predominantly from pro-Kurdish points of view. As such, it is likely that victories and the scale of enemy losses have been highlighted, while defeats and losses among the Kurdish forces have been minimised. Certainly, it seems that the lack of records makes it impossible to know for sure what losses the Kurdish forces really sustained.

Yet more of it has to do with matters beyond the individual battles. The events of 1945 were a classic case of winning battles but losing the war. The Kurdish forces were able to achieve

Revolution

victory in individual engagements, but they could not prevent the diplomatic pressure between those engagements that ate away at their forces. They could not prevent the British from winning over surrounding tribes, could not stop sustained aerial bombardment, and could not take action to decisively win the conflict.

Each of those bears further examination. We know that the British and Iraqi governments maintained sustained diplomatic and legal pressure to try to fragment Mullah Mustafa Barzani's forces. Their scale and strength came largely from his own diplomatic efforts in convincing surrounding tribes that the conflict was one for the whole of Kurdistan. Yet pressure from the British in particular was able to persuade a number of tribes to turn against the revolt, persuading them either that it was a Barzani matter that they should not be involved in, or that it was actively harming their tribes by placing Mullah Mustafa Barzani ahead of their own leaders. It was a move that was able to both pull forces away from the revolt and provide the Iraqi army with guides who could potentially take away some of the peshmerga's advantages when it came to the terrain.

Then there were the attempts to bring officers and police back into the ranks of the Iraqi armed forces, away from those of the Kurdish forces. By promising them that they would not face sanctions, the British and Iraqi authorities sought to make it easy for them to leave the revolt. The extent to which this strategy was successful is unknown, but it seems likely that the more difficult the situation became, the more able it was to achieve results.

The attacks on Barzani targets by the RAF also had a role to play. They allowed the British and Iraqis to inflict casualties on the Barzanis without opening themselves up to risk, but more importantly, they allowed them to attack targets throughout Barzani held areas. It was a strategy that effectively meant that nowhere was safe.

The Idea of Kurdistan

Worse, it was compounded by the essentially defensive nature of the war the peshmerga had to fight. Light, irregular forces might be dangerous in the mountains of Kurdistan, but they are not designed for holding territory, and they certainly could not mount sustained offensive operations in 1945. They were limited to effectively defensive warfare, trying to ambush advancing forces as they came into Kurdish territory. That worked well against light, conventional ground forces, but it left them at a significant disadvantage against air assault or heavier forces.

The biggest factor in the failure of the revolt, however, was almost certainly the timing. Logistically, a revolt in autumn and the beginning of winter made things difficult. While it held the promise of forcing back the attacking Iraqi forces, it also meant that there was the threat of running out of supplies while coming under attack in the longer term. Worse for the revolt, September 1945 finally brought with it the official end of World War Two. With that ending came a new freedom for British forces to add their weight to operations, and Mullah Mustafa must have been aware of it.

We can reasonably say that the rebellion was not defeated militarily, but at the same time, all those involved must have been aware that it eventually would be. That was why, in late September, Mullah Mustafa Barzani finally took the decision to leave Iraq with his followers.

Chapter Five: Republic of Mahabad

Different writers have treated the Republic of Mahabad in very different ways. For some, it was a success story. A precursor of the current region of Kurdistan, and perhaps a sign that it has the potential to be a free country in its own right. For others, it is a historical blip, equivalent to the Paris Commune of 1871; a short-lived experiment that espoused many interesting ideals but ultimately failed too quickly to have had a real impact on the future. What is the truth? Is the Republic of Mahabad just an empty symbol, or did it play a real role in the creation of modern Kurdistan? What impact did Mullah Mustafa Barzani have on the Republic, and perhaps just as importantly, what impact did it have on him? These are all questions we have to answer if we are really going to understand this complex episode in Mullah Mustafa's life.

The Birth of the Republic

The first point worth making about the Mahabad Republic was that it was not Mullah Mustafa Barzani's idea. Although we will be primarily discussing his role in it here, and although he certainly came to play an important role in it, he was not responsible for its creation. Indeed, while it was being created in Iranian territory, his focus was firmly on the north of Iraq.

The Idea of Kurdistan

Instead, the Mahabad Republic was the creation of Qazi Muhammad, a charismatic Iranian lawyer and political leader responsible for the creation of the PDKI (Kurdish Democratic Party of Iran). He was a few years older than Mullah Mustafa, and based in Iran rather than Iraq, but it is worth taking a moment to consider the similarities between the two. Here we have two men, working at the same time in two separate countries, who were doing many of the same things, trying to create a homeland for my people. Qazi Muhammad sought to do it by carving out new territory under the protection of the Soviet Union rather than by declaring traditional lands independent unilaterally, but the effects were similar.

Indeed, to a casual observer, the two must have looked like mirror images of one another, separated only by a few years and the quirks of politics that had placed them on different sides of the Iranian border. Both were, by this point, leaders of political parties dedicated to independence for Kurdistan. Both were in direct opposition to countries whose borders had been 'settled' after World War One. Both made use of their families in key political roles, placing an emphasis on it that continues even today. Both made similar demands for the use of the Kurdish language, and pushed broader social agendas alongside their political ones, modernising even as they sought a return to a past where my people had ruled themselves.

Yet closer up, it is easy to see some of the differences. Qazi Muhammad was a lawyer, an essentially urban and educated man, whose first thought in setting up his republic seems to have been contact with the Soviets, and whose approach seems to have been largely political. Mullah Mustafa, as we have seen, was much more of a military man, spending most of his life either fighting or living with the consequences of those fights. His approach at that time was centred on armed rebellion, generally not backed from outside, with political elements

Republic of Mahabad

perhaps secondary even though he did make attempts at diplomacy between tribes.

Those differences may ultimately have played a role in causing tensions between the two, but they also helped to create two slightly different rebellions. The Republic of Mahabad feels like it was a different kind of thing to the area in the north of Iraq that Mullah Mustafa's rebellion had attempted to declare free. For one thing, it was probably genuinely free of outside influence on a level that the Barzani lands never were. The peshmerga of Mullah Mustafa's rebellion could strike against government forces, could melt into the mountains before retaliation could come, and could make a nominal claim to swathes of territory, but they could not stop consistent bombing by the RAF. They could not stand and hold territory against armour or artillery. They could free areas from control by the Iraqi government by attacking police stations and taking government buildings, but they were not in a position to create a secure mini-state, on the lines of the Republic of Mahabad. One represented a 'freeing from' an existing state of repression, while the other represented more of an act of creation, crafting a new country within the confines of Iran.

Of course, this may be somewhat uncharitable. It is entirely likely that, had his revolt succeeded, Mullah Mustafa would have created a free Kurdistan. That he did not, while Qazi Muhammad briefly did, is a measure more of the relative support that they had, and the success that their revolts temporarily met, rather than of a difference in their aims. Indeed, it is entirely possible that the two may have indirectly influenced one another. The Republic of Mahabad was only officially declared at the start of 1946, but Qazi Muhammad and his supporters had been running Mahabad since 1941, and something resembling a free republic came into being in 1945. It does not seem to have been the culmination of a long revolt, in the way that Mullah Mustafa's declaration of the Freedom

The Idea of Kurdistan

Committee was, but instead seems to have been the outpouring of a movement that was kept carefully underground until then. It seems entirely possible that hearing about Mullah Mustafa's attempt to create an independent Kurdistan in the south might have influenced Qazi Muhammad to go through with his plans to create one further north.

I am not claiming that this was the only influence on Qazi Muhammad, of course. The existence of the political machinery of the PDKI suggests that this was a move that had been in the offing for some time, while in many ways the whole *point* of Mullah Mustafa Barzani's story is that he did not have a monopoly on the desire for independence. We can, moreover, see *both* Mullah Mustafa's revolt and Qazi Muhammad's setting up of the Mahabad Republic as a part of a larger outpouring of nationalist feeling in the region at the end of World War Two. We must remember that Azerbaijan chose that moment to try to gain independence from Iran as well, and that in many ways, this may have been the biggest influence on the Mahabad Republic.

The evidence certainly points to it. The creation of the Mahabad Republic coincided too well with the creation of Soviet Azerbaijan for it to be otherwise. More than that, there is evidence that Qazi Muhammad was sent by the Soviets to talk to the Azerbaijanis when he sought help with his own uprising. Indeed, the history strongly suggests that the Soviets were working under the impression that the Mahabad Republic would eventually join with Azerbaijan, and were annoyed when it did not. Even the principles set out by Qazi Muhammad for the new republic list maintaining strong relations with their Azerbaijani brothers alongside key elements such as the adoption of the Kurdish language and the appointment only of locally born people to official roles.

In that sense, it is almost possible to suggest that the creation of the Mahabad Republic rode on the coat tails of Azerbaijan's

Republic of Mahabad

revolution. To outsiders, and probably to the Soviets in particular, this new Kurdish state was a useful bonus, rather than the main point. Yet for my people, it was the first time in modern times that they had ever had their own state. In that, Qazi Muhammad achieved something that not even Mullah Mustafa had succeeded in doing. Even if Mullah Mustafa Barzani and Qazi Muhammad later had their differences, we must applaud Qazi Muhammad for that moment.

The 3,000

In the previous chapter, I talked about Mullah Mustafa Barzani's decision to withdraw from the fight against the British and Iraqi forces that threatened to overwhelm his people. There were undoubtedly many elements involved in that decision. There was the end of the Second World War and the threat that posed in terms of more troops being available to fight against his forces. There was the approach of winter. There was betrayal by those he had considered to be his allies, as the British and Iraqi authorities maintained a consistent programme of trying to persuade Kurdish tribes that they were being dragged into what the British portrayed as a purely Barzani rebellion. There were the long term advantages their opposition possessed in aspects such as air support.

Yet most of these factors had either been in play throughout the revolt, or could have been resisted for at least a few more months. Mullah Mustafa Barzani's forces had just won victories when he decided that it was the right time to leave. Undoubtedly, the official end of World War Two played a huge part in that, but it also seems reasonable to suggest that the founding of the Mahabad Republic had a part to play.

Mullah Mustafa Barzani wanted a homeland for his people. His declared aims included a Kurdish state, where Kurdish was the main language and Kurds had the opportunity to have a major say in their own governance, and freedom from the

The Idea of Kurdistan

British/Iraqi rule he had grown up under. Until September 1945, it must have seemed to him that the only way to achieve those aims was by fighting for control of the provinces where his family had lived for so long. His forces were engaged in fighting a long, on and off war because it seemed like there was no other option.

The creation of the Mahabad Republic, however, meant that everything he had been trying to achieve for so long existed, just not in the place he had thought it would come. Hearing reports of this new Kurdistan coming into being in the North of Iran, hearing that it was actually backed by the Soviets, and was thus likely to be stable in a way that a country fighting against the British could not be, surely Mullah Mustafa must have decided that it was the future for him and his people? While there was no other option, they fought. Once there was another option, they took that option before the overwhelming force of the returning British army could destroy them.

If we suggest that the withdrawal from Kurdistan was a response to circumstances in late 1945, then it seems likely that Mullah Mustafa did not have much time in which to plan it. Yet there can be no doubt that this *was* a well-planned withdrawal. It was not a hasty or mindless flight to safety for a few people. Instead, it was a staged pulling back that moved step by step, taking with it as many as three thousand other people. Why so many? Part of the answer to that is the scale of the revolt, and the number of people who had to be kept safe now that it was done. Previous revolts had brought with them imprisonments, exiles, and even executions. When this was the largest revolt to date against the Iraqi government, Mullah Mustafa must have assumed that the retaliation at its end would be at least as great.

Another explanation must be the tone of the march to Mahabad. This was not simply a defensive withdrawal, but a mass exodus. It was not simply about getting a few fighters

Republic of Mahabad

away from British and Iraqi forces by slipping across the border or into the mountains where they could not follow. It wasn't about slipping away for a little while until they could come back to their villages later. Instead, it was about moving entire families to new homes and new lives. It wasn't about escaping a failed attempt to produce a homeland, but about populating the one that had been created.

The scale and nature of the withdrawal meant that it had to be well planned. So did another factor: the lingering threat of attack from the tribes who had been persuaded to go over to the Iraqis, in whole or in part. Ordinarily, the British and Iraqi forces would not have known the mountains well enough to represent a continuing threat to the withdrawing Kurdish forces. Nor would they generally have sought to attempt cross border action in a world where the Cold War was just starting to take shape, and where the Soviet Union's interest in Iran was clear. Yet the ability of the British to persuade other tribes to abandon the revolt and join up with the Iraqi forces meant that Mullah Mustafa Barzani had to be careful. Families attempting to reach the Mahabad Republic were potentially under threat the whole way there, both along the roads leading to the republic and from the rear as they started to move. If the peshmerga had withdrawn too quickly, they would have left their families vulnerable to attack.

Instead, we know that Mullah Mustafa Barzani took the time to secure both the route his people would take to get to the Mahabad Republic and the space behind the families who were leaving. The extent to which this was necessary is hard to judge. We know that fighting continued while the Kurdish forces left, but it seems that much of it was aimed at re-taking the positions they had captured earlier in the revolt. We know that the RAF continued sporadic bombardment even as Mullah Mustafa Barzani's forces retreated, but in the absence of heavy ground support, we can only view this as a tactic of harassment designed

The Idea of Kurdistan

to create fear, rather than as a genuine effort to destroy the retreating Barzanis.

Indeed, the nature of the Iraqi forces' actions suggests that they were content to let Mullah Mustafa and his people leave. They moved forward in several areas only after his peshmerga had left, burning villages once they were empty but mostly not moving into ones that were still occupied. That might have had something to do with them trying to avoid running into rear-guard actions. However, the combination of tactics employed by the Iraqi forces seems to have been aimed more at keeping my people moving and preventing them from returning than at destroying them utterly. It was almost as though the Iraqi government of the time accepted that the best way to get rid of Mullah Mustafa and his revolt was to allow him to leave for this new Kurdish land in the North. Certainly, it seems to have been the most efficient way for them to achieve the aim of control over Iraqi Kurdistan.

The British and Iraqis weren't the only ones who seem to have allowed the march to Mahabad. Several writers have suggested that the Soviet Union and Iranians must have been aware of, and complicit in, such a mass movement of people through Iran. That seems likely. Certainly, it seems impossible that any country today would not react to an armed force moving through its territory in such numbers if it knew about it, and it seems unfeasible that any competent military would not know. So if we accept that the Iranians knew, why did they allow the former rebels to travel to Mahabad in safety? Given the way Iran later crushed the republic, it seems odd that they would do such a thing. It makes little sense that they would allow a well-armed, battle seasoned force of peshmerga to join up with Qazi Muhammad and his project.

Why would they do that? Again, there are only limited possibilities. Either they did not know, which as I have suggested seems unlikely, they did not care, which seems just as problematic, or outside pressure prevented them from acting. Which means that the Soviets must have been fully aware of the withdrawal. Indeed, they may even have seen it as a positive thing, because of what Mullah Mustafa Barzani could bring to the Mahabad Republic.

Mullah Mustafa Barzani in the Republic

What impact did Mullah Mustafa Barzani have on the Mahabad Republic? It's an important question, but one that people seem to have been reluctant to explore. Perhaps that is because it seems like a relatively small part of his story, or perhaps it is because the evidence is limited when the new state was swept away so quickly. Perhaps there are even those who are worried about exploring the differences of opinion that existed between Mullah Mustafa and Qazi Muhammad. Yet it is an area that must be explored, if we are to understand not only the life of Mullah Mustafa Barzani, but also the details of the Mahabad Republic.

Let us start with the obvious point: Mullah Mustafa and his people were newcomers, coming into an existing state. He did not help to create the Mahabad Republic. He was not responsible for its political structures, its initial values, or its foundation. I say that both because there is a danger in any biography such as this of ascribing the leading role in all things to its subject, and because there are aspects of the Mahabad Republic (such as its strong Soviet connections) that Mullah Mustafa probably wouldn't have chosen had he been responsible for them. It is worth remembering that Mullah Mustafa Barzani cannot be held responsible for things that happened there before he arrived.

So what about after he arrived? Initially, the answer there was that he didn't do much, both because he was occupied with ensuring that the families who had come with him found places to stay in Iran, and because the Soviets had directly asked him not to. Politically, Mullah Mustafa Barzani was dangerous in 1945–46. He had just fought a very bitter, very public revolt against the British, and now he was going to join up with this new nation, against which Iran was already protesting. Britain was complaining about his involvement in it, suggesting both that the Soviet Union was trying to build an empire for itself in the region, and that it wasn't appropriate for them to give shelter to a man the British still regarded at that time as a criminal.

There may have been another reason that they asked Mullah Mustafa not to try to become too prominent. From 1941 to 1945, Mahabad had been drifting gently along under Qazi Muhammad and his supporters, with Soviet support, while the rest of the world was too caught up in war to notice. They had been at least reasonably content to exist within the political structures of Iran, and if the Soviets had any expectations for their future, it was that Mahabad would eventually form a part of the Soviet Republic of Azerbaijan. Mullah Mustafa Barzani had consistently and openly stood for an independent Kurdistan, free from outside interference. The Soviets must have known that he would no more have settled for them ruling over his people than he had settled for the British or Iraqis doing so. In asking him to keep a low profile, they were asking him not to cause trouble for them as much as anything else.

Yet it seems that ultimately, that was impossible for Mullah Mustafa. He was not a man capable of settling into a quiet retirement while others controlled things around him. His contribution to the Republic of Mahabad seems to have come on three levels, one that most commentators mention, and a couple of others that, surprisingly, do not seem to have been fully explored. The one that writers often comment on is the level of military organisation Mullah Mustafa brought to the Republic of Mahabad. In the Barzanis who had just fought an extended revolt against the Iraqis and British, he brought with him a ready-made military force for the region. He brought with him a knowledge of military tactics and training that gave the Mahabad Republic at least a chance to defend itself, and allowed it to stave off Iranian attempts to destroy it, at least while Soviet support still prevented them from advancing in full force.

It is hard to underestimate the importance of that role. If Qazi Muhammad was the civil leader of the Mahabad Republic, Mullah Mustafa Barzani was very much its military one. This points to a second element to Mullah Mustafa Barzani's impact on the Mahabad republic, which was his symbolic role within it. The soldiers fighting for the Mahabad Republic were told to treat orders from their commanders as though they came directly from Mullah Mustafa, while he spent as much time in early 1946 giving speeches and being seen by troops as helping to develop military strategy. That is not to say that he did not play a crucial role in that military organisation, he helped to put key structures together, brought weapons and implemented training, but I would like to suggest that the symbolic role was in some ways even more important.

Why? Because ultimately, the Republic of Mahabad's armed forces consisted of a few thousand men. Enough to stop a small force, even a division, but against the full might of Iran's army, they were always going to be overwhelmed by sheer numbers. Yet Mullah Mustafa was able to get them to stand and fight anyway. He was able to get them to fight right up until the odds became that overwhelming. He understood his role as the leader of the revolt in Iraq. He understood that people could gain morale just from his presence. Indeed, because of all the ideas he had put forward in the course of his revolt back in Iraqi Kurdistan, I would like to suggest that his very presence changed the nature of the Mahabad Republic.

That is the third way Mullah Mustafa Barzani had an impact on the Mahabad Republic. He changed some of the expectations of it. He changed some of the things it sought to achieve. Before his arrival, it had been going along quite nicely as just one semi-independent region that had merely drifted away from Iran a little. The expectation seems to have been that it would eventually drift into the political orbit of Azerbaijan. Yet in 1946, just months after Mullah Mustafa's arrival, the Mahabad Republic stopped drifting. It declared itself an independent state, aimed at becoming exactly the kind of Kurdish homeland Mullah Mustafa envisioned, and seemed to have no obvious plans to do more than declare a kind of vague confraternity with Azerbaijan.

Yes, there are other possible explanations for the declaration of the republic. The revolution in Azerbaijan undoubtedly played a huge role. Yet the Republic of Mahabad did not officially declare itself then. Nor did it seek the kind of independence that it eventually chose for itself at that point. Instead, it was only after Mullah Mustafa Barzani's arrival that these things happened. It is only after his arrival that it shifted from being quite a limited ongoing project to one that demanded full independence immediately. Can this truly be a coincidence? I do not believe it can. Mullah Mustafa Barzani *must* have had an influence on the shape the Republic of Mahabad took after his arrival. What it became mirrors what he was trying to achieve with the Barzani revolt far too closely for it to be otherwise.

Life in the Republic

What was everyday life like in the Mahabad Republic? To some extent, the answer to that depends on the period we are talking about. If we are talking about the initial phase from 1941 to 1945, then we must remember that we are talking about a situation where people's daily lives had already been disrupted by war, and where the conflict between the warring powers overshadowed any changes being made in the background. Qazi

Republic of Mahabad

Muhammad's people might have been working to build a level of autonomy, but daily life was probably taken up with the more immediate issues of food, shelter, and the potential threat from the war around them. It was not normal, in the sense of being the same as their lives before, but under the circumstances, it seems likely that no one expected anything to be normal.

The phase that concerns us, however, is the one after the arrival of Mullah Mustafa Barzani and his followers. To them, the Mahabad Republic must have initially seemed like a wonderful opportunity to resume normal lives. They spread out through the villages of the region, either being taken in by Iranian families or finding space for themselves. After the constant threat of bombardment and attack that had been present during the revolt back in Kurdistan, it must have seemed almost peaceful.

Yet it probably would not have seemed normal. The Barzanis were far from their homes, and the arrangements made for them, while hospitable, also must have seemed worryingly temporary. They must have known that being scattered throughout the region like that, relying on the kindness of strangers, was not an arrangement that could function long term. They weren't even sure where they fitted into the political arrangements around them, since Qazi Muhammad already had his political party and government in place. Rather than being at the heart of the new country they sought to create, as they had been in Kurdistan, they were suddenly incomers trying to find a place in an existing society.

Even the principles of the republic, when it was officially declared in 1946, seemed to emphasise that. While most of them, such as the use of Kurdish as the official language and its teaching in schools, would have been welcome to Mullah Mustafa Barzani's followers, there was also a declaration that all officials would be chosen from the local area in which they worked. While it was probably a declaration aimed at ensuring that those positions would be filled by Kurds rather than by officials sent in from the heart of Iran, it also had the incidental effect of excluding the newly arrived Barzanis from local posts.

As for life after the declaration of the republic in 1946, that would most definitely not have been normal for the majority of the inhabitants. They were engaged in conflict with Iran almost from the moment of the declaration, fighting low level running battles to defend territory, but also fighting much larger battles to counter Iranian army garrisons at Saqqiz, Baneh and Sardasht. While there is a case for saying that such conflict had become normal for a people who had been engaged in revolt against the British and Iraqis for so long, it was certainly a long way from the life they had come there for.

The forces Mullah Mustafa had brought with him found themselves among the first called up into the military of the new republic, suggesting that in many ways, their lives did not change when they made their journey to Mahabad. They went from fighting one numerically superior foe over the future of a potential homeland to fighting another with only the barest of breaks. Worse, this time it was in territory they did not know, and in circumstances that they could not fully control.

There were also other problems from day to day. Food was initially adequate, thanks both to the resources of the region and support coming through Soviet held Azerbaijan. As time wore on however, and as the international community put pressure on the Soviet Union not to interfere in Iran, food grew scarce. The Mahabad Republic had a dilemma in that respect when it came to the Barzanis. On one hand, they represented vital additional troops to defend the newly formed state. Troops with combat experience and skilled leaders such as Mullah Mustafa. On the other hand, their extra numbers meant that food would run out more quickly. Most writers seem to agree that the pressure of these extra numbers caused resentment among the indigenous population of the Mahabad

Republic of Mahabad

region. Those extra numbers also meant that other resources, such as medicine, were scarce, and disease spread quickly during the conflict with Iran.

The exact numbers who died are, as with so many of those in this period, hard to determine accurately. One estimate suggests that more than two thousand of those who had come with Mullah Mustafa died in a typhoid epidemic in 1946. While consistent with the kind of damage that disease can do, and while it seems certain that only a few hundred followers eventually escaped Mahabad with Mullah Mustafa Barzani when the republic eventually fell, it seems likely that this is more of a general estimate than a precise count. The source may potentially be including battlefield casualties in that number, since it is careful to point out on several occasions the way the Barzanis took no casualties while taking on whole Iranian divisions, which doesn't seem entirely realistic.

Whatever the ultimate causes of their casualties, we can be certain that from the start of 1946, the Barzanis found that their life in the Mahabad Republic was worse than anything they had endured in Kurdistan. Perhaps Mullah Mustafa Barzani saw this, because it certainly seems like he was making plans aimed at an eventual return. The foundation of the PDK in 1946, while obviously a crucial moment in the political history of modern Kurdistan, also points to an intention to return to Kurdistan on Mullah Mustafa's part. It suggests that by then, if it wasn't all along, the Mahabad Republic had become less a place to build a new life than simply one in which to rest before returning to the fight for his people's more traditional lands. The logic here is simple, but hard to resist. If Mullah Mustafa had been intending to stay in the Mahabad Republic permanently, then he would have had no need of a political organisation back in Iraq. Its very existence suggests a continued focus on Iraq.

It is hard to see how that cannot have added to the tension

in the Mahabad Republic. Here were two leaders, in Qazi Muhammad and Mullah Mustafa Barzani, who had very different approaches, and possibly very different aims. Then one of them gave such an obvious signal that he was not purely focused on the Mahabad Republic, but potentially had other plans.

1946 Yalta Agreement

So there were many day to day pressures within the Mahabad Republic. Yet ultimately, can those pressures be blamed for its fall? What share of the blame for its failure must we attach to Qazi Muhammad? To Mullah Mustafa Barzani? They were both leaders of the republic, so are they culpable for its failure? Qazi Muhammad certainly seems to have thought that he was, surrendering to the Iranians in an effort to prevent further violence in a way that is at least a little reminiscent of a captain trying to go down with his ship.

But was he, and does Mullah Mustafa Barzani share any of the blame? We can say that there was one moment in their control that may have contributed to the republic's downfall: its official declaration in 1946. Prior to that, it existed in all but name, within Iran, but the moment the two declared the republic, they created conditions in which they had to know that Iran would do all it could to crush it. We have already seen that the declaration may have owed at least something to Mullah Mustafa Barzani's arrival, to his symbolic value and to his more rigid approach to the idea of a Kurdish homeland. He was very much the figure who would never settle for anything less than a fully independent Kurdistan. While that is an attitude that has proved important to his legacy, in this instance, it may also have played a role in forcing a declaration of independence that ultimately contributed to the Mahabad Republic's downfall.

Yet we must ask truthfully how much of a choice he and Qazi Muhammad had at that point. With Azerbaijan having

Republic of Mahabad

declared its independence, and with Soviet support apparently available, it was their best opportunity to act. International events dictated the creation of the republic at least as much as personal qualities.

International events were also the key factor in the fall of the republic. Mullah Mustafa did everything he could have done militarily. His forces won battles and held ground against the Iranians. They made it so that the Iranians did not wish to advance on those areas they held for fear of the potential losses. He even managed diplomacy with Tehran expertly, managing to visit and then leave to deliver its ultimatums when it must have seemed like the most likely outcome was his arrest.

Yet as with so often for my people, it wasn't enough. It wasn't about them. Mullah Mustafa ultimately had just a few thousand men, defending a country that had been no more than a single region of Iran prior to 1946. After the Second World War, just as after the first, international politics and the manoeuvring of great powers overshadowed any attempts to set up a Kurdish homeland.

Following the First World War, as we have seen, it came down to a combination of a desire on the part of the Great Powers to carve up Kurdistan, and their support for another new country in the form of modern day Turkey. After the Second World War, it was almost about the opposite. The international community wanted to *stop* a land grab on the part of the Soviet Union, sparking the beginnings of the Cold War, while at the same time putting down a new country in the form of Azerbaijan.

Both elements are important. Azerbaijan and the Mahabad Republic were fundamentally tied to one another, however much Mullah Mustafa and Qazi Muhammad sought to avoid being absorbed into the newly formed Soviet Republic of Azerbaijan. The Mahabad Republic received food, finance and military supplies via Azerbaijan, famously including Soviet tanks that proved crucial in keeping the threat of Iranian invasion at bay. Yet when Azerbaijan also came under attack, those resources melted away, leaving the Mahabad Republic vulnerable. Even the tank commanders took their vehicles home, ordered back to the Azerbaijani fronts in order to attempt to delay the Iranian advance. Azerbaijan fell to the Iranians just as surely as the Mahabad Republic did.

Ultimately though, even the fall of the larger Azerbaijan was the result of a larger political game. A game in which the very creation of the newly formed republics had been moves. The Soviet Union had occupied Iranian territory in the course of World War Two. It had agreed to return that territory following the war's conclusion, because other international powers, most notably the United States, did not want it to become any more powerful. It encouraged the creation of the republics, and fuelled the nationalist sentiments within them, not because it truly believed in Azerbaijan's or Mahabad's right to self-determination, but because it felt that was the best way to maintain some measure of influence there and avoid handing them back to Iran.

The ultimate failure of the Mahabad Republic came down not to the willingness of the people to fight, or even to the fact that many tribes sided with Iran in the end. Those only went over to the Iranian side once it was clear that the experiment with a republic had been destroyed at an international level. It certainly wasn't the personal fault of any one man. Instead, the failure of the Mahabad Republic came down to a series of UN Security Council resolutions aimed at forcing the USSR to return the land it had taken and withdraw support for the republics. Going back a step, it came down to the knock-on effects of the Yalta Conference of 1945, where the Great Powers negotiated what they would do with the land they had taken in the war, and where the USSR initially agreed to give back Mahabad.

Republic of Mahabad

It came down, as it so often seems to have with my people, to international issues seeming to be far more important than their lives. Agreement between the USSR and the USA probably seemed crucial to everyone involved. It may even have seemed like the only way to avoid another world war in the near future. Yet the price for it was the creation and then crushing of the Mahabad Republic. It is something that is hardly remembered internationally, where Azerbaijan and Iran are seen as the key areas involved in this first step in the Cold War. If it is remembered, it is remembered as a move in a deadly game of chess between the two emerging superpowers, yet to the people on the ground, this 'move' represented both the crushing of their dreams and an immediate threat to their lives.

The Failure and Success of the Republic

At the start of this chapter, I compared the Republic of Mahabad to the 1871 Paris Commune, suggesting that for many writers, the Republic of Mahabad represented the same sort of thing: a short lived, progressive, but largely unsuccessful political experiment cut off from the rest of the world and quickly squashed from the outside. A historical blip, or a footnote to a bigger story at best. Now that we have had a chance to look closely at the Republic of Mahabad, is this really a fair analysis? To what extent does the Republic of Mahabad resemble the short lived Commune? Can we really say that it was the same kind of minor historical oddity, or did it have a greater impact? Does Mullah Mustafa Barzani's involvement change that impact?

There are some obvious similarities between the two. Both claimed to be republics, but were ultimately at war for so much of their existences that they didn't have the time to put in the full political systems to which they aspired. Both came into existence at the end of wars (the Franco-Prussian war in the case of the Paris Commune, as opposed to the Second World War for the Republic of Mahabad) taking advantage of the

The Idea of Kurdistan

chaos left by those situations to carve territories out of existing countries. Both were short lived, with the Mahabad Republic lasting just a year and the Paris Commune just a few months. Both fell because of outside influence, the Paris Commune falling when the Prussians decided to release French prisoners to fight it, the Mahabad Republic falling following the Soviet Union's withdrawal of support.

In those areas, the similarities are easy to see, yet that does not mean that the two were identical. There were some key differences. The Paris Commune was effectively an attempt to declare a new government in a war damaged country. It was never supported generally, had no powerful outside benefactors, and ultimately seemed doomed from the start. The Mahabad Republic was something very different. It was not attempting to take over a country but to create one, trying to craft the homeland that my people were missing rather than trying to gain power within an existing political unit. It was not mindlessly Utopian in its ideals, either. Although both the Paris Commune and the Mahabad Republic were nominally socialist, we can say that in Paris, that was down to a political commitment to ideals already tested out in fragments of the French Revolution, whereas in the Mahabad Republic, those involved were probably just taking advantage of the Soviet Union's willingness to lend support to those who were willing to espouse its ideals.

That support is one of the crucial differences. It helped to shape the nature of the Mahabad Republic, but it also gave it a real sense at the time that it might be something important. Something that might last. The prospect of a Kurdish nation as a permanent part of the Soviet Union might not have been exactly what my people actually wanted, but in 1945, it may have seemed like the best opportunity for a nation of our own the Kurds were likely to get.

Of course, we know that ultimately, things did not work out that way. The Mahabad Republic fell when the Soviet Union

Republic of Mahabad

withdrew its support, allowing Iran to move in and destroy it. Qazi Muhammad was killed, along with many of the republic's other leaders, while Mullah Mustafa Barzani was forced to flee with his close followers. Does that fact affect the importance of the Mahabad Republic? Does the fact that it was quickly destroyed reduce it to a minor historical quirk, for all its important intentions? Is it ultimately just the same kind of event that the Paris Commune was?

I would argue that the Mahabad Republic is different, because of its knock-on effects on Kurdish identity, and because of the way it has been treated afterwards. It is a classic example of the importance of identity and perception, of exactly the sort that is so crucial to Mullah Mustafa Barzani's story. Where the Paris Commune is treated as just a minor historical moment by the French, the Mahabad Republic is remembered as something far more crucial by my people. It is remembered as a crucial first attempt at an independent nation. It is remembered as almost a blueprint for independence, as well as a cautionary tale about the dangers of relying completely on outside help to maintain a country.

Mullah Mustafa Barzani's involvement in the Mahabad Republic is also crucial here. Although it was not his idea, and he did not do the work of setting it up, he and his followers did play a crucial role in helping to maintain it. More than that, his involvement in the Mahabad Republic has helped to create a sense of continuity between the republic of 1945 and the modern Kurdistan. Without his involvement, the Mahabad Republic would indeed feel like a historical oddity, unconnected to anything else. With it, that connection exists, so that the modern Kurdistan feels like a step along the same road. It feels like a necessary step between the 1943–45 revolt and the attempts to set up an independent region within Kurdistan that came later. Mullah Mustafa Barzani may not have helped to create the Mahabad Republic, but he was undoubtedly crucial in connecting it to the story of Kurdistan.

That role in Kurdistan's wider story is a crucial one for the Republic of Mahabad. Without it, the only functioning Kurdish nations would have been ancient ones, long gone from the world and seemingly impossible to resurrect. With it, there was an example of a relatively modern Kurdish state, running along what seemed at the time like up-to-date political lines. The Republic of Mahabad didn't work; perhaps it never *could* have worked; but it suggested that possibly one day, another attempt might. That is a message that has been crucial to the development of Kurdistan as a whole, and that must have been crucial to Mullah Mustafa Barzani as he continued to try to bring it about.

Chapter Six: The Soviet Union

Once more Mullah Mustafa Barzani found himself forced to flee following a failed attempt to bring about an independent Kurdish state. He couldn't return to Iraq in 1946, but he certainly couldn't stay in Iran either. Not when Iranian forces were entering Mahabad in large numbers, with the obvious intention of killing the leaders of the Mahabad Republic. Not when tribal leaders were once again changing sides around him, killing officials within Azerbaijan to demonstrate their loyalty to a regime that looked like it would inevitably be victorious.

As with all of the withdrawals through his life, Mullah Mustafa Barzani saw what was coming in time to plan and evacuate families stuck in the path of the Iranian advance. Where some revolutionaries through history quickly found themselves killed through an insistence on fighting to the death in situations they could not win, Mullah Mustafa Barzani seems to have had the knack of spotting the point where a situation became untenable and ensuring that his people survived to fight another day. He understood that countries and ways of life were not changed in a day or a year, and was prepared to withdraw when it meant the survival of those around him.

Negotiation

Perhaps this approach was one of the reasons the Iranian army did not try to strongly engage the Barzanis. Perhaps they knew that if the situation became impossible, they could be persuaded to leave without having to engage a fighting force that had been in almost constant battle for years. Alternatively, perhaps they saw that while the Barzanis potentially had the capacity to harm them in a way that Mahabad's other forces could not, they were also fundamentally cut off from their homes, with little intrinsic attachment to the region, and thus little reason to stay. Perhaps they were working from an understanding of the previous occasions on which the Barzanis had been forced to leave behind revolts in order to preserve their way of life.

Whatever the reason, the Iranian commander was willing to engage in negotiation, at least at the start. He presented demands to the Barzanis, first requiring their surrender, then suggesting that they would be resettled on farmland within Iran. Mullah Mustafa Barzani even went to Tehran briefly to discuss these requirements, returning because he was able to persuade the government there that he was needed in order to put the conditions to Sheikh Ahmad and his followers. This was a tactic that he employed several times in his lifetime, using Sheikh Ahmad both as a reason to return to his people after talking with enemies and as a reason not to give a definitive answer to their demands.

Was there ever any suggestion that the Barzanis might have gone along with the Iranian government's suggestions? It seems unlikely that they would have surrendered, but perhaps the refusal to consider the offer of resettlement elsewhere needs some explanation. It would seem to have offered a peaceful, safe conclusion to the revolts that they had been involved in for decades at that point. But it does not seem to have been seriously considered. Why not?

Part of it must have been an awareness of the hostility of the

The Soviet Union

Iranian government. After many months of armed defiance of their insistence that Mahabad belonged to them, could Mullah Mustafa really believe that they had any intention of bringing about a peaceful resolution to the situation? His previous experience of governments and their promises in Iraq probably suggested to him that such promises could only be trusted for as long as the government in question found it convenient. So on that level there was no reason to accept the offer of resettlement.

The other part of the reason was almost certainly Mullah Mustafa Barzani's commitment to his cause. These days, it is easy to be cynical about the world and anyone whose commitment to a cause seems so absolute, yet there can be no doubt that Mullah Mustafa was completely committed to the idea of an independent Kurdistan. Giving that up to become a farmer, and a part of another country with no hope of ever achieving his aims, must have been inconceivable.

But he must have known that at the start of the process of negotiation. Just as it is hard to believe that the whole of the Iranian government can have been so foolish as to be unaware of how Mullah Mustafa Barzani worked. Neither side can truly have expected the negotiations to yield much. So why go through with them?

The answer seems to have been time. Mullah Mustafa Barzani was fully aware that the negotiations were unlikely to produce anything useful, but he was also aware that the other options were worse. They couldn't hope to win a sustained campaign against the full forces of the Iranian military, they couldn't return safely to an Iraq that had been calling for the arrest of the rebels since the revolt there, and they couldn't flee to the Soviet Union thanks to the severity of a winter that had blocked many of the mountain passes. Since at that point, those were the only three options available to his forces, they needed to buy enough time for conditions to change and one of those options to become more viable.

The danger was that more time meant that the Iranian forces had more opportunities to wear down the rest of the Mahabad Republic's forces and isolate the Barzanis. While delaying was initially successful, eventually it became obvious that another tactic was needed. Between them, Sheikh Ahmad and Mullah Mustafa Barzani made the decision to return their people to Iraq.

The Escape

That return took place on the 19th April 1947. At least, that is the date on which they crossed the border between Iran and Iraq, although the movement of such large numbers of people must inevitably have taken time and effort. Why return to Iraq? It seems likely that Mullah Mustafa Barzani didn't have much of a choice left to him at that point. The alternatives still seemed impossible.

Which left the task of returning to Iraq and trying to defend themselves there long enough for something to change. Mullah Mustafa Barzani probably felt that it was a better option than trying to take on the Iranians, since at least he and his forces knew the mountains in Iraq well. There was also the point that the Iraqi government probably didn't expect them to return, and that bought them time while it tried to mount a response. Reaching out to the Iraqi government to attempt to discuss terms for their return bought more time.

It was time in which Mullah Mustafa Barzani made what is now a famous decision. He knew that he and many of his fighters would be unacceptable to the Iraqi government. He must have guessed that their presence placed the civilian families with them in greater danger, by giving the Baghdad government an excuse to take military action against their villages. He must also have known that the presence of those civilian families was one of the things that had made the way to the Soviet Union so impassable before.

The Soviet Union

Ultimately, the decision was simple. He and those fighters most in danger if they stayed would head back into Iran and attempt to get from there to the Soviet Union. My uncle was one of those involved, and he left with Mullah Mustafa even knowing exactly how arduous the trip was likely to be. My grandfather would have gone, but he had been injured in the Mahabad Republic, and knew he would potentially hinder the rest of the group. He stayed behind, keeping one of his sons with him to look after the rest of the family and sending my uncle, as my uncle tells it, as a gift to Kurdistan's cause.

Those who left knew that staying would almost certainly mean death, so even the risks of the mountains were better for most of them. Not all. Some of the fighters stayed, either because they believed that they would be given an amnesty by the government, or because they could not bring themselves to leave their families. Many of those who stayed found themselves arrested, put on trial and executed.

Yet things were hardly easier for those who left with Mullah Mustafa. The initial phase of the journey required moving through the mountains, heading in directions that were believed to be impassable to avoid the Iranian forces that would undoubtedly try to cut them off if they tried more conventional routes. They had to cut steps into mountain ice and snow to cross them, and found themselves moving in single file through conditions that could easily have proved fatal had they not been prepared.

More than that, almost the entire march was undertaken under constant threat from the military forces of the surrounding nations. Iraqi bombers attacked them while they stopped in the village of Dari, while Turkish troops attempted to prevent them from crossing the border, forcing Mullah Mustafa's men to slip past them through surrounding forests.

They sought help from the tribal villages they came to along the way. At almost all of these, the men were welcomed warmly,

The Idea of Kurdistan

even while the Iranian government tried to gain news of them and a location at which to capture them. Previous biographers have suggested that this was indicative of their devotion to the cause of independence. That might be putting things a little strongly, especially since on at least two occasions, individuals attempted to betray them. Yet it is probably fair to say that the largely Kurdish population of the Iranian mountains had no real love for their rulers, and that Mullah Mustafa's forces would have been symbolic of a wider struggle to many of them.

We know of one major conflict in the course of the march, around Mako and its bridge over the Zangi River. Iranian forces waited there, obviously knowing that if Mullah Mustafa Barzani's people intended to cross into the Soviet Union, they would need to pass that way. The fighting was described as fierce, and it is typically suggested that it was a surprise even for the Kurdish forces that they managed to drive the Iranians back from the bridge. Yet the essentially defensive nature of the Iranians' approach probably gave the marchers at least one advantage, allowing them to choose the timing and method of their attack. More than that, there is the difference in their aims and objectives to consider. The Iranians were there to kill or capture the Kurdish forces, while the Kurds only had to succeed in getting past the Iranians.

They did so after a day's fighting, pushing their way over the river and then moving forward to the Araxes river on the border of the Soviet Union. At that point, it must have been obvious to those involved in the march that they had succeeded. They might even have believed that they would finally be safe once they crossed the river. Things, however, would not prove to be that simple.

Azerbaijan

The first stop for the retreating peshmerga was Southern Armenia. After the constant fighting in Iran and Iraq, it must

The Soviet Union

have seemed like a safe haven. Here they were, in a country prepared to give them sanctuary, which was strongly backed by the Soviet Union in a way even the Mahabad Republic hadn't been, and so was unlikely to fall the same way. For the first moments after their arrival, it must have seemed like things would be perfect.

Yet we know that the initial welcome for the men who had made the journey was not a pleasant one. Mullah Mustafa Barzani, made ill by the long march and the strain of leading the men on it, needed several weeks to convalesce. In that time, he was away from his men, which meant that there was no one to argue their case effectively when the Armenian authorities decided to intern them in what was effectively a prison camp built around them, complete with barbed wire and limited rations.

Today, that probably seems like an entirely unacceptable way to treat new arrivals in a country, yet consider the circumstances. The Armenians had just seen a force of armed, and by that point probably quite dishevelled, men arrive in their country. Men who had a reputation for guerrilla warfare, and whose intentions weren't immediately clear. From where they were standing, it must have looked as much like an advance force sent to attack the region as a collection of refugees. It is hardly surprising, put like that, that the Armenians wanted to take precautions.

In any case, we know that once Mullah Mustafa was recovered, he was able to persuade the authorities that his men were not a threat, and that the fences should be removed. He was able to use a visit to Baku to secure a place for them within Azerbaijan, and the methods he used are of interest here, because they typify his Soviet experience. He sent letters to Soviet leaders, asked for direct meetings with them, and in both his message was the same. He and his men were fleeing repression, and wanted to train in the Soviet Union in order to be able

The Idea of Kurdistan

to raise the profile of their cause and ultimately free their country.

Both parts of that approach are important. Mullah Mustafa never shied away from approaching major political leaders directly. He seemed to think it was obvious that, as an important leader within the revolts he had been a part of and as a potential leader of his country, he should be able to contact the likes of Stalin, and later US leaders. That level of confidence, and of directness, meant that he was often able to avoid the political machines that seemed almost designed to limit access to those leaders, and that he was consequently able to gain support for his cause at levels that might otherwise never have heard of it. We will see examples of this approach throughout his stay in the USSR.

The second part of that was just as important, however. Throughout his time in the USSR, Mullah Mustafa Barzani sought to emphasise that he and his men were there in order to learn and promote their cause. That they needed training in order to be able to return to Kurdistan and succeed where they hadn't been able to before. This may well have been true. It may well have been the case that Mullah Mustafa genuinely was there because he thought it was the best way to advance the skills and knowledge of his men, as well as securing support. Yet we have also seen that there were other reasons for them to be there, not least amongst which was the likelihood that if they had stayed in Iraq, they would have been arrested and executed.

That was not the side of things that Mullah Mustafa emphasised, however, and in that, it feels like he showed considerable awareness of the political realities of the Soviet Union under Stalin. He had the option to portray his men one of two ways: either as a group fleeing a failed revolution and seeking asylum, or as a group seeking to improve itself and spread revolution again. Mullah Mustafa must have known that the first option

The Soviet Union

would have been seen just as a drain on the resources of the nation they arrived in. The second made them sound like they were still of use to the Soviet cause, and so encouraged those he contacted to provide assistance. We will see shortly the difference that approach made to their lives in the USSR.

Mullah Mustafa also understood the importance of political organisation on the Soviets' terms. Although the PDK was already in existence, he agreed to the formation of a political leadership for the Kurdish nationalist movement in Iraq, created alongside one for Iran at the Baku conference of 1948. It is possible to argue that this was not strictly necessary, with a political party in existence back home, and that this was simply an attempt by Mullah Mustafa Barzani to maintain his leadership within the movement, but there are two things to consider here. One is that while the PDK did exist, this was a period in the aftermath of the Baghdad government putting down the last revolt. Mullah Mustafa had no way of knowing how free it was to operate, or how much it could achieve. Secondly, the official nature of the conference points to it being a move aimed at least in part at pleasing the USSR, and forming connections with them that would improve the safety and stability of the situation for Mullah Mustafa and his men.

The conference and its aftermath did not entirely succeed in that, however. While it undoubtedly created links with the Communist Party, the same feeling that had been present towards the Mahabad Republic remained, that the Kurdish movement should be only a part of the larger Azerbaijani one. Mullah Mustafa was no more about to agree to that arrangement than he had been in Mahabad, which inevitably caused friction with the Azerbaijani leader, Mir Jafar Baghirov. So did repeated insistences by the Iranians that the Azerbaijanis should hand Mullah Mustafa over. Even though the Soviets refused those requests, it was a combination of conflict between the two leaders and a possible threat that could not be ignored.

Uzbekistan

The solution Mullah Mustafa Barzani found was to request a transfer for his people to another country within the Soviet Union. That country was Uzbekistan where, initially, it seemed that things were going to go well. Mullah Mustafa's men started to get the training they had asked for, while their living conditions improved. It wasn't to last, however.

In March 1949, Mullah Mustafa found himself tricked into separation from his men by the promise of a meeting with Stalin. He was taken instead to a secure location near Lake Ural and closely watched, effectively placed under house arrest. The rest of the leaders he had brought with him were taken to similar locations, but spread out as widely as the Soviet political machine could manage. Their men were also been spread out, split up into groups and assigned to work camps, effectively imprisoned and forced into hard labour.

Mullah Mustafa's previous biographers have tended to assume that this was purely a plot by the leaders of Uzbekistan, working in collusion with Baghirov back in Azerbaijan. That is certainly the explanation that was given to Mullah Mustafa in 1951, and that the committee that investigated it found. How much can we trust that explanation? Was it just a personal vendetta, or was there something more to it?

It is certainly conceivable that it could have been personal. Stalin's USSR was notorious for officials using their positions to settle scores, for the use of labour camps and exactly the sort of tactics that Mullah Mustafa faced. Yet in that case, we have to ask why it didn't happen while he was in Azerbaijan, and how so much of the Soviet Union was used to spread out the men. Partly, the answer to that is simply that the Azerbaijani and Uzbek officials *were* officials, and thus had access to significant resources.

Yet there must also be some sense in which that approach was accepted on official levels. Yes, the situation was quickly

The Soviet Union

turned around once it got Stalin's attention, suggesting that he was not involved, but the whole investigation has the feel of scapegoating those involved, backtracking on something that far more people had known about than was later admitted to. Why would that be the case? What reason would the Soviet machine have to ignore such actions against Mullah Mustafa Barzani and his men?

The answer there may be that the Soviets felt Mullah Mustafa and his men were just seeking asylum. That they felt that their attempts at revolution were done, and that there was nothing to be gained from them in the future. Because if there is one thing we can say with certainty about Communism under Stalin, it is that it rarely if ever acted from a sense of altruism. If Communist officials thought that the odds of Mullah Mustafa returning to Iraq to revolt again were low, if they felt that his presence was an international embarrassment because of the way it upset relations with Iran, then it seems almost obvious with the internal logic of the system in place at the time that the Communists would want to make Mullah Mustafa, or at least his men, disappear.

I have added that qualifier because it is notable that Mullah Mustafa was not forced into the same conditions as his men. He was watched, but he was relatively well treated. Certainly, he was not made to do hard labour in the same way that those who had travelled with him were. In many ways, that is one of the biggest points against this being a personal vendetta. The man with whom Baghirov and the Uzbeks would have had the vendetta seems to have received the best treatment.

Why? Because on one level, Mullah Mustafa may have seemed useful in a way that his men were not. His presence within the Soviet Union meant that the Soviets could effectively control his image, using the idea of Mullah Mustafa if necessary. There was a *New York Times* report speculating that he might be somewhere on the Soviet–Iranian border, ready to invade. That could just have been a wild rumour dreamed up in a news room, but it sounds far more like the kind of thing that might have resulted if the Soviets had let the idea leak, specifically to make use of Mullah Mustafa's reputation to see what would happen.

If that way of looking at events seems implausible, remember that it is entirely consistent with the way the Soviet Union acted over the Mahabad Republic. There was that initial welcoming of the revolution, but with a slightly embarrassed edge to it and a suggestion that it should be part of Azerbaijan. There was a measure of support for exactly as long as it seemed to be in the Soviet Union's interest. There was an emphasis on the propaganda value of the republic, but again, it only lasted so long. The moment the situation seemed set to create embarrassment on an international level, the Soviets stepped back to allow the Iranians to invade, knowing full well the likely consequences. Imprisoning a few hundred men once it seemed that they wouldn't achieve much more in terms of revolution seems like a relatively small action for the Soviet Union compared to that.

Whatever the reasons for the imprisonment, we know that conditions were about as far from those the peshmerga had expected when they set off as could be imagined. They were all prisoners, and the ordinary fighters were held in often terrible conditions, half-starved and forced to work in circumstances that killed untold numbers throughout Stalin's presidency.

Faced with those conditions, many of the men engaged in strikes and disruptions. That seems inevitable. They were, almost by definition, not men willing to take injustice quietly. The very journey they had undertaken to be there showed that. Nor was Mullah Mustafa likely to stand by and ignore the situation when his whole political life had been founded on standing up to repressive authorities.

The Soviet Union

Stalin and Kruschev

Mullah Mustafa started to write letters to Stalin, setting out the situation and asking that it be set right. It is, in some ways, a curious move for him to have made. This was a man who had made his name through armed rebellion after armed rebellion. Who had always seemed to be the more active, military, hawkish figure when set beside partners such as Sheikh Ahmad and Qazi Muhammad. It seems somehow odd that at a time when he was imprisoned, at a time when his men were doing the closest thing to rebelling that they could manage, the man who had brought an entire region up in arms was reduced to writing letters.

Yet we shouldn't forget that this was also a man who had been in exile before. Who had been effectively imprisoned in a strange city as a child. Who was only in the Soviet Union because he understood as well as anyone that there were situations that he could not win with force. Attempting to rebel at that point would only have given his captors and opponents a potential excuse to kill him or imprison him more severely. At that point, even letters would not have been possible.

Besides, letters represented in many ways the most effective approach open to Mullah Mustafa Barzani. And it is notable again that he did not bother with approaching any lesser members of the Communist Party. He aimed his letters straight at the top. Again, it seems that he had the confidence and the certainty in his own authority to do so when many others would not have dared. Remember that Stalin was a man responsible for millions of deaths, with seemingly no compunctions when it came to having dissenters or opponents killed. Yet Mullah Mustafa was perfectly prepared to write to him to complain about the treatment of himself and his men. More than that, he was prepared to keep writing, even when it must have been obvious that his first few attempts had not made it through.

He eventually reached Stalin by giving a letter to one of his

The Idea of Kurdistan

rare visitors and asking them to get it to him. The letter returns to my second point about Mullah Mustafa's tactics when it came to his Soviet adventures, which was that it stressed that he and his men were there to train, promote their cause internationally, and eventually bring about a revolution to free Kurdistan. It emphasised his and his men's usefulness to the party and the wider Communist movement, while de-emphasising the part that was asking for help.

It was a sensible move. One that resulted in freedom for Mullah Mustafa and his men, along with a wider inquiry into the circumstances in which they were imprisoned. The inquiry blamed a 'gang' at the heart of the Azerbaijani and Uzbek regimes, although it is notable that Baghirov retained his place until Stalin's death in 1953. Again, that seems to lend some weight to the possibility that the wider government knew about what was happening to Mullah Mustafa Barzani and his men.

Certainly, Mullah Mustafa made a point of establishing good relations with the incoming government after Stalin's death. He travelled to Moscow and sought a meeting directly with Nikita Khrushchev, the new General Secretary of the Communist Party and leader of the country.

In some ways, it is a move that probably should not have worked. The idea that someone could just walk up to the leader of one of the world's superpowers in a period when the Cold War was in full flow seems almost impossible to believe. Yet perhaps in some ways that is why it worked. The sheer audacity of the move made it one that was almost guaranteed to catch Khrushchev's attention, although it could easily have backfired. Yet because Mullah Mustafa was prepared to take the risk, he was able to gain time with the new Communist leader, and restate his case that he and his men were in the Soviet Union to receive training and to place themselves in a position to bring about change in Kurdistan.

With Khrushchev, it was a message that proved extremely

The Soviet Union

successful. Mullah Mustafa found himself enrolled in the Communist party's political and military schools, while his men received military training to supplement the skills they had already gained through practical experience of combat.

Were there any differences between Mullah Mustafa's relationship with Stalin and his relationship with Khrushchev? Indeed, to what extent can we say that there was a relationship there? Clearly, to Kurdistan, Mullah Mustafa remains a key figure, but how important would he have been to the leaders of one of the world's two major superpowers?

On one level, perhaps not that important. After all, he was not the leader of a country. Nor was he in a position to effect an immediate revolution within Kurdistan, or to provide a significant military advantage to the Soviet Union. Stalin and Khrushchev would probably not have seen an equal when they met with him. Yet they *would* have seen someone of interest. Someone with qualities that perhaps reminded them of themselves, in that drive and zeal for what they wanted to achieve.

They seem to have played similar roles when it came to Mullah Mustafa. There were relatively brief meetings with them, and based on those meetings, Mullah Mustafa and his men achieved better conditions. Yet there were differences, in that Stalin was merely correcting an already unacceptable situation, whereas Krushchev seemed to be attempting to forge the possibility of a longer term relationship between the USSR and Mullah Mustafa's independence movement.

In some ways though, the biggest difference seems to have been in Mullah Mustafa Barzani, between Stalin's reign and Khrushchev's, he had learned how to play the Communist system. He had learned the importance of its leader, despite its talk about equality and party decisions. In that sense, any difference between the way he interacted with the regime under Stalin and that under Khrushchev seems to have been largely down to the way he approached each one.

Mullah Mustafa Barzani and Communism

Mullah Mustafa Barzani's time in the USSR is interesting, but it also throws up a lot of questions. Several writers have, over the years, questioned the extent of his involvement in Communism, often with a view to suggesting that it is an influence that somehow carries over to the PDK. So we need to ask two slightly different questions here. We need to ask what kind of a relationship Mullah Mustafa had with the USSR and its politics. Then we need to ask about the influence, if any, his time there had on the development of modern Kurdish democracy.

There have been suggestions from some quarters that Mullah Mustafa became a loyal Communist during his time there. There has been a photograph of him in full Red Army uniform advanced as proof of this. Yet the photograph probably doesn't mean as much as it initially seems to. I have been told privately that the photograph in question was taken as a joke, essentially as a kind of tourist piece or memento rather than as a serious statement of a political position.

It is far less important, in other words, than the fact that Mullah Mustafa Barzani was enrolled in the Communist party's schools for military and political leadership. It is impossible to deny that those involved large elements of indoctrination and attempts to politicise the students. It seems extremely unlikely that years around Communist thinking, being taught by Communist teachers, would have had no influence at all on the thinking of the men who made the trip to the USSR.

Some aspects of those influences were relatively clear to see in the later episodes of Mullah Mustafa Barzani's life. The military and political structures he used owed a lot to the lessons he had learned in the USSR, while the tactics he employed in the 1960s and beyond also seem to have been influenced by his time there. There was also a left leaning concern for equality and opportunity in his later politics, although it is also possible

The Soviet Union

to argue that those concerns had always been there to some extent.

Yet it seems hard to argue that Mullah Mustafa ever truly became a Communist. Yes, he was involved in the Soviet backed Mahabad Republic, but it was Qazi Muhammad who sought that assistance initially. Yes, he chose to go to the USSR, but that seems to have been largely because it was the only safe place for him to go. His requests to Stalin and Khrushchev, while they could be interpreted as wanting to spread revolution, actually read more like requests for help with essentially nationalist revolts. His later political intentions remained focused on independence, and were again largely nationalist in tone.

The big question we have to ask, of course, is why it matters. Why is it important whether Mullah Mustafa Barzani was ever a Communist or not? The answer tells us a lot about the ways in which his time in the USSR influenced the later course of Kurdistan. It is important because attempts to counter the spread of Communism were, for much of the period leading up to the creation of Kurdistan, one of the major forces affecting the politics of the region.

The whole region was at the heart of what was one of the most concerted struggles of the Cold War. The USSR and the USA used large portions of the Middle East as a major area to play out their conflicts by proxy, striving for influence over some of the largest oil producing nations there. Kurdistan initially gained assistance from the USSR, but later received more support from a USA interested in stopping the influence of Communism. Even in recent times, the USA has been one of Kurdistan's bigger international supporters.

Is it any wonder, therefore, that writers have either sought to play down any political link to Communism, or sought to make it out to be more than it was, depending on which side they represented? This has been more than a spat between writers with different opinions. Kurdistan's political parties have

The Idea of Kurdistan

been shaped by these pressures, generally having to take pains to show that they have not been influenced by that aspect of Kurdistan's history. Mullah Mustafa's time in the USSR has influenced modern Kurdish politics, therefore, by giving the region's political parties something that they need to carefully avoid appearing to be.

It may also have influenced foreign attitudes towards the region in other ways. We know, for example, that the USA was prepared to abandon Kurdistan's attempts at self-determination following the Algiers Accord in 1976. Most of that was probably dictated by the political pressures within Iran and Iraq, but could memories of that vague connection to Communism have coloured the decision? At the very least, it is a connection that may have created the impression that Kurdistan was willing to work with any partner, rather than being wedded to the ideals of the USA.

Yet that is a relatively tenuous connection. Do we have evidence for Mullah Mustafa Barzani's time in the USSR having any more direct effects on modern Kurdish politics? Possibly. I think it is fair to say that modern politics are influenced more by the lives and needs of the people in the region today than by an adherence to the past, but there are some elements that might be said to have been affected by Mullah Mustafa's time in the USSR.

For one thing the PDK is somewhat more left leaning than many nationalist parties around the world. It has a commitment to equality and freedom as a part of its main concerns, and indeed, that translates over to the region as a whole through its constitution. Yet can we say that is the influence of socialism sixty years ago, or simply the effects of modern thinking on those subjects? Perhaps we can say that there are some socialist influences in the desire for public works, and in the assumption that it is the state's job to make things better for the population, rather than relying on the private sector to achieve it.

The Soviet Union

Yet mostly, the biggest influence of Mullah Mustafa's time in the USSR shows itself in Kurdistan's international relations. It has achieved close connections with many countries, including the USA, but there is also a certain caution there that comes from its earlier connections to outside forces. A certain ability to balance the demands of the outside with what is actually best for the region. We have seen that Mullah Mustafa was not afraid to put Kurdistan's case forward even in the face of imprisonment by one of the world's superpowers, and that attitude still seems to be present in Kurdistan today.

Chapter Seven: Return to Kurdistan – The 1960s

Mullah Mustafa Barzani's stay in the Soviet Union was never intended to be a permanent thing. From the moment he arrived there, he emphasised to the authorities he met that he and his men were there to receive training and spread the word about the cause of Kurdish independence, with a view to eventually returning to Kurdistan. He emphasised the fact that he was still focused on the fate of Kurdistan, and wasn't about to subsume that desire into the more general ideas of someone else's cause. Even after years in the Soviet Union, he was still prepared to reiterate that point to Khrushchev, re-stating that desire to go back to Kurdistan and fight for its freedom.

In part, as we have seen, that was a political move. It emphasised the idea that Mullah Mustafa and his men would still be of use to the Soviets and were not just asking for charity. Yet it was also no more than the truth. After everything he and his followers had already been through in the name of Kurdistan, Mullah Mustafa wasn't about to give up on the aims that had brought him to the Soviet Union in the first place. He fully intended to return, just as he had returned from exile earlier in his life.

He probably didn't think that it would take quite so long, however. Mullah Mustafa Barzani and the men who marched

Return to Kurdistan – The 1960s

with him to the Soviet Union ended up spending more than a decade there. A decade would have been enough time for many people to build a life and settle down. It was certainly a long time for the men to be away from the families they had left behind in Kurdistan. Yet with the Baghdad government still remembering Mullah Mustafa's uprisings, he couldn't return until things changed.

Then, in 1958 things *did* change, more completely than anyone could have foreseen.

Return

The origins, aims and effects of the 1958 revolution have been discussed again and again by writers on both Iraq and Kurdistan. I do not propose to re-examine all the details of the revolution, except inasmuch as they are relevant to the life of Mullah Mustafa and the knock-on effects of the revolution on the current Kurdistan.

The character of the 1958 revolution is important. It is easy to portray it as a popular socialist revolution, and indeed, more Marxist writers have tried to show it as exactly that. In some respects, it probably was both of those things to an extent, but not completely. It was popular, or at least populist, in that it achieved a measure of popular support once it was running. Some of its stated aims, such as seeking a republic, claimed to benefit the whole population. Even some of the political issues that seem a little arcane and convoluted to modern eyes, such as the question of Iraq's position on the Hashemite Union with Jordan, were important ones to many of Iraq's inhabitants. It enjoyed a high degree of cross party support too, with the National Unity Front at the heart of the revolution containing four of the main political parties in the country. The PDK was not directly involved in it, but enjoyed strong connections to the National Unity Front (NUF) at the time.

It was also socialist in the sense that many of the parties

The Idea of Kurdistan

involved had at least nominal socialist leanings, they had connections to the Soviet Union, and the main thrust of the revolution was the removal of the country's monarchy along with those around it. Indeed, most of those involved probably thought that it was the socialist revolution it aimed at being, and for a few years at least, it may even have been that.

Yet in many respects, there were elements that point to a somewhat different character for the revolt. The military was heavily involved, for example, with many of those who ended up in power having strong military connections. General Abdul Karim Quasim was at its heart, along with a group of 'Free Officers' who formed the backbone of the attempt to overthrow Iraq's then king.

Then there is the wide range of grievances the revolution sought to address. Economic factors were involved, but so were international political ones and essentially nationalist ones, trying to remove the influence of outside countries over Iraq. None of these elements points to the socialist revolution that some writers have tried to portray the 1958 revolt as.

One point about the revolution is crucial here: it was an essentially Iraqi revolt. Where the previous revolts Mullah Mustafa had been involved in had been Kurdish revolts against an Iraqi or British run government, this was about Iraqis overthrowing their own government. The PDK was not a full part of the NUF, and the stated aims of the revolt did not include a free Kurdistan. Which in some ways begs the question of why Mullah Mustafa Barzani returned then. What was it about the 1958 revolution that brought him back?

There were several things. The first was the thought that the destabilising effect of the revolution might potentially provide an opportunity for Kurdistan to become free. That, with Iraq in turmoil, with the country attempting to rebuild itself from the inside, there might be an opportunity to break free from Baghdad's control.

Return to Kurdistan – The 1960s

That is not just a thought that was present for Mullah Mustafa Barzani and the PDK. The Soviet Union seems to have thought it was possible too, because they were the ones who suggested that he should return. They were the ones who organised the logistics of his return to Kurdistan, through a circuitous route that took in Cairo. They were the ones who insisted that the situation was one that could benefit from his presence. Other countries also seem to have believed that Kurdish independence was a real possibility. Britain in particular seems to have been concerned that it might happen, and that in the event that it did, Turkey would take the opportunity to invade.

That international opinion, coupled with the rhetoric of the revolution, may have been enough to convince Mullah Mustafa Barzani that the opportunity was better than it appears to have been with hindsight. Perhaps we can also say that even if he wasn't certain whether there would be immediate independence for Kurdistan, he must have seen that Iraq was at a moment of rebuilding. To be a part of that rebuilding, to help create an Iraq in which Kurdistan could eventually become free, Mullah Mustafa had to be there. Perhaps he could not immediately declare independence, but returning to Iraq gave him an opportunity to help determine what kind of country Iraq would be in the future.

There were simpler elements to Mullah Mustafa Barzani's return too. The fall of the monarchy in Iraq represented in many ways the first *opportunity* he had to return. Although it had been the military that had been responsible for putting down his previous revolts and the military that was at the heart of the current revolution, he must have felt that the change of government represented the best chance for a return that he would get.

That is the key point here. Although there may have been an aspect of returning to renew the struggle for independence in Mullah Mustafa's return to Kurdistan, much more of it must

The Idea of Kurdistan

have been simply about coming home. For the first time in twelve years, he was able to return to the land he had fought for over such a long period. He was able to see family members he had not been able to meet in more than a decade. He was able to return to the villages he had been forced to leave so abruptly in 1945. We must not underestimate the desire to come home on Mullah Mustafa's part, and the role it played in his return. He was a man who loved Kurdistan, who continually restated his desire to return while in the Soviet Union. It seems obvious that he would return at the first opportunity he had to do so.

There has been some debate over Mullah Mustafa Barzani's reception when he returned. There have been those who have said that any positive reception was carefully arranged by his supporters, and that for the majority of the population of Kurdistan, certainly of Iraq, it was a non-event. I find that hard to believe. Is it really conceivable that, in the aftermath of a revolution, the return of Kurdistan's most famous revolutionary would really go unremarked? That seems impossible, and indeed, the evidence seems to suggest that large crowds met Mullah Mustafa on his arrival.

This episode is important partly because it suggests that even after a decade away from the country, Mullah Mustafa's reputation was still intact, and partly because it suggests that even at that stage, his image was almost as important to Kurdistan as the man himself. If it had just been about Mullah Mustafa Barzani as a man, then presumably people would have largely forgotten about him in the time he was away. A decade would have been easily enough time to forget. Instead, if anything, his reputation *increased* during the time he was away, which explains something about the nature of his reception. By the time Mullah Mustafa returned to Kurdistan, he was there not just as himself, but as a symbol of an entire movement.

Return to Kurdistan – The 1960s

After the Uprising

If Mullah Mustafa Barzani had hoped that his return home would be a peaceful one, any such idea was quickly pushed aside. The period after the 14th July Revolution was a complex, unstable, and often violent one. It needed careful handling, as well as adaptation to a completely new set of political realities within Iraq.

One of those realities was that, for the first time since its creation, the PDK was considered a legal, legitimate party by Baghdad. Although it hadn't formed a part of the NUF, it had been close enough to it that it was considered an ally by the new government, and looked set to form a part of the political landscape in the new political system that was coalescing.

It must have been a strange experience for Mullah Mustafa Barzani, being within the official political system rather than fighting against it. His time in the Soviet Union had been spent with the assumption in mind that any return would result in a struggle, probably an armed struggle, for independence. Indeed, when the Soviets suggested to him that the time might be ripe to return, they must have been thinking the same thing. He returned expecting a fight against the government.

Instead, he and his party ended up fighting on its behalf on several occasions. The period following the revolution was a turbulent one, and several figures felt that they could use it to advance their individual agendas. They sought to use the opportunity to either break away from Iraq on a local level or to start a counter revolution that would place them in control of the country.

It must have seemed ironic to Mullah Mustafa Barzani that he and the KDP were involved in putting down several of these revolts. They were involved in Kirkuk, in Mosul and beyond, lending the weight of their peshmerga to government forces to stop Iraq from disintegrating. Those were violent, brutal days, but the PDK was one of the key forces involved in stabilising the situation.

The Idea of Kurdistan

Why? Why did the PDK allow itself to be caught up in the violence? Why did it help to support the government in Baghdad rather than simply trying to secure Kurdistan? Why didn't it immediately try for independence, using the situation to break away from a government that still claimed Kurdistan as its territory?

Perhaps part of the reason was Mullah Mustafa's past experiences. He had been shown repeatedly that violent insurrection tended to be a way to delay failure rather than a way to bring about success. Perhaps we can suggest that this time, he felt that a political solution, working *with* the Baghdad government, was more likely to bring about independence.

Certainly, he had every reason to think so. After all, this was a revolutionary government. One whose constitution for Iraq formally recognised the Kurds as one of the two peoples for whom the country was a homeland. It was not a foreign government with an interest in controlling the whole region. It was not a king, jealous of his power over the territories he claimed. Perhaps it seemed, for the first time, like there was a government in place to whom Mullah Mustafa could talk.

If so, that does a lot to explain the role of the PDK and peshmerga in putting down insurrections. Having seen how rare it was for a government to seriously discuss Kurdistan's situation, they would have been unwilling to see one that looked like it might do so overthrown. Then, of course, there is the point that at least some of these insurrections were occurring in Kurdistan. Even if the PDK had not wished to stabilise the overall situation, it still had an interest in keeping Kurdistan stable, and in maintaining its position within areas such as Kirkuk. Even if it had been planning on a violent separation from Iraq from the start, it would still have had to fight the battles it did there.

So, if Mullah Mustafa and the PDK initially attempted to contribute to the stability of Iraq, if they felt that Abdul Karim

Return to Kurdistan – The 1960s

Quasim was someone they could do business with, how did that transform into a situation where the two sides were ready to go to war with one another? Was the initial assessment of the situation that badly wrong, or did things change so utterly? Was it, as some historians have suggested, a case of elements with their own agendas pushing Mullah Mustafa and Abdul Karim Quasim apart? Or was it simply that they had been able to paper over the cracks between them until then?

Some of it is perhaps that the instability of Iraq appeared to give Kurdistan what it wanted. At a time when the whole country was in turmoil, the Baghdad government wasn't in a position to exert any kind of control over the region. It seems likely that the PDK mistook this inability to act in the region for a lack of will to do so. They thought that they had found a government willing to give them near autonomy, when in fact, they had merely found one that hadn't consolidated its position. They sought to help to stabilise the government, perhaps thinking that it would place that government in a position to grant them greater freedoms. Instead, doing so merely placed Baghdad in a better position to resist calls for independence.

Yet that probably wasn't the only element involved. Part of it seems to have been that both sides were talking at cross purposes from the start. There seems to have been a particular difference of interpretation when it came to Article Three of the new constitution. That declared that both Kurds and Arabs formed the main peoples of Iraq, and that the constitution would state their national rights under Arab unity. Kurdish nationalists seized on this as a promise of an independent state. Arab leaders in government seem to have taken it more as a statement of Kurdistan being a part of Iraq, emphasising the latter half of the article. While such a confusion of intentions could survive for a time, eventually it was inevitable that it would pull things apart.

The Idea of Kurdistan

So would the situation within Iraq. The popular mood in the south seems to have been firmly against Kurdish independence, and even against the idea of a separate Kurdish cultural identity. Several articles at the time suggested that the cultural destruction of the Kurds and their absorption into an overarching Arabic culture was a desirable thing. This was not unique at the time, and in fact mirrors the kind of policy of cultural obliteration Turkey actually put in place, but it was still explicitly hostile to the aims Mullah Mustafa and his followers had espoused for so long. Perhaps someone else could have stood by while Kurdish officials found themselves replaced by Arab ones, or while the Baghdad government started to make claims over Kirkuk, but with Mullah Mustafa there, conflict seemed inevitable.

In that, we must make a point that may seem controversial: Mullah Mustafa Barzani's presence in Iraq probably contributed to the breakdown of relations with the government. It probably wasn't intentional, but it was almost inevitable. By that stage, he was one of Kurdistan's biggest symbols of independence, known as a man who would not compromise on that issue. His very presence was an ultimatum, a statement that the Baghdad government could either give Kurdistan the autonomy it desired or face insurrection.

Worse in the Baghdad government's eyes, this symbol of Kurdish nationalism now had connections to the Soviet Union. Connections that had already supported one Kurdish breakaway state with Mullah Mustafa intimately involved. Connections that had the power to potentially be a major threat in a politically unstable situation. Just by being there, Mullah Mustafa Barzani carried with him the threat of potential Soviet intervention. When he returned to the Soviet Union in 1960 to seek support for both the new Iraq and Kurdistan's place within it, that move can only have added to the Abdul Karim Quasim's fears.

Those fears started a vicious cycle of mistrust. Since he did not trust Kurds or Kurdish officials who might have been a part of any move towards independence, he sought to remove them from public life where he could, as well as seeking to reduce the use of the Kurdish language. That made it look like the worst fears of Mullah Mustafa and the PDK were coming true, which in turn encouraged them to take a more aggressive, less forgiving stance on independence. Both sides fed off the reactions of the other, moving over the course of 1960 and 1961 to a position where they couldn't be reconciled, and the only answer was violence.

Revolts

In September 1961, it became clear that the government was never going to accede to even partial Kurdish independence, let alone the full independence that was Mullah Mustafa Barzani's long term aim. With increasingly violent action from the government, and democratic elections that never quite came about to give the PDK a chance to make its case in the region, eventually the only option left was armed struggle.

The uprising seems to have followed the pattern of most of the ones that had preceded it, with an initial rising to take control of the region and the removal of central government officials from their posts in Kurdistan. From there, as so many times before, the battle was to hold on to the gains that they had made, using the terrain of the mountains to their advantage, fighting a war of ambushes and sudden engagements that promised little in the way of decisive results, but was at least enough to prevent Baghdad from exerting full control over the region.

How much support did this revolt have? Inside Kurdistan, we can suggest that it was a popular one. Perhaps unusually, Mullah Mustafa had been one of the more conciliatory voices in Kurdistan. He was the one who sought to engage peacefully with the government for as long as possible, even tolerating some negative comments from more aggressive members of his

The Idea of Kurdistan

party because he felt that the effort was worth making. By the time he was ready to fight, his people were more than ready to fight with him.

Support abroad was more hit and miss. Thanks to his trip to the Soviet Union, Mullah Mustafa was assured of their political and logistical support. Yet, at what was a very unstable time for the Cold War, with the USA worried about the domino effect, it was not in a position to intervene more directly. The Vietnam War was already starting to show that the US was willing to counter any moves in that direction. Perhaps Mullah Mustafa would not have wanted the USSR to intervene in any case. Throughout his time in the Soviet Union, he had emphasised that he wanted Kurdistan's independence, not for it to be subsumed into another Soviet republic.

That message didn't quite make it over to America though. To the USA, he was the man who had just spent a decade in the Soviet Union. Who had come from it at a time when Iraq was unstable, and who had gone back to it for additional support. Although it is now clear that Mullah Mustafa Barzani was not a Communist, the American press portrayed him as one in the early 1960s. They feared that his uprising was the first stage in an expansion of Soviet interests in the region, or portrayed it as a tribal uprising that had nothing to do with nationalism and everything to do with personal interest. That combination was enough to destroy any US support at the time.

Which meant that ultimately the success of the revolt would come down to factors within Iraq and Kurdistan. Without outside support, Mullah Mustafa's forces were not in a position to win definitively, but at the same time, the Baghdad government was not in a position to put the revolt down either. It had increasing divisions throughout Iraq to contend with. Divisions that it had previously been able to count on the support of its Kurdish allies to deal with. By alienating them, the government had put itself in a position where it could not deal with other revolts and conflicts. Which in turn meant that it couldn't commit the resources needed to fully put down the Kurdish rebellion.

Perhaps Mullah Mustafa Barzani saw the way things were going. Perhaps he realised that in such a fragmented situation, all he needed to do was hold on until it collapsed completely. Perhaps he realised that, if a stable situation had been what allowed the Baghdad government to repress his people, holding on to an unstable situation was the best opportunity for relative autonomy. Then again, it was an approach to warfare that he and his fighters had used throughout his life to date, so perhaps it was simply that he was repeating those tried and true tactics.

Whatever the reason, it meant that the revolt was still going on when circumstances changed. Previously in Mullah Mustafa's life, those changes had tended to mean the collapse of his rebellion as other forces came to bear. This time though, the circumstances worked to his advantage, because the government finally fell. The 1963 coup by the Ba'ath party took a lot of the pressure off the Kurdish revolt, and indeed allowed for a truce shortly afterwards.

Yet it did not make things straightforward for Mullah Mustafa Barzani. Threats remained. First, there was the threat that came from the Ba'athists being in power. It had been Ba'athists that the Barzanis had helped to put down previously, brutally so in Mosul. It was an action that was consistent with the violence of the times, but Mullah Mustafa must have known that in that violent world, retribution might be coming.

He also had worries within his own party in the form of a splinter group under Jalal Talabani, who went so far as to hold his own party conference, and who courted Baghdad, accepting a role there close to the new regime. It looked like an attempt to close Mullah Mustafa out of his own party, attempting to

The Idea of Kurdistan

re-focus it in a more urban, intellectual direction with closer links to the Iraqi government.

For almost two years, these problems were enough to occupy Mullah Mustafa Barzani's attention. Then in 1965, another revolution struck Iraq. The changes of the 1963 revolt were undone at a stroke, the old regime was back in place, and the Kurdish forces found themselves fighting against the government once again. Did that come as a surprise? It must have, on some level, because if they had expected the counter revolution, they or the regime might have been able to do something to stop it. Yet the possibility of further violence must always have been there in general terms.

This time, it was violence supported from beyond the country. Both Israel and Iran sent significant support in terms of money and weapons, giving Mullah Mustafa's men enough that they could sustain a war against multiple divisions of the Iraqi army well into the late 1960s. The benefit to Kurdistan was obvious. The benefit to the peshmerga's sponsors came in the form of entangling the Iraqi army, preventing it from acting against them. The best part of that situation from the Kurdish point of view was that their current sponsors had an aim that was long term. Where a superpower might try to achieve a short term aim or use Kurdistan to set up a position elsewhere, these smaller powers had an interest in tying the Iraqi army up for years to come. Yes, it meant sustained conflict for Mullah Mustafa and his men, but that was only consistent with everything they had experienced in the previous decades. It was what they were used to.

There was an unexpected side effect of that conflict. It tied the Iraqi army up to such an extent that it could not act abroad, but it also prevented it from acting internally. As with the first revolt of 1961, this second revolt created the conditions for someone else's revolution.

Return to Kurdistan – The 1960s

1968 Ba'ath Coup

The 1968 coup by the Ba'ath party in Iraq was probably one of the most significant moments in recent history for my people. It brought to power a political party that would ultimately attempt to wipe out the Kurdish people through a combination of cultural repression and mass murder through the use of chemical weapons. A party that would murder 8,000 Barzani men in 1983, and imprison their women and children, before going on to the horrors of the Anfal later in the decade.

Yet at the time, the coup was a relatively bloodless one, avoiding the chaos that had accompanied the transition from monarchy to nominal republic ten years earlier. The party's previous period in power must have suggested to the fighters in Kurdistan that peace was a prospect, as it had been in 1963. Yes, there were the obvious memories of violence and contention between the PDK and Ba'ath parties, but there must have been the feeling in 1968 that the change in circumstances might bring about peace.

At least initially, however, it did not. If anything, the period immediately following the coup brought an upsurge in violence, as the new government sought to demonstrate its power by crushing the revolt. The previous government had allowed its conflict with my people to fade to a steady drip after around 1966, as worries about the army led Iraq's leaders to avoid giving it too many resources, and as the war for independence ground on into a long term conflict. The incoming Ba'ath Party probably thought that with their greater support from the army, they were better placed than the previous government to win the conflict. Certainly, after they systematically purged the Iraqi army of more than two thousand officers believed to be potential opponents, they must have felt confident in their ability to control it.

Yet the escalation in violence also came in part from the Kurdish side in 1968. As we have seen above, foreign powers had taken to backing the peshmerga on several occasions during the previous decade, supplying them with arms and finances to prolong their struggle and thus tie up the Iraqi army so that it could not be used elsewhere. The 1968 coup had brought with it a new selection of enemies for the Ba'ath party; enemies who wanted to see the conflict with Iraq continue to prevent any expansionist threat from the country's new rulers. Iran in particular felt that Kurdistan represented its best opportunity to conduct a war by proxy, and control the military ambitions of its most dangerous immediate neighbour.

America also had an interest in seeing things unstable in Iraq. The Ba'ath Party had an apparent commitment to socialism in its stated political ideals, which was a significant worry for an America worried about the spread of the USSR's power. It was at the height of the Vietnam War, freshly reeling from the effects of the Tet Offensive, and so wasn't in a position to intervene directly, but it was in a position to act indirectly through encouragement and the supply of logistical support.

Which meant that, for Kurdistan, the 1960s ended as they began, in conflict with a newly formed government in the south. Yet there was one event that overshadowed even that. In 1969, Sheikh Ahmad Barzani, Mullah Mustafa's older brother and for years the leader of the Kurdish cause, died. Although we have been focusing primarily on Mullah Mustafa here, Sheikh Ahmad's influence on Kurdistan is also undeniable. He was so often a stabilising influence, less military in approach than his brother, but able to give the cause of Kurdish independence a second, civilian face with which to negotiate. Even his presence somewhere in the background proved important. Time and again, Mullah Mustafa was able to meet with his enemies and walk away simply because he claimed to need to put their demands to Sheikh Ahmad to make a real decision.

Sheikh Ahmad's death had a potentially huge impact on the

Return to Kurdistan – The 1960s

shape of things in Kurdistan, and certainly on Mullah Mustafa Barzani's position. Although he had been the leader of the PDK for years, there had always been the presence of Sheikh Ahmad somewhere there in the background. Another authority to refer to. Again and again through Mullah Mustafa's life, even with his march to the Soviet Union, he sought Sheikh Ahmad's final permission before acting. Now, full responsibility for decisions that could affect his whole people fell on him.

In some ways, that complicated things. It meant that Mullah Mustafa could no longer afford to be an essentially military leader, but instead had to balance that with more of a civil role as well. There was no longer the ability to delay talks through the question of having to speak to Sheikh Ahmad about the decision. Yet in other ways, things became simpler. Mullah Mustafa was the leader of the Kurdish Independence Movement and of the Barzanis from that point in formal terms as well as in practice. It was clear that he was able to offer terms, which made for quicker decision making.

Yet ultimately, we must ask how much things really changed at that point. It seems clear that, while Mullah Mustafa continued to consult with Sheikh Ahmad to some extent, he was definitively in charge of the independence movement following his return to Kurdistan. The creation of the PDK had solidified the movement as national and political, rather than local and tribal. Mullah Mustafa was the (only occasionally disputed) head of the party, and thus the figure to whom the rest of the movement looked for leadership. Sheikh Ahmad had been a key figure in the revolts up to 1945, but in the 1960s he was in a kind of semi-retirement. Still there. Still important for who he was. Yet ultimately not heavily involved in the day-to-day running of events.

So on that level, the transition probably wasn't as major as it appears from the outside. Yet it must still have been a key symbolic moment. The moment when Mullah Mustafa was

The Idea of Kurdistan

effectively in sole charge of Kurdistan's destiny. The only question was what he would do with it.

The 1960s and Kurdistan Today

For a lot of writers, the 1960s form a starting point. They are the point where people start talking about modern Kurdish and Iraqi history, as though anything before then is mere detail. Specifically, a great many of them start their narratives in 1968, with the Ba'ath party coming to power. While it is possible to see why some of them might do so, I feel that it is a mistake. It suggests that Saddam Hussein is somehow the only thing that matters in either Iraq's history or Kurdistan's, when there are so many other points that matter at least as much. Yes, Saddam's crimes against my people matter (my previous book was devoted to the Anfal and Kurdistan's recovery from it) but they took place in a specific historical situation that must be understood. More than that, the ways that Kurdistan has developed since have at least as much to do with the past before then as to do with the years since 1968.

So, where do the 1960s fit in? What influence do their events have over Kurdistan today? Is there a case for saying that they had as much, if not more, influence on the structure of modern Kurdish democracy than many of the events that came later?

The 1960s were a decade of conflict for Kurdistan. They began in the wake of revolution, and they ended the same way. Mullah Mustafa's return in 1958 meant that he was in a position to directly influence events in Kurdistan for the first time in a decade, but many of those events were so chaotic and uncontrollable that in many ways all he could hope to do was keep the region safe until the danger passed.

Yet in some ways, the chaotic transitions of the 1960s were crucial in defining Kurdistan's place for the next thirty years. The revolutions and counter revolutions moved Iraq away from the stable monarchy that had been both powerful enough to hold

Return to Kurdistan – The 1960s

Kurdistan in a fixed relationship to it and inimical enough to Mullah Mustafa Barzani that he could not return home. Without the transitions in and around the 1960s, there is a case for saying that Mullah Mustafa might never have been able to return to his homeland, and that he certainly would not have been able to resume the position of influence he did when he returned.

One consequence of this, and one of the most crucial things to happen in the 1960s, was the reintegration of Mullah Mustafa's brand of armed revolt with the region. Mullah Mustafa's absence in the 1950s had meant that in many ways that kind of struggle for independence was no longer associated with the region. It, like Mullah Mustafa, was something waiting outside somewhere, while the region itself stayed stable and ruled from Baghdad. There may have been pressures towards independence, but it was in the 1960s that Kurdistan showed it was still prepared to fight for its autonomy.

That is important, because it would have been easy for Kurdistan to fade in the 1960s. It had already been relatively peaceful in the 1950s. If it had not risen up in the 1960s, when there were revolts going on throughout the rest of Iraq, it would have created the impression that it was no longer interested in securing its own freedom. The momentum of the fight for independence would have stalled, and the odds of Kurdistan achieving any of what it has today would have been dramatically reduced.

Yet it was also in the 1960s that Kurdistan really started to define itself in opposition to the government in Baghdad. Yes, it had risen up before, but generally only defensively, seeking to prevent the extension of influence from the central government. In the 1960s, revolt became more complex, as outside forces started to try to sponsor the efforts of Mullah Mustafa and his men, seeking to limit the ambitions of Iraq. That had beneficial effects at the time, making it possible for them to sustain their revolt in a way that forced successive new governments to the negotiating table, yet it also may have contributed to a climate in which Kurds came to be seen as the enemy by later governments.

Indeed, no matter how hard we try, it is impossible to escape the thought that the 1960s paved the way for many of the atrocities that came later; the pain out of which Kurdistan was eventually born. It was the 1960s that returned my people to a position of near continual revolt. It was the 1960s that first placed them in opposition to the Ba'ath party, trying to work with the then government to put down rebellion in Mosul. These small seeds of hatred would build to inhuman consequences in the decades to come.

There were other moments that foreshadowed the future. The divisions within the PDK in this decade pointed to the fractious nature of Kurdish politics that spilled over into civil war in the 1990s. The divisions over the interpretation of Article Three of Abdul Karim Quasim's draft constitution pointed to more modern wrangles over the interaction between Kurdistan and Iraq's constitutions and what their terms implied for their peoples.

Yet for all their violence and disruption, the 1960s were also crucial on one level: they represented the first movements towards a modern political system in Iraq. A system in which the main Kurdish party, the PDK, was briefly legal. Yes, it was a broken system with only the barest of nods towards real democracy, but it was the first time that politics in Iraq had been defined in terms of real parties and representation. Yes, the PDK was already in existence as a political unit, but this was the moment that moved it from being a group somewhere in opposition to the system, or just a name for a political position, to being a party within a political construct. Political parties and a multi-party system seem like such obvious things that they almost appear to arise of themselves, yet with this moment the 1960s were crucial in bringing about Kurdistan's modern political system.

Chapter Eight: Revolution in the 1970s

The 1960s gave way to the 1970s in a state of turmoil and transition. Kurdistan and the Baghdad government were still at war, the Ba'ath government in Baghdad was only newly arrived, and the Kurdish leadership, particularly the Barzani leadership, was still acclimatising to life after Sheikh Ahmad. At that stage it seemed like the last thing that might happen was peace.

1970 Peace Accord

Yet in 1970, suddenly, there were peace talks on the table. Mullah Mustafa found himself, after years of conflict, in discussion with one of the most important men of the new regime: Saddam Hussein. Hindsight makes it seem insane that he of all people should ever be sent on a mission of peace, and yet to some extent that is one of the problems of history. We see it through the prism of today. We look back, knowing what happened next, and we assume that the peace attempt cannot have been a genuine one.

Yet why not? It seems obvious that peace was of more use to the Baghdad regime of the time than continued conflict with my people. They wanted to save their military resources if they could, and to stabilise their hold over Iraq. The Soviet Union,

The Idea of Kurdistan

moreover, was pressing for peace between the country that claimed to have a socialist government and the region whose most important leader had spent so much time there. From the point of view of the people on the ground at the time, it must have seemed entirely possible that they may have been negotiating in earnest.

The story Saddam Hussein liked to tell of the negotiations was of heading up to Kurdistan personally, putting down a blank piece of paper and refusing to leave the peace talks until they had found a way to bring an end to the conflict between the Iraqis and the Kurds. It was an obvious piece of propaganda aimed at self-aggrandisement, and yet I have argued in my previous book that it may also be a story that provides clues as to Saddam's hatred of my people, because it meant that any future conflict between the Baghdad government and Kurdistan must have seemed like a personal affront. A personal 'betrayal' of the kind that evil men seem to be so ready to see in others even when they are the ones doing the betraying.

Yet there is also another aspect to this story which is interesting, because in the direct approach, the emphasis on personal contact, the refusal to give in, there are mirrors of episodes in Mullah Mustafa's life. His contacts with Stalin and Khrushchev in particular seem reminiscent of this approach. It is a story of two men who, in terms of their intentions for the Kurdish people, were polar opposites, yet who probably shared that sense of directness, that steely determination to achieve their aims, and even a certain charisma. There must have been a certain grudging respect there, even as Mullah Mustafa was obviously wary of the kind of promises from the central government that he had seen broken so many times before.

And he *was* wary. The evidence for that from the time is clear. Not only were there widespread fears when the Ba'ath party came to power over potential retaliation for Mosul, but the continuation and escalation of the war in 1969 were

Revolution in the 1970s

discouraging signs. Mullah Mustafa actually said that he suspected it was all a trick, while his earlier experiences with Abdul Karim Quasim in 1958 must have taught him the dangers of engagement with the regime without enough caution.

So why did Mullah Mustafa Barzani agree to peace? Part of it was that things were moving in that direction anyway. Jalal Talabani had formed connections with the new government, accepting a post from it and moving into the media. That might have signalled to Mullah Mustafa that the Ba'athists were prepared to do business with members of his party, and it might also have created the political threat of being shut out of future discussions, since Talabani had already attempted something similar once. With that, the danger was that a deal might have gone ahead anyway, and not one that was to Kurdistan's advantage.

Another part of it might have been the threat of what might happen if the negotiations failed. Particularly with the Soviets talking to Baghdad to force them to the negotiating table, there must have been the sense for Mullah Mustafa Barzani of things shifting about internationally somewhere behind the scenes. It was a feeling that must have been familiar to him, with so many of his previous revolts being undermined by shifts in the international political landscape.

And then, ultimately, there was the fact that the deal was such a good one. Maybe too good to be true, and certainly Mullah Mustafa had his suspicions about it. After all, it is easy to promise the world when you don't intend to deliver it. Yet in a way he found himself trapped. Trapped by both his own actions and by the image that he had built up over the years. He had spent decades to that point fighting for a free and independent Kurdistan, where Kurdish language and culture were allowed to thrive, and where Kurdish people could have the opportunity to rule themselves, rather than having officials from outside placed over them. More than that, he'd spent much of that time fighting governments over articles and definitions that seemed to promise different things depending on how they were looked at, and by whom.

So when Saddam unequivocally proposed that Kurdistan become an autonomous region, free to use the Kurdish language in education and public life, with its own officials and relative freedom from control by the central government, Mullah Mustafa Barzani was put in a position where he couldn't do anything other than accept. To have turned down the offer would have been to force the continuation of a war past the point where its objectives seemed to have been achieved. Doing so would have cost Mullah Mustafa significant support, and might even have caused the rebellion to collapse.

He had to accept, but he could at least put conditions in place to try to protect the agreement. With long experience of governments not keeping to their deals, Mullah Mustafa put a time limit in place: the full implementation of the peace accord by no later than 1974. It was a necessary move, but also in some ways a dangerous one, because it presented the Baghdad government with an ultimatum while also telling them exactly how much time they had to prepare for the potential consequences.

1971 Assassination Attempt

In theory, the 1970 peace accords should have heralded a period of peace in Kurdistan. They should have been a major success for Mullah Mustafa Barzani, too. After all, they seemed to give him much of what he had been fighting for in the previous decades. They seemed to guarantee Kurdistan's political and cultural autonomy, and set clear limits on the implementation of the agreement's terms. Some of the initial signs, such as a willingness on the part of the government to work with Jalal Talabani, were promising. The PDK had seemingly achieved a good portion of what it wanted, and the violence of the revolt

Revolution in the 1970s

was at an end for the time being. The initial mood probably should have been one of optimism from both sides, even if it was cautious optimism.

Instead, the main mood in the wake of the agreement seems to have been one of waiting for things to go wrong. Everybody involved seemed to know that there was something about the situation that wasn't likely to work in the long term, and they all seemed to be looking out for the moment when the other side would betray them. Mullah Mustafa seems to have been certain that eventually the government would betray its promises the way so many had before, while there is also some suggestion that Saddam's government was working under the assumption that of course a hardened revolutionary like Mullah Mustafa Barzani would eventually return to the business of revolt.

Perhaps that was down to a recognition of the essentially opposite desires the two sides had, with the government wanting control over all 'its' territory, and the PDK wanting that territory's independence. Yet to some extent it was also a self-fulfilling prophecy. In wanting to be ready for the moment when the other side betrayed them, each side built up its readiness for a fight, which in turn made the other side trust them even less. It was a slow spiral down, where everyone seemed to know what was coming but everyone also seemed to want to cling on in the hope that it would turn out differently to the way they expected.

One of the most serious moments after the peace agreement came in 1971, when there was an attempt to assassinate Mullah Mustafa Barzani through the use of explosives. The Ba'ath party had persuaded a group of imams to travel to Kurdistan to act as go-betweens in the ongoing peace process, and the drivers they provided had suggested to them that they should take a 'recording' device so that they could get a true picture of what went on. That device turned out to be an explosive one, however, one that killed several of the clerics, while their drivers

The Idea of Kurdistan

were killed by Mullah Mustafa's guards when they tried to attack with more explosives and handguns. With all the visitors dead, it was impossible to prove the source of the assassination attempt, but it seemed obvious that such an action had to come from the top in such a totalitarian Iraq. Two more assassination attempts came in the months that followed, each more desperate than the last.

Why? What did Saddam and his regime hope to achieve through such direct assaults on Mullah Mustafa and his family? If the aim was to destroy the independence movement, then surely something larger than the assassination of one man was needed?

Perhaps not. Certainly by that point, Mullah Mustafa Barzani had become almost synonymous with the movement he led. Perhaps the Baghdad regime felt that the movement would collapse without him, or that it would at the very least make it far easier to crush militarily. After all, Mullah Mustafa's reputation was as an exceptionally skilled leader in war, so removing him would have represented a considerable advantage to a regime building towards it.

Of course, there is another possibility. It is possible, just possible, that the Baghdad regime felt that the best way to maintain the peace was to eliminate Mullah Mustafa. I have already talked about the self-fulfilling prophecy of mistrust prevailing at the time. Perhaps the Iraqi government felt that Mullah Mustafa, this war leader, this man who had revolted so many times before, would inevitably do so again. Perhaps they felt that by killing him, they would reduce the momentum towards revolt, forcing Kurdistan to continue on their terms.

Perhaps they even felt that killing Mullah Mustafa would result in a change of leadership. After all, Jalal Talabani was far closer to the new regime than Mullah Mustafa was, having accepted the kind of government sponsored sinecure that Mullah Mustafa had been given under Abdul Karim Quasim in the

1. A young Massoud Barzani with Iraqi Prime Minister Abd al-Karim Qasim
2. Mullah Mustafa Barzani, Spring 1965, photo by William Carter
3. Standing proud in 1932
4. With his brother, Sheikh Ahmed Barzani, 1958
5. Leading a group of peshmerga (Kurdish militia) in 1963

6. Peshmerga en route, by William Carter
7. Peshmerga, those who confront death.
8. With UN representatives in 1972

9. Loyal followers of Mullah Mustafa Barzani visit his grave
10. General Mustafa Barzani
11. Idris Barzani, first son of the immortal Mustafa Barzani

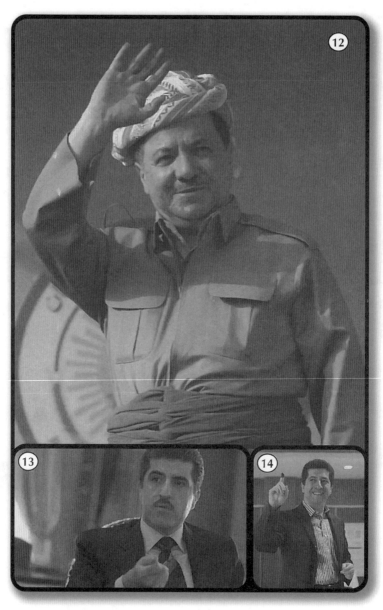

12. Masoud Barzani President of Kurdistan.
13. Kurdistan Prime Minister and KDP deputy president, Nechirvan Barzani.
14. Masrour Barzani, head of the Kurdish region's National Security Council.

1960s. He had also already made one play for the leadership of the PDK. It is possible that Saddam and his people felt that if they succeeded in killing Mullah Mustafa, his family, and/or large portions of the PDK's leadership, they might be left with a Kurdish leader who would be more interested in dialogue than the possibility of fighting in the mountains. They might even have thought that, if they succeeded in killing the man whose legend had grown so much, they would frighten any successor sufficiently to force him to cooperate.

Whatever the reasons, we must ask one more question. Why didn't the assassination attempts immediately result in war? The answer to that may have something to do with the lack of definitive proof about the origins of the attacks. It may have had something to do with one revolt having only just finished, and the difficulties of persuading the whole of Kurdistan to dive straight into another. I think, though, that the answer was rather simpler than that: neither side felt that it was ready for war in 1971. Which meant that from then on, it was a race to see which side could get to full readiness first.

Preparations for War

From 1972 to 1974, both Kurdistan and the Iraqi regime started making preparations for what was to come. Some of those preparations were military. The Baghdad government started to build up its armed forces, using the peace to reverse the losses it had suffered and increase its numbers, while adding more advanced military technology in the form of greater air power. Mullah Mustafa Barzani sought to increase the numbers of peshmerga, while seeking arms from abroad. Specifically, he went back to the Shah of Iran, seeking military assistance from the only potentially friendly power in the region able to match Iraq.

That shows the important thing here, which is that the preparations for the possibility of future violence were not just

The Idea of Kurdistan

about the accumulation of men and weapons. They were about social and political elements too, building into positions that would provide major advantages in both warfare and in any negotiations that followed. It wasn't just about war, because for both sides, a peace on their terms was probably preferable. The trick was forcing the situation into a position where any peace *would* be on their terms, and not on those of their opponents.

One of the most important elements of that process was building alliances abroad. Iraq wanted to deprive Kurdistan of the foreign support that had allowed it to sustain its previous revolt for so long. It probably felt that it would be dominant in any conflict that was between its entire armed forces and those of a simple region. Kurdistan wanted to build a broad base of alliances, to avoid the scenario of losing those allies in the future.

For the Baghdad government, that meant courting the Soviet Union. Some sources make that courtship sound like an easy thing, citing a continuous relationship between Iraq and the USSR since 1958. That, however, underestimates the effects of the revolt of 1968 on those relations. Yes, there had been friendship between Abdul Karim Quasim's government and the USSR. Yes, they had signed a deal over oil rights as late as 1967, but the Ba'ath party was an entirely new government. One that had just overthrown the Soviet Union's previous allies in the country. It took time for them to persuade the Soviet Union that they were allies, and to build up the friendship needed for the pact of 1972. That pact was a declaration of friendship between Iraq and the superpower, stating that neither would work against the other's interest, and that crucially, neither would offer support to those hostile to their new allies.

That element effectively removed any chance of support from the Soviet Union for future revolts by Mullah Mustafa. Apparently, his time in the USSR meant nothing by that point.

Revolution in the 1970s

Or perhaps the Soviets were saying with that peace accord that they wanted the pattern of rebellions within Iraq to stop. That the USSR felt that Kurdish revolt was no longer in its interest, and that it wanted peace between the two nominally socialist groups within Iraq. In doing so, it ignored both Kurdistan's interests and the fact that Saddam had his own agenda.

To counter this loss of allies, Mullah Mustafa sought closer relations with the Shah of Iran. More than that, he sought assistance from the United States, which seemed both like the only power that could balance the USSR's involvement and like an ally that was unlikely to abandon them when it became convenient. After all, the USA had been founded on breaking away from a repressive regime in the name of freedom, hadn't it? His messages to the USA went by indirect routes, but it still seems that several of them reached their intended recipients.

The Shah of Iran seemed interested in using the Kurdish cause to tie up Iraqi forces, and at his urging, the USA decided to back the PDK to balance the increased connections between Baghdad and the USSR. Partly, that was because it had an interest in stopping the Soviet influence in the region, and partly, it was because Iran was in favour with the US, so it tended to get the support it wanted.

That meant that support flowed Kurdistan's way, yet that support came primarily in the form of money and small arms, rather than heavy military technology. The Shah of Iran got advanced fighter jets and tanks from the Americans, but he did not pass that ordinance across the borders. Slowly, a gap in military capabilities began to open up between Baghdad and Kurdistan.

Baghdad also started to make preparations socially. It was in 1972 that it started work on a concerted 'Arabisation' of Kirkuk, encouraging, even forcing, Arabs to take up residence in the city while trying to force Kurds to move away in order to alter its ethnic makeup. This process suggests that Baghdad was

The Idea of Kurdistan

interested in 'winning the peace' as much as going to war, but it is certain that military preparations went on alongside this process.

At the same time, Baghdad was engaged in a process of consolidating its grip on Iraq. It needed solid control of its own territory before it could risk threatening Kurdistan further. Indeed, the Ba'ath party had already learned that lesson the hard way when it lost power in 1965. Yet by 1972, they felt secure enough in their position to nationalise Western held oil interests in the country. That is a symbol of their control over the country, but it also served to increase the power of their position, providing them with massive resources to use in the acquisition of further military capacity.

Taken together, those elements meant that as time went on, the Baghdad government's position only improved, while that of Mullah Mustafa Barzani and his men seemed to remain almost static. By 1974, Saddam's government had enough of an advantage that it could risk acting.

1974

1974 was the year that saw Kurdistan and Iraq spiralling into conflict once again. Why then? Why not earlier, when both sides seemed to know that further conflict was coming? Part of the answer to that seems to have been that neither side was completely set on violence at that point. Each suspected that the other wanted it, but both seem to have been in a position where they would have preferred to avoid the damage to their own position that violence would bring.

More of it, however, has to do with the presence of a natural starting point in the form of Mullah Mustafa Barzani's 1970 ultimatum. In the peace deal he was able to conclude then, he stipulated that the Baghdad government had to implement its side of the deal no later than 1974. The moment he did that, he created a deadline that both sides could use as a target. He had guaranteed peace until 1974 almost regardless of what happened, but had created a real possibility of that peace failing once 1974 came around.

What is perhaps most surprising is that the Baghdad government did make an attempt at providing Kurdish autonomy in 1974, producing an autonomy law that provided for a quasi-independent Kurdish region with its own government and rulers. Why? Why make the effort to produce such a law if it was set on violence at that point?

There are a couple of possibilities. One is that perhaps Baghdad was not as set on conflict as some commentators have believed. Please understand, I am not suggesting that Saddam's government was somehow working from a sense of altruism. It was a military regime, demonstrably unafraid to use even the most horrific violence when it suited its aims.

Yet that is the key phrase here. Violence was a tool for the Baghdad government, but not its only tool. If it could achieve its aims of stability and control without military action, then that was simply more efficient and safer. It held a reduced risk of instability within Iraq, a reduced risk of being drawn into an extended, draining conflict, and a reduced risk of negative publicity with the international community. If they could have peace on their own terms, then that was only to their benefit.

The other possibility is that Baghdad put the autonomy law in place because they had to be seen to be trying to keep their word, by their allies, by the wider world, and by others within Iraq. By crafting an autonomy law that they must have known Kurdistan could not agree to, they created a situation where it seemed that the PDK were the ones being unreasonable, going to war when it seemed that Baghdad had given them 'everything' they asked for. It was about going to war while appearing to be in the right, allowing the Iraqi government to maintain its support with its allies, while potentially removing some of the Kurdish fighters' support.

The Idea of Kurdistan

Or perhaps it was a combination of the two, in the kind of realpolitik that was so common at the time. By waiting until 1974, the Baghdad government created the potential to deal with the rebellious Kurds to its north without having to fight, while giving itself the appearance of the moral high ground if that failed.

The proposed autonomy law was actually a good attempt to implement the 1970 agreement on a lot of levels. It provided for an autonomous region, divided into three zones centred on Erbil, Sulaymaniyah and Dohuk, for the use of the Kurdish language in public life, and for Kurdish officials. There was even an attempt made at Kurdish language television. Yet one issue meant that Mullah Mustafa Barzani could never have accepted the deal as it stood: Kirkuk.

Kirkuk was clearly a part of the territory Mullah Mustafa intended when he talked about the possibility of an independent Kurdistan, and today, it stands as a key part of Kurdistan's economy. Yet in 1974, the Baghdad regime sought to separate the city from the autonomous region they were proposing. They sought to use the argument that it was an Arab city, citing a population balance affected by their ongoing policy of Arabisation, as well as falsified census records. The real reason was the same reason that Kurdistan could not afford to let Kirkuk go: oil. It had, and still has, some of Kurdistan's most important oil resources. Resources that were vital to the life of the region, but which Baghdad wanted for itself, the same way it had seized Western oil interests in its own territory.

The result was, almost inevitably, war. From the start, as had been the case so many times through Mullah Mustafa Barzani's life, it was clear that the Kurdish forces could not win a conventional war. They had plenty of money from their allies, but no heavy armour or artillery. Once again, they were forced into a guerrilla war in the mountains, seeking to prolong the conflict long enough through an essentially defensive war that they would be able to force the government back to the negotiating table. Indeed, when they had been so close to getting what they wanted from the autonomy law, with only Kirkuk left out, there must have been a note of optimism there. Just one more push, backed by the USA, and they might be able to bring about the free Kurdistan they had been working towards for so long.

Yet ultimately, that was not to be. Forced into a defensive war in the mountains, Mullah Mustafa was almost certain that he could out-wait the Iraqi army. With his support from abroad, he had the supplies and the political will behind him to keep going for as long as he needed. Yet in 1975, despite all his precautions, the unthinkable happened, and once again his support melted away like it had never been there.

Algiers Accord

There have been many moments of betrayal for Kurdistan involving the international community. The Treaty of Lausanne is typically the most cited, for the way in which it abandoned the promises made to Kurdistan following the First World War. It was a moment where the Great Powers of the world placed their own interests ahead of those of Kurdistan and its people. The Yalta Conference of 1945 saw the world's major powers ignore Kurdistan's position again in the wake of the Second World War. The Soviet withdrawal of support for the Mahabad Republic in 1946 led almost directly to its collapse. In that sense, another moment where international allies abandoned their support for Kurdistan should hardly have come as a surprise.

Yet in a sense, the Algiers Accords of 1975 were one of the biggest surprises of all for Kurdistan. In 1970, it would have seemed impossible that something like that could have happened again. The Kurdish peshmerga under Mullah Mustafa Barzani had deliberately sought a wide range of international support,

The Idea of Kurdistan

including discussions with the USSR, the Iranians and the Americans. They had played the part of revolutionaries for hire, willing to tie up Iraq's military resources in return for aid, and in doing so, they had managed to create a broad base of support that looked like it could not all fall away at once. That might sound like a cynical way to look at the situation, but after years of being used and then abandoned by international partners, it was really only an understandable level of caution. The Kurdish authorities were well aware that other countries wanted to use them, so it only makes sense that they sought to use those potential patrons in return, to fuel their attempts to gain independence.

As the 1970s moved on, it seemed like a wise strategy. We have already seen how the Soviet–Iraqi pact linked the Baghdad government with one of the major patrons Mullah Mustafa Barzani had cultivated, effectively taking away the possibility of support from the USSR. It would have been attacking one of its own allies. If the PDK had been dependent on just that single source of support, it would have quickly found itself without the opportunity to match the government's forces. Instead, it still felt that it had adequate levels of support available where necessary from the Iranians, and through them from the USA. If anything, the stronger links between the USSR and Iraq seemed to guarantee that US support in future, thanks to the pressures of the Cold War. During the revolt that followed the failure of the 1974 autonomy law, that support was essential in maintaining the Kurdish position, allowing the peshmerga forces to pull back to zones on the Iranian border to avoid taking on the Iraqi army head on. Their ability to harass and tie up the supposedly socialist Iraq became a miniature expression of the Cold War, while allowing Iran to fight its side of the ongoing Iran–Iraq conflict without a major commitment of its own troops.

The Algiers Accords changed all that at a stroke. They came

about when Iraqi and Iranian officials met one another at an OPEC (Organisation of Petroleum Exporting Countries) conference in early 1975, at the behest of the United States. That meeting place was significant, because it was by that point just about the only situation in which the two sides could meet. Yet it was also significant because it was a situation in which Kurdistan had no voice.

The talks paved the way for a number of treaties and agreements between the two countries in the months that followed, yet for Kurdistan, the crucial moment came in that first meeting, when under pressure from the US, both sides agreed to stop supporting peshmerga fighters to attack one another. Both sides. The wording of that seems almost laughable today. Perhaps it was an attempt to make it look like a compromise agreement, or to save face by ensuring that the Iranians weren't the only ones agreeing to something, yet even the United States must have known that only the Iranians were supplying the peshmerga. The withdrawal of support by 'both sides' was in fact an abandonment of Kurdistan by the Iranians, giving Saddam's forces carte blanche to move in and crush the Kurdish revolt.

Let us be clear: the Americans knew that would be the case when they made the decision to remove support. When they put pressure on the two sides to meet and come to a peaceful resolution, they did not do so unaware of the possible consequences for Kurdistan. Henry Kissinger famously commented on the situation that one should not mistake covert action for missionary work. Or to put it another way, America had achieved its objectives in the region, and did not see a reason to continue its involvement simply out of kindness or charity.

Even so, we must assume that there were reasons of some sort for the decision. The most basic seems to have been that conflict between Iraq and Iran was no longer desirable. America

The Idea of Kurdistan

wished to build bridges with Iraq, having realised that it was nowhere near as socialist in tone as it claimed, and deciding that talking might be a better option for limiting the USSR's influence there than direct action. The needs of the Cold War also played a part in that sense, since continued action that could be traced back to the USA risked pushing Iraq more towards the USSR's embrace.

Yet there was also a sense of concern about Kurdistan at the time. Reports from the time make it clear that Kissinger at least had no interest in Mullah Mustafa Barzani succeeding in his revolt, only in the revolt continuing long enough to create a favourable situation for Iran at the negotiating table. Earlier reports from the 1960s had been particularly unfavourable to Mullah Mustafa, playing up his time in the Soviet Union and calling him a 'Red' (a Communist). The whole Kurdish independence movement was effectively seen as suspect by the Americans at the time, and so they were only too ready to abandon it when it suited their interests.

Iran

The result was the collapse of the Kurdish revolt, so rapidly that it must have seemed at the time like it was made out of paper. The Kurdish forces did not have the equipment to match the Iraqi army in conventional warfare. Their only hope had been to use the mountains, to use the possibility of retreat into Iranian territory, to conduct the kind of guerrilla war they had fought so many times before. Yet without Iranian support, without the supply lines from the Iranian side of the border, they were effectively put in a position where there was no hope of sustaining that fight for long. And in guerrilla warfare, the essence of it is the ability to sustain the conflict longer than the opponent, being willing to keep fighting past the point where they become sick of the conflict and seek to negotiate, or so worn down that you can shift to a more conventional assault.

Revolution in the 1970s

We can have no doubt that Mullah Mustafa Barzani understood the implications of the situation. He had seen it again and again. He had lived through it repeatedly, in Iraq and Iran, in the Mahabad Republic and Sheikh Ahmad's earliest revolts. Each failed revolt had led to only one thing, the thing that inevitably faced his people now: flight and exile.

Yet this was not some small scale escape. This was not a march with a few hundred men. Nor was it the evacuation of just his family and a few thousand immediate followers, which had seemed like such an immense undertaking in 1945. Instead, more than a hundred thousand people left Kurdistan in 1975. A hundred thousand refugees from the oncoming wrath of the Iraqi army, all of whom needed to be organised as they fled to Iran, all of whom required homes, food, and the permission of the Iranian government to enter their territory.

In many ways, the organisation of this mass movement of his people stands as one of Mullah Mustafa Barzani's greatest achievements. He was not able to win a free Kurdistan for them, but he was able to ensure that huge numbers of them were able to escape the violence that was to follow. He was able to negotiate a way into Iran for thousands upon thousands of those who had followed him, and with hindsight, knowing everything that happened afterwards, we can safely say that it was an action that saved their lives.

We know that all this happened quickly. The Shah of Iran informed Mullah Mustafa of his withdrawal of support on 11th March 1975, and gave his people just thirty days to cross into Iran if they wished. After that, the borders were to be closed. In fact, the border stayed open until the end of April, but that was still a pitifully short time.

That Mullah Mustafa initially declared that he would keep fighting and sent his sons to keep up the fight perhaps reflects the desperation of the situation. He needed to maintain some semblance of resistance to avoid the Kurdish cause simply collapsing. Yet a week after the meeting with the Shah, he was ready to declare that the revolt was done, and that escape was the only option.

Escape to *Iran* was the only option. Turkey had already closed its borders by that point, making it clear that its soldiers would turn back any Kurds who attempted to cross into its territory. That was hardly surprising. It had its own problems with Kurdish insurrection, and had historically shown a greater hatred of the Kurds as an ethnic group than almost anywhere else. There was never any suggestion that it would simply accept an increase in the number of my people within its borders.

There was a supposed amnesty offered by Saddam's forces to the south and west. Those forces blockaded the southern and western sides, making it almost impossible to flee to the rest of Iraq, while accepting the offered amnesty was at best an act of desperation, trusting to the word of a Ba'ath party that had already broken its word on several occasions, and that had already begun a progressive campaign of Arabisation that pointed towards its attitudes to my people. Many people were forced to take up the amnesty by circumstances, but it was rarely anyone's first choice.

The decision of whether to stay or go divided my people. Whole families found themselves split in half, separated by their ability to make the journey into Iran, and their willingness to trust that nothing bad would happen, based on their experiences of previous reprisals for rebellions. For Mullah Mustafa Barzani and his immediate family, the decision was simple: they had to leave. Saddam had been willing to try to murder Mullah Mustafa even at a point where they were supposedly at peace. In the aftermath of a rebellion, it seemed certain that Iraq's ruler would have him killed.

So, for what was to prove to be the final time, Mullah Mustafa Barzani crossed the border into Iran. There, he and his family were given a house in one of the compounds of the Iranian secret police. It was a move that amounted to the same sort of house arrest he had suffered as a boy in Sulaymaniyah, bringing his series of revolts full circle. He was in comfortable conditions, but was watched constantly, presumably on the basis that the Shah did not want to risk him escaping and returning to Iraq yet again.

In this, the Shah and his men seem to have assumed that after so many escapes and comebacks, Mullah Mustafa would try for at least one more. Yet at this point, he had lived out a full life of revolts. He had dedicated his life to the Kurdish cause, spending year after year either fighting or in exile. In instructing his sons to continue the fight, he had effectively passed over the baton of revolt. He was, finally, ready to stop.

USA

Yet there was one final attempt to rally support before the end. By 1975, Mullah Mustafa Barzani had a number of minor medical problems, including a permanent limp that his doctors believed was from a trapped nerve. Yet when that came to be accompanied by chest pains and other symptoms, they started to believe that something more serious might be behind the problems. They urged Mullah Mustafa to seek medical treatment in Iran.

Astonishingly, he refused, stating that he would only seek medical treatment in the United States. Ostensibly, this was because he trusted the impartiality and skills of American doctors more than those who would be provided by the Shah. Yet even at the time, it seems that everyone knew that he wanted to make one last attempt at securing support for Kurdistan. Both the Iranians and some among the Americans seem to have been unwilling to let Mullah Mustafa travel to the US, fearing that he would create a public relations nightmare for them if he let the way they had abandoned Kurdistan be known.

Yet ultimately, that was the reason they had to let him travel,

The Idea of Kurdistan

because Mullah Mustafa had enough connections in the USA, including one of its senators, Senator Jackson, that the story of him being stopped travelling would have become public had they done anything else. So he was sent to the Mayo Clinic in the USA for treatment of what turned out to be lung cancer.

Yet if he had hoped that the trip would permit him access to key political figures, he was disappointed. Both the CIA and members of the Iranian secret service watched him and those around him, seemingly specifically to prevent the kind of direct approach that Mullah Mustafa had used to gain support in the USSR. They tried to distract Mullah Mustafa's entourage by taking them on sightseeing tours around different areas of the country, but when asked to do things like take Mullah Mustafa to the White House, they would only drive past it, pretending to misunderstand.

Crucially, they refused to give Mullah Mustafa or his people any direct access to Henry Kissinger, the US Secretary of State. After much effort on the part of the Barzanis (and specifically former Iraqi diplomat Mohammed Dosky), they were able to secure a meeting with one of Kissinger's under-secretaries, Joseph Cisco. Even that meeting, however, was designed simply to defuse the situation, not to provide any real help. Cisco hadn't been involved in any of the decisions the US made regarding Kurdistan, didn't have the power to make any binding commitments, and had been specifically instructed to do no more than placate them.

In October 1975, the US returned Mullah Mustafa Barzani to Iran, apparently certain that they would not see him again. Yet in 1976, Mohammed Dosky was able to secure a return to the USA for him, on condition that it was purely for medical treatment, not to talk with the press. The USA was still highly sensitive about the role it had played in the failed revolt.

In theory, the CIA were not to watch Mullah Mustafa while he stayed in the US, but it did with greater or lesser consistency as Mullah Mustafa attended the Mayo Clinic for treatment and met with US officials, including several senators. In 1977, he was finally able to speak to journalists, thanks to the efforts of Roberta Cohen in arranging a meeting where *technically* he only spoke to her, just happening to do so in the hearing of a whole group of journalists, and thanks to a change in the US administration.

Yet these efforts ultimately were not able to change US policy. At best, they allowed for refugees from the conflict to flee to the USA, and paved the way for US assistance in the future when it became convenient to them again. Ultimately though, from 1977–79, Mullah Mustafa found himself caught up in the battle against his illness as fully as he had been engaged in any of his previous conflicts.

Finally, in March 1979, Mullah Mustafa died. He had outlasted the reign of the Shah who had withdrawn his aid, but did not live to see some of the worst excesses of Saddam's regime against my people. His body was taken back to Iranian Kurdistan and laid to rest just outside Mahabad, in Oshnoviyeh.

The Impact of the 1970s

The death of Mullah Mustafa Barzani obviously makes the 1970s incredibly significant for Kurdistan, in the same way that the end of the 1960s was made poignant by Sheikh Ahmad's death. Indeed, there are mirrors in the ways the two decades finished, with the deaths of key leaders, Kurdistan in a potentially difficult position, and the future looking very uncertain.

Yet while Mullah Mustafa Barzani's death was a landmark moment for Kurdistan, it was far from the only way in which the events of the 1970s had an impact on the future of the region. Indeed, there is a case for saying that many other moments in that decade had a greater impact, as Mullah Mustafa, in life, made his last decisions regarding his homeland.

The 1970 peace deal was one of those crucial moments. Its

The Idea of Kurdistan

impact at the time was obvious: it stopped the on again, off again rebellions that had consumed Kurdistan for much of the 1960s, allowing for a period of rebuilding, and even pointing briefly towards the possibility of future peace. Its impact on the modern Kurdistan has been even greater though.

Why? Because the original peace deal set out something remarkably similar to the Kurdistan that exists today. It provided for an area roughly equivalent geographically to the one that currently forms Kurdistan, and set out a formula for that Kurdistan to achieve a measure of independence within the context of a wider Iraq. Again, that sounds extremely similar to the situation that exists today, with Kurdistan being effectively self-governing while still remaining as a part of a federal Iraq. It is arguable that such a situation could not exist without the precedent set out by the 1970 agreement.

The 1974 autonomy law and its aftermath were also crucial. This was a moment that could potentially have led to a stable Iraq. Yet that is the problem. It would have been Iraq, with no sign of Kurdistan in the long term. Agreeing to the 1974 law would have led to a Kurdistan incapable of being anything more than a few scattered sub-states. It would certainly have left Kurdistan's government without the resources it needed to invest in infrastructure or building projects, and would have thus resulted in a very different Kurdistan today.

Rejecting the 1974 law was necessary, but the rebellion it sparked resulted indirectly in some of Kurdistan's worst troubles in the future. It appears to have been the moment when Saddam decided that he could not solve the conflicts with Kurdistan through peaceful means, and was the starting point of a chain of events that led to displacement for my people, to the mass murder of Barzani men, and ultimately to the chemical horrors of the Anfal. It was the rebellion that set Kurdistan firmly at odds with Saddam's government.

It was also the rebellion that helped to shape some of

Revolution in the 1970s

Kurdistan's foreign relations, thanks to its betrayal by its allies. It taught Kurdistan to seek out multiple foreign partners, rather than being overly reliant on just one. To put its military in a strong enough position to protect itself rather than relying on other people. The events of the 1970s directly shaped attitudes that continue to have an impact on the politics of the region today.

Chapter Nine: Kurdistan in the 1980s and 1990s

The period following Mullah Mustafa Barzani's death was a complex one. I do not propose to discuss the 1980s and 1990s in Kurdistan in full detail here, but only give an overview of their events. This is partly because such complex events would require more space than we have here to discuss in full, partly because they fall outside our frame of reference in Mullah Mustafa's life, and partly because there is much existing scholarship on the period, including my own previous work *Kurdistan: Genocide and Rebirth*. Nevertheless, there is enough space in this work to give a general guide to events, and show how the position at the end of Mullah Mustafa Barzani's life was able to transform into the democracy currently enjoyed in Kurdistan.

The Late 1970s: Preparation

It is impossible to understand the events of the 1980s without understanding that even in the late 1970s, preparations were underway for violence towards my people. Even as Mullah Mustafa was being forced into exile and facing his fight against the illness that would kill him, Saddam and the rest of the Iraqi government were cracking down on those who had been involved in the revolts.

Kurdistan in the 1980s and 1990s

The first step was the movement of further troops north, taking advantage of the collapse of the Kurdish defences after 1975–76 to move massive numbers of troops into Kurdistan. They filled military bases, surrounded villages, and instituted strict border controls that included the use of exclusion zones in which people could be arrested or shot simply for being there. The exercise was branded as a counter-insurgency one, but its practical effect was to create a division between those of my people who were able to escape across the border to Iran, and those forced to remain in their villages, knowing that something worse would be coming in the future.

And it seems likely that they *did* know. Everyone I have spoken to from the period suggests that they were fully aware that there would be some kind of reprisal from the government. The only thing that varied at the time was opinion on how bad that would be. After all, my people had weathered the periods after failed insurrections before, dealing with crackdowns by the British, by Iraqi royalty, and by the earlier governments of the 1960s. They had seen the Mahabad Republic destroyed and that had not stopped their desire to keep going with pushing for independence. Nor had arrests or executions. Mullah Mustafa had been a symbol of that spirit in so many ways, pushed into exile or retreat again and again, but somehow always coming back to try again.

Yet by the late 1970s, even before the news of his death, it was clear that he would not be coming back. Other things were changing too. Saddam Hussein had been the de facto military ruler of the country since 1976, but in 1979 he became the ruler in every other sense. It gave him a freedom to act that was dangerous for my people. That was combined, from 1979, with severe difficulties for anybody who succeeded in making the escape into Iran, as it was in that year that a fatwa was issued there against my people. The result was entire families split in half.

The Idea of Kurdistan

The mood in the late 1970s was a dangerous one, therefore. It quickly became even worse for those who had to stay behind. Although people speak of the destruction of the Anfal, many of the tactics employed then had already been trialled in the 1970s. More than six hundred villages belonging to my people were destroyed. Not just attacked. Destroyed outright. Their people were rounded up and transported to prison camps, using Russian made trucks, or were sent away deep into the south of the country. Those who tried to fight back were killed.

When the people were gone, the very infrastructure of the villages was destroyed. Houses were pulled down with bulldozers and phone lines were pulled up. The aim seems to have been, not just to move people on from their villages, knowing that they would only return when the army was gone, but to make those villages effectively uninhabitable. It was a tactic of controlling Kurdistan by destroying those areas of it that had given the Baghdad government the most trouble in the past.

The whole process included two policies whose effects can be felt in Kurdistan today. One was a continuation of the Arabisation of Kurdistan, extended by that point from Kirkuk to the rest of the region. It is a policy that has contributed to the debates over the ownership of Kirkuk, but also to racial and ethnic tensions within the region, as Kurdistan's government has sought to address the issues created by such forced alteration of the ethnic balance of the region without alienating those Arabs who were born and raised in Kurdistan, and who consider it their home.

The second policy was one of urbanisation. The destruction of villages was partly a direct attack on those places that had been involved in rebellion before, but it was also an attack on an entire way of life. The Baghdad government seems to have felt that since all the earlier revolts were centred on villages and fighting from the mountains, the most effective solution would be to concentrate my people in cities where they could be more conveniently controlled by Iraqi officials. There may also have been a recognition that such a concentration of people might make it easier to attack them in future.

As a result, those families who were removed from their villages either escaped and found themselves forced into the cities by the widespread destruction of other villages, or they were taken to hastily built camps. Most were not even finished before the first people were brought to them, and they had to effectively build their own prisons. Initially, large numbers of families were clustered together in general holding camps, but then slowly those came to be split up, distributing the interned families more widely around camps throughout the region. Some were even sent south, beyond Kurdistan, while many were made to 'disappear' completely.

This period is often seen as somehow separate from the atrocities that followed, because it was aimed at limited areas and particular tribes more than my people as a whole. It is seen as a counter insurgency campaign rather than as the beginnings of genocide. That is a mistake. Although people might see the use of chemical weapons during the Anfal as qualitatively different, for the most part, many of the tactics involved were the same. The destruction of villages, the mass displacement of people... I feel that it is better to see these initial actions in the 1970s more as a prototype or a trial run for what was to come in the 1980s. It was a period of preparation, and once those preparations were complete, horror followed.

The Early 1980s: The Beginning of Violence

When people talk about the 1980s in Kurdistan, they typically refer to the Anfal. The Anfal is important, and we will be exploring it shortly, but it lasted for only a few months in the late 1980s. To concentrate solely on its atrocities is to ignore a campaign of repression lasting through the entire early part of the period.

The Idea of Kurdistan

That campaign was ongoing. After all, many of my people began the decade in prison camps, given only limited food, water and shelter, hemmed in by guards, and with no access to the outside world. Saddam's men did not regulate the day-to-day lives of those within the camps, preferring mostly to sit at the edges and keep everyone in, but they did make 'raids' into the camps where they would come in and beat or kill people, perhaps dragging them away and making them disappear. The children of the camps were educated, but only as a part of an ongoing process of indoctrination, aimed at making them loyal to Saddam even while he ordered them imprisoned. All lessons were delivered in Arabic, while we were required to sing songs praising Saddam as the country's ruler.

It was a relatively small step from imprisonment to murder. In 1983, Barzani forces had joined with Iranian ones as part of the ongoing conflicts between Iraq and Iran. They had harassed Iraqi troops seeking to fight in the north, continuing their policy of guerrilla warfare from the mountains against them. That is generally cited as the provocation for what came next, but the truth is that it was at best a mere excuse for the government. An opportunity for escalation that would have always come along in some form.

I argued in my last book that Saddam seems to have been trying to 'solve the problem' of Kurdish rebellion in increasingly extreme ways, each more disproportionate than the last. He began with treaties, moved on to warfare, then to imprisonment and the clearing of the borders. Each new moment of rebellion (usually sparked by the cruelty of his methods) seems to have convinced him that his last approach was not extreme enough, and that he should escalate to a more concerted attack against my people. Certainly, that is an approach that seems to explain the rapid escalation from warfare to imprisonment to mass murder to the use of chemical weapons in full blown genocide.

In 1983, the 'solution' of the time was the murder of all

Kurdistan in the 1980s and 1990s

Barzani males deemed to be of fighting age. There was no specific age attached to it, although several commentators have attempted to connect one to it. Instead, my recollection is that the process was done by size, so that I had larger friends the same age as me who were taken. In tactics reminiscent of those used in many other war crimes, the men were forced into trucks and driven away, never to be seen again. Some were able to escape by hiding or running, particularly outside the camps, but thousands were not. Eight thousand men and boys were taken away in August 1983.

Although the details will probably always be unclear, since 2005 we have had a good idea what happened to those men. More than 500 of their bodies were found in a mass grave in Iraq's southern deserts, having been machine gunned. Combined with the stories that have emerged piecemeal over the years, it seems likely that all 8,000 were murdered in similar ways, shot in various corners of the desert and buried in mass graves using bulldozers.

It is a crime that is often forgotten when it comes to the history of Iraq, or even the history of Saddam's atrocities. It was not his first mass killing, since he had ordered family and tribal groups murdered earlier. It was not his largest, because the 182,000 dead of the Anfal eclipses the scale of this atrocity many times over. Yet for me, it remains a vitally important moment in Kurdistan's history, and not just because it was Barzani men and boys being murdered.

Instead, the importance of 1983 comes because it represents the moment when the Baghdad government flipped over to the use of mass murder as a possible 'cure' for Kurdish rebelliousness. It represented both the moment when Saddam's people started to go beyond the kind of tactics that had been employed by the British or the Iraqi's before, and the moment when they first showed a commitment to large scale murder in connection to the situation in Kurdistan.

Yet in 1983, the violence still had not reached its zenith. Although Kurds continued to be taken from the streets by the repressive regime, much of the work against my people in the years immediately following this moment was more cultural in scope. It tried to force my people to love Saddam, and to be more Arab. Perhaps the idea was that, after attempting to destroy the Barzani's capacity to fight back in one brutal moment, they might be able to take the next generation and raise it in a way that would make its members into the loyal, pro-regime citizens Saddam wanted.

It was a process that meant ongoing misery both for those in the camps and for those stuck outside, wondering about their friends or relatives. There were limited communications with the camps, consisting of messages smuggled in by peshmerga at great risk, since the areas around the camps were almost always exclusion zones, where people could be shot just for trespassing. For a while, it looked almost like that would be the extent of the violence. Like the regime would simply keep my people locked up in prison camps on a permanent basis, letting out only those young people they could brainwash enough to get them to join the army.

Yet as the decade wore on, even that approach wasn't enough for the regime. It decided to move on to something larger. To the Anfal.

The Anfal

It is hard to see how someone could sit down and plan the murders of 182,000 people. It is barely comprehensible that anyone could kill so many people, in a region that had only a relatively small population at the time. Yet the regime did kill those people, using a mixture of chemical weapons and more conventional tactics. Tactics that figures like Ali Majid Al Hasan planned in great detail, so that the killing became almost industrial in its approach. There have been only a few instances

Kurdistan in the 1980s and 1990s

of mass murder in modern history that have killed or 'disappeared' more people.

There are several things that it is important to remember about the Anfal. The first is that it was not one event, but instead consisted of multiple operations, spread out over the course of several months. Each phase seems to have used slightly different tactics, as the efficiency of the mechanisms of murder evolved. The earliest attacks began with almost pure chemical weapons use, as at Halabja, using bombers or artillery to attack civilian targets under the pretence that they were targeting peshmerga. As the phases of the Anfal went on however, the use of chemical weapons began to be combined with units of the Iraqi army on the ground, waiting outside the areas targeted by chemicals to capture or kill those who fled. Remember that the final figure for the Anfal's death toll does not include those many thousands who were added to the prison camps in that period.

It is also worth remembering how thorough the Anfal was. It was not just a campaign of mass murder. It was a campaign to wipe my people out in Iraqi claimed territory, at least in any of the rural areas that had given the regime so much trouble over the years. The fifth phase of the Anfal was ordered repeated because it had not killed enough 'insurgents' for Saddam's liking. In terms of tactics on the ground, whole villages were destroyed, extending the tactics employed in the late 1970s. Houses were bulldozed or destroyed with artillery, infrastructure was torn up, and even livestock was slaughtered. The attacking Iraqi forces did this partly to ensure that any of my people who fled would be unable to take the resources with them that they needed to make it to safety, and partly to ensure that my people could never return to those villages. In the modern Kurdistan, it has taken concerted programmes of investment and building to resettle some of the areas that were affected.

It is also worth remembering that the Anfal was accompanied

by an extended propaganda campaign. Even the name, meaning 'The Spoils of War' was an act of propaganda, trying to imply that this was merely looting and pillaging by an Iraqi army that had been fighting against the Kurds as a part of the war against Iran. Trying to disguise the greater evil of mass murder by implying a lesser evil.

Disguise was at the heart of the propaganda campaign around the Anfal. Previous propaganda efforts within and around Kurdistan had been based on the notion that with enough persuasion that Saddam was my people's friend, at least a percentage of the population would begin to believe him. Before the Anfal, the idea was that the sustained use of propaganda would result in the integration of my people with the Arab population. Once the focus shifted to my people's destruction, that was no longer needed.

What was needed was enough distraction that the international community would not notice what was happening, or if they did notice, enough that they would not act. So we find moments of propaganda around Halabja, for example, that even had many people within Kurdistan convinced that it had been the Iranians who had attacked the city and not the regime. Other propaganda tried to convince the world that Saddam was merely fighting the kind of counter-insurgency war that the British and others had already fought in Kurdistan, rather than conducting a campaign of mass murder. It tried to play on the fears of the international community regarding their previous experiences in wars such as the Vietnam War, suggesting that getting involved in a long, bloody conflict involving guerrilla groups would not be to anyone's benefit.

Perhaps that reasoning explains why some of the international community were complicit in the spread of that propaganda. Messages from the United States embassy, and communiqués from the USA to other countries, asked about Iran's involvement in events, particularly in Halabja. In doing so, the USA helped to confuse matters, planting the seed that Iran might have been involved. It even persuaded the UN to add to the wording of its Security Council resolution requiring *both* Iraq and Iran to cease the use of chemical weapons. By spreading the blame, the USA seems to have been determined to avoid any suggestion that there was a genocide going on.

Why? Because genocide is one of the few things in international law that not just allows for outside intervention in a state's affairs, but actively demands it. In theory, the moment genocide is declared to exist in a country, the UN's members are obliged to intervene to stop it. It is a rule that is designed to prevent a second Holocaust from ever happening, and yet in practice it often means that those members who do not wish to find themselves caught up in war twist and turn to find ways of denying what is in front of them. It is only recently that several of the countries involved have come to recognise the Anfal for what it was.

That lack of recognition meant that the Anfal was able to go on largely unchecked for several months. It meant that Saddam Hussein was able to stay in control of Kurdistan in its wake, and that many of my people remained in prison camps even if they had not been killed. It was a lack of intervention that meant far more suffering for my people in the brief time that remained in the decade.

Uprising and Escape

Yet eventually, those of us caught in Saddam's camps were able to escape. How did the situation change so much, and over the course of just a short space of time? Typically, the change is ascribed to the after effects of the first Gulf War of 1990–91. The war is seen by some outside observers as weakening Saddam to the point where my people could become free, or their freedom is seen as a side effect of American action.

Yet this does not represent the truth of what happened. The

The Idea of Kurdistan

Gulf War did not directly affect the situation in the north of Iraq, being more closely aimed at the situation in the south. Indeed, its justifications were primarily about the Iraqi invasion of Kuwait, rather than to do with the atrocities that had been perpetrated against my people in the previous two years. Those were mentioned almost as an afterthought, perhaps because focusing more on that aspect would have created too much of a precedent for the US to have to stick to in other cases of mass murder or genocide.

At the time though, it certainly seemed to my people like the military intervention might blossom into more. The prevailing hope in Kurdistan was that the vastly more powerful military forces of the Americans and their allies would remove Saddam completely, thus paving the way for Kurdistan to be free. It was a war where the Americans officially lost only 294 troops, more of them to non-combat accidents than to enemy action, compared with the more than 20,000 casualties they inflicted on Saddam's military. It seemed almost obvious that with such a clear advantage, the US and its allies would complete the job by removing Saddam.

Yet they chose not to, for reasons that seem to have had at least as much to do with the internal politics of the US government as with the situation on the ground. Once again, Kurdistan found its expectations of the United States let down. Instead, it seemed that the US expected Kurdistan to free itself. Certainly, in 1991, US backed radio stations called for the Iraqi people to rise up and overthrow Saddam. It was an attempt to do with words what the more hawkish elements of the US government had been prevented from doing by their political opponents. And in 1991, Kurdistan *did* rise up with much of the rest of Iraq.

That uprising was so nearly totally successful. Within days, a combination of rebel groups from different parts of Iraq had managed to take over cities and government buildings, so that

Kurdistan in the 1980s and 1990s

it looked for a moment like Iraq might be able to do for itself what the outside military forces had not been willing to do for it. Kurdistan rose up with the rest, and peshmerga were quickly able to secure the cities there. It must have seemed like freedom had finally come.

The problems began when, in the south, no one was able to take Baghdad. Because the attempted revolution consisted of numerous different groups attempting to work together only in the vaguest of ways, it could only really succeed if it succeeded quickly. The longer it wore on, the more time there was for factions to fall out with one another, for the lack of organisation to result in logistical problems, and for the regime to start to pick groups off piecemeal.

That certainly seems to have been what happened in the south. The regime's remaining military forces went after the militia groups one by one, using their continued superiority when it came to heavy armour and air support. Almost as quickly as it had come, the attempted revolution fell in the south, leaving behind thousands of dead in its wake. In Kurdistan, things lasted a little longer, yet ultimately, the 1991 revolution was merely an opportunity for escape for many people. It resulted in more than one and a half million of my people fleeing Kurdistan, approximately half to Iran, in what became one of the biggest humanitarian efforts seen at the time. Many people found themselves escaping prison camps in Iraq only to find themselves stuck in refugee camps just the other side of the Iranian border, running only a little ahead of Saddam's jets and helicopters.

The peshmerga held back the Iraqi army as best they could, and succeeded in keeping the pressure off the refugees for long enough that the world could finally take notice of what was happening and impose a no fly zone over the north of Iraq. That no fly zone gave the refugees a measure of security, preventing the use of aerial bombardment against them as they fled.

Yet even as so many of my people were forced to flee, others were still fighting. They might have lost control of the cities, but they were able to extend the conflict for another six months, fighting the regime's military to a standstill in a way that did two things: first, it threatened to destabilise the regime by taking away resources that it still needed to control the rest of the country. Second, it created the threat of more foreign intervention if Saddam continued to attack his people.

Because of this, and perhaps because Saddam knew that my people were the one force in Iraq with a clearly defined territory and set of aims, he found himself forced to accede to the creation of the kind of autonomous region that he had promised all the way back in 1970, and which would become the current region of Kurdistan. It was a moment of surprising success in the middle of a period of brutal violence.

Civil War

Yet sadly, the violence was not to stop, because while the various elements of Kurdistan's political parties were able to agree for a time, eventually they found themselves pressured to a point where their differences could not be contained. Those differences turned into fractures, and the fractures eventually exploded into civil war.

It is hard even today to write about the civil war in Kurdistan. The reasons for it are easy to see with hindsight. As a part of Iraq, the new autonomous region of Kurdistan was subject to the same embargoes as the rest of the country when it came to official international trade. Saddam's regime compounded that with an unofficial embargo on contact with the south of the country that effectively laid siege to Kurdistan. It meant that for the political parties who were dominant in an area to ensure that people were fed and able to have access to resources, they effectively had to control the smuggling routes out of the country. With such pressures on all sides, war was almost inevitable.

Kurdistan in the 1980s and 1990s

Again and again, history has shown the tragedy of civil wars. In a war against an outside aggressor, there is at least a sense of unity forged against that attacker. There is a clear sense of who the opponents are, what they represent, and how the war is likely to end. An outside attacker either overruns a country or is pushed back. They destroy or they are destroyed. And at the end, there is often a single clear authority with which to negotiate a peace.

Civil wars are not like that. They pit people against one another based only on differences of political beliefs that cannot be seen. They frequently take place between sides with no uniforms, no ways of identifying one another, and no obvious command centres. One cannot drive out the other side in a civil war when it is the person living next door, or the family living down the street. It is a set of circumstances that frequently makes the tactics employed brutal, and the hopes of a resolution seemingly impossible.

Worse, civil wars destroy trust. There is a sense in them that no one can trust anyone beyond themselves and possibly their family. Their closest friends could turn out to be on the other side, and the wrong word said in the wrong place could result in death. It is little wonder in some ways that the present political parties of Kurdistan have developed the habit of employing family members. They remember the civil war well, and what could happen if they trusted anyone else.

I do not want to rake over the rights and wrongs of the events of the civil war. I think it is fair to say that all the sides involved did things that they now regret, and that there were no real winners when it was the innocent people of Kurdistan who ended up suffering in the violence that followed.

The worst part of the civil war was the way it created opportunities for Kurdistan's enemies to seek to extend their interests in the country, either by allying themselves with factions within the sides involved, or by taking advantage of the inability of the peshmerga to focus on regional defence to send troops into Kurdistan. Turkey, Iran and the Iraqi regime all interfered in the civil war, with Turkey and Saddam's regime sending in troops to try to take advantage of the situation. Turkey entered with the ostensible aim of rooting out members of the fringe PKK party, but used the excuse to attack civilians and try to take territory. The regime was simply trying to take advantage of the situation to impose its will on Kurdistan.

The result was that a simple series of outbreaks of violence became a complex, multi-sided conflict, with temporary alliances wherever they could be forged and more difficult battles against more heavily armed opposition. With embargoes and the no fly zone still in effect, there were limits to the tactics that could be employed, but the addition of the new enemies made the war far more complex and dangerous than it had been. It had gone from being a war over the direction that Kurdistan would take to one over its very existence.

In some ways though, it was the outside incursions that helped to bring an end to the war. The presence of the Iraqi army in Kurdistan prompted air strikes from the Americans, forcing it to retreat in a way that left the path open for the PDK to gain control of Erbil. The move reminded everyone that there were worse threats out there than the other political parties in the region. The same is true of the Turkish incursions. Although they were limited in scope, targeting supposed PKK positions, they served to remind the sides involved in the conflict that there was the potential for larger attacks if they weren't able to stabilise Kurdistan and defend its borders more effectively.

The effects of the civil war on Kurdistan are probably out of proportion with its actual death toll. That stands at approximately three thousand casualties, including civilian deaths. While a tragic number, and deserving remembrance, it is also many fewer deaths than occurred in any of Saddam's assaults on the region, or in his massacre of the Barzanis a decade before. Even in the midst of civil war, most of the violence was relatively low level, occurring in sporadic clashes and raids rather than fixed engagements.

The real damage that the war did was to trust within Kurdistan. It created a situation where the region was politically fragmented, with effectively total control over individual cities passing to the dominant parties in them. It created political wounds that are still only just healing, and attitudes to public life that were born out of the necessities of a violent situation rather than the ideals of a peaceful democracy. Kurdistan is slowly working to move on from the situations created in the civil war, but such deep-seated effects take time to change.

Peace

How did peace finally come about? There were multiple ceasefires in the conflict, some imposed from outside, some responding to other threats and some coming from within. The one that finally lasted came in November 1997, coming unilaterally from the PDK under Massoud Barzani as they decided that a peaceful solution was a far better option than damaging Kurdistan as they fought over it. The other parties in the conflict quickly went along with the ceasefire, even if they didn't formally declare a position on it.

The actual peace negotiations took most of the next year, but by September 1998, both sides of the conflict were ready to sign the peace agreement. Why did this attempt at peacemaking succeed when other ceasefires had failed? It was probably down to a combination of circumstances, concessions from outside, and the difficult nature of the civil war.

In terms of the circumstances the sides found themselves in, the situation had improved somewhat from the early phases of the war. The parties involved had stable claims on relatively coherent territories within Kurdistan, so that neither felt that its position would collapse if it didn't keep fighting. Both sides

The Idea of Kurdistan

had adequate access to the infrastructure and resources that existed at the time. The two sides were, in short, balanced enough in what they had gained to make peace.

Circumstances outside Kurdistan had shifted as well. The threat of potential invasion by Kurdistan's neighbours was one spur to make peace, creating a need to defend Kurdistan's borders that was greater than the conflicts between the two sides. Ultimately, no one wanted to see Turkey making repeated incursions into Kurdish territory, and the continuation of the civil war would only have allowed them to do so.

Perhaps a more important element was the relaxing of outside embargoes on the sale of oil, allowing both sides to legitimately buy in the food and resources they needed without having to fight over the control of more limited black market outlets. At a stroke, this move effectively removed much of the pressure from the war, by creating legitimate ways for both sides to ensure the wellbeing of their supporters.

Yet I would argue that there was also another element to the peace, one that I think shows through in the readiness of both sides to accept the initial ceasefire. That is simply that the war had gone on long enough. After years of violence, and after decades of outsiders inflicting violence on them, my people were simply sick of the fighting. They could see the damage the war was doing to Kurdistan, so when an opportunity arose to end it in a way that was beneficial to both sides, they took that opportunity.

Of course, it was a long transition from a tentative peace to the democratic near country that Kurdistan is today. The first step on that road was the consolidation of power within Kurdistan, ensuring that Iraq could not take back the gains Kurdistan had made. In the wake of the civil war, those efforts quickly made Kurdistan one of the most stable regions of Iraq.

The removal of Saddam Hussein in 2003 was the next step. With him still ruling over Iraq, there was always the feeling

Kurdistan in the 1980s and 1990s

that eventually he would try to finish what he had begun in Kurdistan. That he was simply waiting for international attention to flag again to allow his troops back into the region. While he ruled, Kurdistan was stuck in an in-between state where it could not move any closer to a settled, democratic political system. Saddam's overthrow prompted a re-evaluation of the political system throughout Iraq, and created an opportunity for Kurdistan to rebuild itself politically as completely as it had rebuilt itself in terms of its housing and infrastructure.

Doing so has thrown up conflicts with the Baghdad government. Some of those tensions have come from economic issues and conflicts over Kurdistan's borders, but just as many have come from purely political questions over where Kurdistan's political system fits into the broader Iraqi one, and which areas of decision making belong with which body.

Those are issues on which even Kurdistan's political parties are not always united, and yet all of the main parties have maintained a commitment to the peaceful pursuit of their causes within the political process, rather than seeking to impose their will through violence. That might seem like an obvious way to go about things to those readers living in stable, long established democracies, but one look around many of Kurdistan's neighbours shows that it is not a universally accepted approach.

It took Kurdistan a civil war to accept the peaceful, democratic approach as the right one. To accept that putting up with those views you don't like is better than trying to kick over the whole political system. All of Kurdistan's main parties have seen the violence that can lead to, and the opportunities it opens up for other countries to take advantage of Kurdistan.

In that sense, while the civil war was a tragedy, it is one that has brought some good for the region. The people of Kurdistan had already seen the dangers of outside tyrants, kings and conquerors. The civil war allowed them to see that imposing a position on Kurdistan from inside wasn't any better. In many ways, it is *because* Kurdistan had to fight such a brutal civil war, because it had those years of struggle as it started to come into being as an autonomous region, that it has the stability that it does today. We can only hope that all those within Kurdistan continue to remember the lesson that the civil war taught us, so that the peace forged afterwards can continue to last.

Chapter Ten: Family and Kurdistan

Arguably, Mullah Mustafa Barzani's greatest legacy when it comes to Kurdistan is his family. Although he did not live to see the form the modern Kurdistan has taken, his family continue to be involved in all walks of Kurdish life, and particularly in Kurdish politics. Indeed, throughout the events this book covers, Mullah Mustafa Barzani's family have played crucial roles. Although this book has focused on Mullah Mustafa, we must not forget those efforts made by other Barzanis in the past, or the ones that have built on his legacy since his death. Accordingly, this chapter explores the roles of several key Barzani family members, their relationships with Mullah Mustafa Barzani, and the extent to which current family members continue in his footsteps.

Sheikh Ahmad

In one obvious sense Sheikh Ahmad doesn't form a part of Mullah Mustafa's legacy: he was older, and was working towards Kurdistan's freedom while Mullah Mustafa was just a child. Yet it is worth exploring the relationship between the two of them for several reasons. First, Sheikh Ahmad was crucially important to Kurdistan, even if he has not been my main focus in this work. Second, the ways that he interacted with Mullah Mustafa

The Idea of Kurdistan

Barzani had key impacts on both the ways in which Mullah Mustafa was able to act, and on the things he learned about the process of rebellion. Those were lessons that he passed down to those who followed him, and which continue to affect Kurdistan today.

Some of the earliest rebellions that Mullah Mustafa found himself caught up in were under Sheikh Ahmad's command. He found himself leading the Barzanis in the uncertain period at the end of World War One, and again in the rebellions of the early 1930s. It was only in the 1940s that we can really say that Mullah Mustafa Barzani came to the military forefront within the Barzanis, effectively taking over the tactical side of things from his older brother.

We can have a good idea of what life would have been like for Sheikh Ahmad in that period. He had been given leadership of the Barzanis after the execution of Sheikh Abdul Salam, in the middle of a revolt, with the responsibility for keeping his people safe now resting squarely on him. He had grown up in revolts, and had been taught from an early age to resist outside interference. Yet there was also a part of him that wanted to achieve wider social goals and to use the process of independence also as a mechanism of social growth.

If that sounds familiar, it is no coincidence. It is inevitable that Sheikh Ahmad and Mullah Mustafa, growing up in the same family, exposed to the same influences, would have many of the same attitudes and goals. Indeed, one of the reasons that I am including Sheikh Ahmad in this section is to show just how strong that familial influence can be, reinforcing the influence that Mullah Mustafa probably had on those Barzanis who came after him.

Yet, for all that they shared so many things in common, Sheikh Ahmad and Mullah Mustafa Barzani were not the same. They had differences in their approaches, in what they were looking to achieve, and even in the patterns that their lives followed.

Family and Kurdistan

The most obvious difference of approach seems to have been in how focused on military action they were. How much violence they were prepared to risk to achieve their goals. From the moment that he attained leadership of the Barzanis, Sheikh Ahmad seems to have emphasised minimising the extent of open revolt, resorting to violence only where no other option was available, and even surrendering if he felt it was in the interests of his tribe. He was, after all, the one who stayed behind to face the consequences of the 1945 rebellion while Mullah Mustafa made his long march to the Soviet Union. He was not the man who could take on the single heroic action, but he was the man who could consistently engage in dialogue, even when those around him were bent on war.

This proved, as I have argued elsewhere, to be a useful thing in combination with Mullah Mustafa Barzani's more militarist approach. It meant that there was always one member of the family who could serve as a point of contact for peace, even while there was the balancing threat of Mullah Mustafa's military skill if that peace should fail. On several occasions, Sheikh Ahmad's presence gave the Barzanis time in which to make decisions that saved them from being overrun militarily.

Of course, it is important not to make too much of this distinction. There were times when Sheikh Ahmad felt it was necessary to fight, just as Mullah Mustafa was willing to achieve his aims through diplomacy in the Soviet Union, and in the peace agreement of 1970. It was a difference of degree rather than a complete opposition of approach. Yet Sheikh Ahmad wasn't just different from Mullah Mustafa Barzani in being focused on dialogue. We can see other differences in emphasis and approach in other areas.

He was, for example, much more defensive and local in approach than Mullah Mustafa. When he came to the leadership of the Barzanis in the First World War, his approach was not immediately to seek freedom for the entire area of Kurdistan, as Mullah Mustafa did towards the end of the second. Instead, it was to secure the traditional lands of the Barzanis against outside interference. This is not a criticism. Instead, it merely serves to demonstrate that he and his brother were trying to achieve different things. Mullah Mustafa was trying to seize freedom for everyone, Sheikh Ahmad to preserve it for a few.

There were some elements to Sheikh Ahmad's approach that proved to be crucial to Mullah Mustafa Barzani, and that have continued to have an influence even into the modern Kurdistan. His early rebellions included a stated concern for the environment, wanting to preserve the wildlife and resources of Kurdistan. Today, even as a major exporter of oil, Kurdistan takes its environmental responsibilities seriously, trying to ensure that it will still have a functioning environment to hand to its children even while it strives to make that land separate.

Sheikh Ahmad was also one of the first Kurdish leaders to emphasise the role of women, and to insist on respect for women's rights. It is a respect that Mullah Mustafa embraced, and which has continued into modern Kurdistan, making it far more progressive in its attitudes to women than many of the states around it, and even guaranteeing their place in society in ways that many states further afield would not.

Sheikh Ahmad undoubtedly had an influence on both Mullah Mustafa Barzani and Kurdistan as a whole. More than that though, he points to a sense of continuity among the Barzanis that hints at the continuing influence of Mullah Mustafa on events today.

Idris Barzani

Idris Barzani was born in 1944, two years before his brother Massoud. He was for years one of the key figures in the PDK, until his death in 1987 from a heart attack. As one of Mullah Mustafa's sons, he found himself caught up in the events that followed the demise of the Mahabad Republic, sent to Southern

Family and Kurdistan

Iraq with those members of his family who were not able to escape to the Soviet Union with Mullah Mustafa. By the time the revolts of the 1960s came, he was ready to make a name for himself, first militarily, as a member of the peshmerga, and then later politically.

By 1970, he was an important figure within the PDK, working closely with his father in the peace talks that led to the ultimately ill-fated peace agreement of that year. Crucially, in a mirror of the many times his father acted that way on behalf of Sheikh Ahmad, he was the key delegate to the discussions over the implementation of the peace agreement in 1974.

When the 1974 discussions spilled over into war, Idris Barzani was one of the major military commanders alongside his father and his brother Massoud. He was involved at all levels in planning for the military operations involved, and was a crucial part of the rear-guard actions that allowed for the evacuation into Iran when the war ultimately failed. He accompanied his father to the USA, but ultimately returned to Iran to work on behalf of the Kurdish refugees there, and then later returned to military and political action, both as a peshmerga continuing the fight against Saddam, and as a key member of the PDK alongside his brother Massoud.

His most important contributions probably came as the PDK sought to rebuild itself in the wake of losing the 1975 war. He played a key part in restructuring the party, helping it to become something close to the form it takes today, with the result that he is often regarded as the 'father' of the PDK. Crucially, Idris Barzani was willing to go beyond just his own party, working to establish the Kurdistan Front as an organisation for communication and cooperation between parties working for Kurdish independence. Perhaps we can say that the modern, coalition based style of Kurdish politics owes something to that.

Had Idris Barzani lived, it would have been interesting to see what role he would have played in the modern Kurdistan.

It is possible that, as the older brother, and as one who had played such an important political role, he might have ended up as the head of the party. It seems certain that he would have occupied an important role, and that he and Massoud Barzani would have continued to cooperate on Kurdistan's future.

Yet his death came too early to see the new Kurdistan, and in that, we can see him almost as a bridge between Mullah Mustafa's generation and the generation that did get to see the region gain its current autonomy. As fitting somewhere between Mullah Mustafa and Massoud Barzani, even though he was only a couple of years older than Kurdistan's current president.

Hamael Mahmoud Agha Zebari

It is so often true of history that it focuses on men's stories more than those of women, and I suppose I hardly get to make that complaint in the middle of something that is largely a biography of a great man. Yet women played a crucial role throughout Mullah Mustafa Barzani's life, and they continue to play a large part in modern Kurdistan. Lady Hamael Mahmoud Agha Zebari, Mullah Mustafa's wife, played important roles through much of this story, even if those roles were not always publically visible.

She was a mother to his children, including current Kurdish president Massoud Barzani. Because of Mullah Mustafa's effective exile in the Soviet Union, we can say that Lady Hamael played arguably the key role in Massoud Barzani's early life. Certainly, she was present in a way that Mullah Mustafa Barzani was not able to be for that first part of his son's life.

That measure of separation shows that it cannot have been easy to be Mullah Mustafa Barzani's wife. The aftermath of his rebellions touched his family as surely as it touched him. His family found itself at various times imprisoned, exiled and attacked. Lady Hamael had to live with the consequences of

Family and Kurdistan

Mullah Mustafa's actions as surely as he did, while at the same time finding ways through it to protect her family, sometimes in Mullah Mustafa's absence.

It is hard to measure her influence on the formation of Kurdistan's political parties and climate. While today, women are at the heart of Kurdish politics, through much of the period we've been discussing in this work, that wasn't true, just as it wasn't true for most other societies around the world in the early to mid-twentieth century. We can suggest, based on the closeness of Lady Hamael's ties to key individuals in this story, that she almost certainly had a great deal of informal influence, and that she would have been in a position to make her opinions felt over time, yet we cannot demonstrate her formal involvement in events in the same way that we can for her husband. This is a difficulty for much history, and not just Kurdish history, and one that hopefully other authors will be able to address.

Yet there are some things we can say. We know that Lady Hamael had links to one of Kurdistan's key tribal groups in the Zebari, and so helped to rebuild those links after the damaging events of the mid-twentieth century rebellions. We have seen many times in these pages how damaging it can be on those occasions when Kurdistan pulls itself apart in violence, and Lady Hamael by her very presence helped to heal one division.

We can also say that in many ways, Lady Hamael's story mirrors that of many Kurdish women later on under Saddam, who found themselves forced to bring up their families without their husbands or other male relatives in the wake of the murders and forced exiles that split many from their families. In this, her earlier experiences when Mullah Mustafa Barzani was forced into exile in the Soviet Union may have provided an example to follow. Certainly, Kurdistan owes a great debt to the many women who held their families together in that later period, often in almost impossible conditions.

The Idea of Kurdistan

It is at least partly because of that debt that Kurdistan is one of the few places within the wider region around it that is actively seeking to improve the situation of its women from day to day. We have an active interest in political life from women, and many female members of Kurdistan's parliament. We have female members of the defence forces and the police, Kurdistan's academic institutions and its civil groups. While I would like to think that part of that is simply that Kurdistan has started to move towards a more equal society, that still begs the question of why it has done so. There might be those who would point to outside influences, but truthfully, haven't plenty of societies with decidedly unequal treatment of women had the same outside influences? What makes Kurdistan more receptive to it, I suspect, is that it has experienced those periods where in many areas, there were no men around. There were no men because they were fighting, in exile, or dead. It is an experience that is common to much of Kurdistan, but that Lady Hamael provides one of the best examples for.

Her presence provided a link to the past in many ways, too. While Mullah Mustafa Barzani was not able to see the growth of the modern, largely autonomous Kurdistan, it was of tremendous symbolic value that his wife could do so. In living until 2011, Lady Hamael was able to see the growth of what has become a new country in all but name, with her son at its head. The symbolism of that is in many ways an extension of the emphasis on the symbolic value of many actions throughout this work.

It is, as I have said, hard to pin down the exact influence that Lady Hamael Mahmoud Agha Zebari had through her life. The nature of the history available to us makes it likely that we will never truly know. Yet everything around her life suggests that she did have an impact. She had an impact on her husband. She had an impact on her sons. And she undoubtedly had an impact on the role of women in Kurdistan as it exists today.

Family and Kurdistan

Massoud Barzani

One of Mullah Mustafa Barzani's biggest legacies to Kurdistan comes in the form of his son, Massoud Barzani. At the time of writing, Massoud Barzani is the President of the Kurdistan Regional Government, the leader of the PDK, arguably the most powerful man in the region, and a key voice in the ongoing debate over Kurdistan's future.

Previously, he has been a crucial component of Kurdistan's resistance to Saddam Hussein's Iraq, picking up the fight against those who would attack the Kurdish people where his father left off, being a part of the extended guerrilla war and then exile of the 1980s, then managing to protect civilians as they fled Kurdistan in the early 1990s. Some of his most notable military achievements including commanding the peshmerga who held back the Iraqi army while many of those who had escaped from Saddam's camps fled to Iran.

Yet, perhaps to an even greater extent than his father, Massoud Barzani has combined political leadership with that military capability. His leadership of the PDK has allowed it to flourish in the emerging Kurdistan, becoming the dominant political force in the region and striving to represent the whole of Kurdistan's people, not just a single small group. But it has also allowed Kurdistan to remain secure in the face of challenges from outside Kurdistan.

Those challenges have been considerable. The Iraqi government continues to push Kurdistan for more control over the region, which is directly at odds with the aims of Kurdistan and its government. It has continued to try to assert control over Kirkuk, and to shut down ways for Kurdistan to fund itself. Some of the surrounding regions have also tried to apply pressure to Kurdistan, either because of continuing conflicts with their own Kurdish populations, or because they feel that the region's resources make it a prime target.

Massoud Barzani has consistently sought to resist those

The Idea of Kurdistan

pressures, and in that he has emulated his father's example in knowing where the red line issues are for Kurdistan; the ones where compromising would result in irreparable damage to the region. He has refused, for example, to allow the giving away of Kurdish sovereignty over its own affairs, but has been prepared to foster social and economic links with the south of Iraq where those have been likely to increase peace with it.

He has also sought out international partners. Massoud Barzani has been very successful in contacting other governments, including the United States, UK and Japan, seeking what amount to bilateral international relations with them and using Kurdistan's natural resources to initiate that contact. He has also been prepared repeatedly to travel abroad to engage foreign governments directly. In that, he is following the example of his father again, since Mullah Mustafa Barzani sought on several occasions to build relationships with foreign governmental partners, bringing the Kurdish cause to their attention.

Politically, he has led the PDK for many years now, and where other regions sometimes descend into dictatorship or undemocratic processes, Massoud Barzani has shown a commitment to democracy that it could be argued stems from his father. He has fought and won elections, but has been prepared to work with his electoral rivals in Kurdistan's parliament where needed. He has also sought to stamp out corruption where it has been found in Kurdish public life. Crucially, he has been behind the moves to keep Kurdistan's presidential elections as a popular public vote, rather than reverting to a simple selection by parliament, where the wider public would get only the most indirect of voices.

Yes, there are those who scoff at these ideas. Who say that as one of the richer men in Kurdistan, Massoud Barzani must automatically be corrupt. Who point to things like the two year extension to his final presidential term as some sort of proof that he secretly wants to be a dictator. Yet neither of these

Family and Kurdistan

things is true. He is wealthy because he comes from a family that has always been wealthy and powerful in the region, with access to many business opportunities. As for the extension to the presidential term, that was intended to cover a period when it seemed that Kurdistan would be in flux both in terms of its wider relations and constitutionally. The idea is for Massoud Barzani to oversee the normalisation of both Kurdistan's constitutional arrangements and its relations with its neighbours, allowing him to hand over the region to his successor in a state where they will be clear about their position and that of Kurdistan's political processes. He certainly has no intention of going against Kurdistan's constitution.

In some ways, we can even say that Massoud Barzani has learned from his father's experiences when it comes to foreign affairs. He has sought out international links for Kurdistan, and international investment, but has always done so on a broad base. Those links he has built have been founded on issues such as trade and mutual investment, rather than on just the needs of Kurdistan's people and their cause. What that means is that Kurdistan is not dependent on a single international partner in the way it became dependent more than once under Mullah Mustafa Barzani. More than that, Kurdistan's current foreign partners are gaining something substantial and tangible from their relationship with the region, meaning that Kurdistan is not dependent on the kind of goodwill that points to either charity or an unseen political agenda. Both of those, as Kurdistan saw on several occasions, can disappear all too quickly.

To what extent is this down to the legacy of Mullah Mustafa Barzani's actions, and to what extent can we say that all this is down to Massoud Barzani himself? It is a complex question, made particularly complicated by how little Massoud Barzani was able to see his father in some key years. When Massoud Barzani was a child, his father was in the Soviet Union. At points during the later years of Mullah Mustafa's life, he was caught up continuing the fight for Kurdistan, as his father had asked him to.

Yet there can be no doubt that Mullah Mustafa had a profound influence on his son. He inculcated in Massoud Barzani the desire to see Kurdistan free, and placed him in a position to carry on that fight. He may not have been able to be there when Massoud Barzani was a child, but his example certainly helped to form the man who works on behalf of Kurdistan today. Without Mullah Mustafa Barzani, there would be no PDK for Massoud Barzani to lead. More than that, there would probably be no Kurdistan left for him to lead it in.

Masrour Barzani

Masrour Barzani is Massoud Barzani's elder son, born in 1969, the year before the ill-fated peace deal that set the course for Kurdistan for the ensuing decades. He was involved in the struggle for independence from a young age, joining the peshmerga at just sixteen and participating in the struggles against Saddam Hussein's army that followed in 1988 and 1991. It was when those struggles forced a withdrawal to Iran that he was able to complete his studies, travelling to the UK and USA to further his education.

He returned to Kurdistan in 1998 to enter politics, being elected first as a part of the PDK's central committee and then its main leadership. He has since become the head of Kurdistan's security and intelligence services, seeking to defend Kurdistan from foreign and domestic threats while providing security for public institutions. His tenure as head of the security services has seen an expansion of women within their numbers, as well as a transition to a greater number of open, public duties.

It seems likely that in the long term, he is seen by the PDK as a potential successor to his father and uncle as a part of the Barzani political dynasty. So how much has he been influenced by that dynasty? How much of the influence of Mullah Mustafa Barzani can we see in him?

Well, it is clear that he shares that mix of the military and the political, having served in the military and now commanding the more civilian security personnel. There is in that the same trajectory that both Mullah Mustafa's life and his father's career followed, moving from a position of armed opposition to a more diplomatic and political role focused on public service.

There are similarities in Masrour Barzani receiving his education abroad, although it was in the USA rather than in the USSR as Mullah Mustafa did. That time in the USA also allowed him to seek to promote an understanding of my people's situation, and is again in line with the approaches Mullah Mustafa attempted. Those connections have helped to foster some of the business and personal links between the USA and Kurdistan.

In the future, it seems likely that Masrour Barzani will continue to play a political role within Kurdistan. His role in the security services is an important one, and so one that is likely to continue into the immediate future, but in the longer term, his family heritage, and his recognisable public profile, might point to him continuing the family traditions in the upper echelons of government.

Mansour Barzani

Mansour Barzani is Massoud Barzani's younger son. His current role in Kurdistan is in its military, within the peshmerga's Special Forces units. There, he has been involved in military operations designed to protect Kurdistan from outside threats in what continue to be potentially turbulent times in the wider zone immediately around the region. Although his role is currently primarily a military one, he has also had the opportunity to meet with officials on several occasions, and has played important roles in building relations with groups outside Kurdistan.

It is notable here that once again we have the pattern of

The Idea of Kurdistan

Barzani brothers in different but connected walks of life within Kurdistan. Although it would not be right to suggest that Mansour and Masrour are in some way equivalent to Sheikh Ahmad and Mullah Mustafa, there is the similarity of one essentially military brother and one working in a more civilian, political field. It is a combination that has shown up again and again for the Barzani family, and while part of the reason could be family tradition as to the fields open for the family's sons to go into, I suspect it also has practical implications.

Kurdistan has been, certainly through the whole of the time this work covers, a region where violence was a possibility. Successive Iraqi governments have attacked the region at different times, and it has been necessary to have individuals who have been prepared to resist that violence, and even to work militarily towards Kurdistan's independence. Yet the political role has also been crucial. It has been essential throughout the history covered here for Kurdistan to maintain a dialogue with the outside world, and even with its military opponents. In low level guerrilla warfare in particular, it has been crucial for Kurdistan to combine that with a willingness to negotiate. Having a mixture of political and military roles has always been important.

Why brothers though? Why couldn't that combination have come from complete strangers, taken from almost any family? Part of the reason is simply that the Barzani name helps with some aspects of achieving a position. It is a recognisable name in Kurdistan, and one that seems to convey a genuine advantage with voters. Yet historically, it has always been more than that. It has been about trust. Often, the individuals we are talking about were working in times that were potentially very dangerous for them. Working with a stranger might have potentially opened up opportunities for betrayal or factionalism. Working with family simply ensured that those involved in often life or death struggles could be trusted.

Family and Kurdistan

Nechirvan Idris Barzani

Nechirvan Barzani is Kurdistan's prime minister at the time of writing, and a key figure in the PDK. He is the grandson of Mullah Mustafa Barzani, being the son of Mullah Mustafa's son Idris Barzani. As with Massoud Barzani, it seems highly likely that his connection to Mullah Mustafa was crucial in driving him into politics, yet he also represents a younger generation of Kurdish politics, having only come into senior positions within the PDK since 1989.

This makes for an interesting comparison, since it means that Nechirvan Barzani is from the very last generation of politicians who came up while Kurdistan was still struggling to come into being as an independent region. He straddles the line between the last days of the struggle against Saddam and the modern Kurdish political environment, where violence is not the usual currency of politics. Indeed, he was not even born until many of the early rebellions in Kurdistan had passed, in 1966. Even for the revolts of the 1970s, he would only have been a child, meaning that his first real opportunities to act came just as Kurdistan was suffering the worst horrors perpetrated on it, in the 1980s.

Nechirvan Barzani is in an interesting position politically. He is Kurdistan's prime minister, having served one period in office previously and being reappointed in 2012. He is undoubtedly a major political figure, serving in key delegations to the Iraq government and abroad. He is also arguably the driving force behind some of Kurdistan's most important policies.

Yet there is also a sense in which he is still waiting for his opportunity. He represents the next generation of the Barzani political dynasty after Massoud Barzani, and since the KRG's president is limited to only two terms in office (in line with many other presidents around the world), there is a sense that he is perhaps being put in line to run for that office when Massoud Barzani has served his terms.

The Idea of Kurdistan

Such a move would represent a continuation of the Barzani name in Kurdistan, but would it represent a true continuation of Mullah Mustafa's legacy? Does Nechirvan Barzani continue to stand for the same things that Mullah Mustafa did? I would argue that in a lot of cases, he does.

The core point seems quite clear: he believes in the sovereignty of Kurdistan, and is willing to resist outside pressure from Iraq, militarily if necessary. That seems to be fully in line with everything we have seen of Mullah Mustafa Barzani throughout this book. He has worked towards a high level of independence even within the confines of the Iraqi constitution, and seems committed in the long term to the possibility of full Kurdish independence, so long as it can be achieved without damaging Kurdistan in the process.

When we look at his methods, there are more parallels with Mullah Mustafa. There are many trips abroad, working to secure support for Kurdistan. There is a lot of work trying to come to peaceful agreements with the Baghdad government. There is even an echo (consciously or unconsciously) of the relationship between Sheikh Ahmad and Mullah Mustafa in the way he represents Kurdistan. He travels, and does much of the negotiation with potential foreign backers, while Massoud Barzani increasingly deals with Kurdistan's domestic and constitutional issues.

In terms of Nechirvan Barzani's methods, there are obviously some clear differences from Mullah Mustafa. He is a politician, not the leader of an armed group of peshmerga. He embraces interviews and contact with the press in a way that Mullah Mustafa often wasn't able to because of outside restrictions. He is working within a more modern version of the party, with a more comprehensive set of social and other positions in addition to a focus on independence.

And yet, often his actions suggest a combination of the new and the old. The legacy of Mullah Mustafa is there even in

Family and Kurdistan

cases where it seems clear there are aspects of a situation that he would not have embraced. Take the oil pipeline to Turkey, which is one of Nechirvan Barzani's pet projects. It seems likely that Mullah Mustafa would have been surprised to say the least at the choice of partners, because in his time, Turkey was openly hostile to even the idea of Kurds existing. They were the first country to close their borders in 1975, and were the main reason Kurdistan did not come into being in the wake of the First World War.

Yet he would have recognised the importance of Kurdistan gaining economic and strategic partnerships where it can, and he would definitely have approved of the idea of Kurdistan gaining a measure of economic independence by being able to export its own oil. The principle of Kurdistan having control over its own natural resources, and then being able to turn that control into a level of economic independence fits exactly with the legacy Mullah Mustafa Barzani left.

So does the idea that Kurdistan would require partners to achieve stable independence as a landlocked country. This is an idea that Nechirvan Barzani has stated in several interviews, and while there are obviously landlocked countries throughout the world, his point is probably a fair one.

It is also a point that suggests the continuing influence of Mullah Mustafa Barzani's ideas today, because we have seen that he consistently sought foreign partnerships in his attempts at independence. He sought them, in some cases, even from countries that didn't necessarily have Kurdistan's interests at heart, knowing that for as long as they gained something of equal value from the relationship, they would continue to be involved in Kurdistan's cause.

Nechirvan Barzani has essentially refined this strategy, by focusing on a resource in oil that is likely to be present for more than just a few years, and by targeting one of the major regional sources of opposition to the idea of Kurdish independence. If Turkey sees that Kurdistan represents a better economic partner free than connected to Iraq, there is every chance that it might put aside its opposition to Kurdish independence.

The Barzanis and Mullah Mustafa's Legacy

Mullah Mustafa Barzani's family is one of his biggest legacies when it comes to Kurdistan. His personal impact on the shape of the region is easy to spot, but it is dwarfed in many ways by the influence that his legacy continues to have through his family's involvement in Kurdish life and politics.

That influence is often what has allowed Mullah Mustafa's effect on Kurdistan to be so great. In several cases, things have ended up the way they have, not just because they happened to be the way Mullah Mustafa wanted them, but because his family have remembered that, or because they have used his example in seeking to help Kurdistan be everything it ought to be.

Kurdistan's flag is an obvious example. Yes, it is taken from the flag of the Mahabad Republic, and before that from hints of other Kurdish flags reaching back into the past. Yet why did Kurdistan pick that particular flag? Would respect for the Mahabad Republic have been enough if figures such as Massoud Barzani had not pushed for its political acceptance?

Why did Massoud Barzani push for the acceptance of the flag in its current form? Partly because he had been born in the Mahabad Republic in 1946, but mostly, because it was a continuation of his father's legacy. The story was there that Mullah Mustafa had received the flag from Qazi Muhammad, and this seemed like the logical continuation of that passing along of the spirit of Kurdish independence.

There are other ways in which Mullah Mustafa's family have been responsible for the continuation of his legacy. The most obvious is in some of the values that they have brought to

Family and Kurdistan

Kurdistan, and to the PDK. Political parties in particular are very easily reshaped by the individuals within them. It would have been easy for the PDK to lose sight of many of the values that it had held under Mullah Mustafa, from the core issue of not giving up on the possibility of independence to social issues such as the role of women within the party. The involvement of Mullah Mustafa's family in the party has helped to provide a strong link to the values he fostered in them, and so has helped to ensure that the party has maintained its core values even as it has adapted with each new generation.

It is worth stating that those Barzanis who become involved in public life are very much aware of the political legacy they carry. It would be impossible for them not to know the depth of feeling in Kurdistan towards their famous predecessors, and the importance of continuing the work that figures like Mullah Mustafa began. If many Barzanis seem to be involved in Kurdish politics, then that is at least partly because many of them feel that the example of the past *requires* them to be involved. That in standing back from working on Kurdistan's behalf, they might somehow not be living up to everything Mullah Mustafa and their other ancestors did. They are fully aware that they will be held up, not just to the usual standards demanded of politicians, but to the standards Mullah Mustafa set, and they are entirely aware for the most part of the difficulties of living up to those standards, but they still feel that they must try.

That is one of Mullah Mustafa Barzani's most enduring legacies for Kurdistan. One that looks set to continue for generations to come.

Chapter Eleven: The Idea of Kurdistan

On 12th April 1606, King James I of England (who was already James VI of Scotland), did something unusual. He proclaimed a flag for a country that did not exist. He fused elements of the flags for the countries he ruled to create a flag for a place he called 'Britain' after the old Roman word for the island they had found so far away and isolated. At the time, people found the whole affair very strange. England and Scotland were clearly not one country, and they never would be. They were just two places that happened to be ruled by the same king. Just over a hundred years later, however, the Act of Union brought the United Kingdom of Great Britain and Ireland into being. While there where many factors leading to that moment, the flag was certainly one of them.

Why? Because countries are not just places. They are symbols. They are ideas. They do not exist because some fluke of geography makes an obvious border, or because they have run out of room to expand. That notion of natural borders is one that has been used by dictators and warmongers throughout history. They do not exist purely because of political processes, or because of the dominance of a particular ethnicity in a region. Borders in many countries are often not well marked, while the experience of my people shows that it is possible for people of

The Idea of Kurdistan

a single ethnic group to be spread across a number of countries. A country might contain notions of all of those things in its construction, but isn't any one of those things.

A country is an idea. A kind of shared dream. An ongoing process of persuasion. Not just Kurdistan. Any country. The USA, or Russia, or the furthest reaches of Malaysia. They exist essentially because they have persuaded people that they do. Often, that persuasion has involved violence, but violence alone is not enough to hold a country together in the long term. Just look at the ways in which the various former Yugoslav republics splintered when there was no longer the force there to hold them together after the fall of the USSR. Or look at the ways in which countries came together in the more ancient past. Yes, there was conquest, but the countries and empires that held together, whether Babylonian or Roman, Egyptian or Sumerian, were the ones that took the places they controlled and persuaded them to buy in to the broader idea of their culture. That recognised the importance of identity and symbolism in the construction of nations.

Even today, when there are formal legal processes for recognising nations, that symbolism is crucial. The UN does not generally carve new nations out of nowhere. Instead, it recognises situations that already exist, where there is either a cultural and political separation so strong that it is impossible not to think in terms of a new country, or where there are sufficient divisions within a country that it seems impossible that it can hold together anymore. Yes, we could turn around tomorrow and say that legally, a new country exists, linking together Syria and Turkey as one place, but no one would take it seriously. The idea is more important than the stamp that gets put on it. Indeed, that moment of legal recognition is itself a symbolic moment; one that is significant primarily because it helps to solidify the idea of a country in the minds of the international community.

The Idea of Kurdistan

What I want to suggest in this chapter is that Mullah Mustafa Barzani's importance isn't limited to the practical gains that he made for Kurdistan during his life. Indeed, in many ways, those practical gains don't amount to that much. His attempted revolutions failed time and again, with the result that the free and autonomous Kurdistan he envisaged didn't come into being during his lifetime.

I want to argue that in a lot of ways, Mullah Mustafa Barzani's greatest impact was on the *idea* of Kurdistan. That he helped to influence it in crucial ways, to keep it alive in the face of opposition from governments that would have tried to wipe it from people's minds entirely or to reduce it to a mere fantasy. He helped to maintain and shape the notion of Kurdistan as a real place, a country worth fighting for and working towards. He helped to build elements of that idea that are crucial to the ways in which the modern Kurdistan functions as an autonomous region today, and that will probably continue to shape it for years to come.

I am sure that there are those readers to whom this will not sound like much. There are undoubtedly those for whom the preservation of an idea might not sound like anything concrete, which is why I started this section by talking about the ways in which countries form. I wanted to make it clear just how important a contribution the shaping of the idea of Kurdistan was. Just how important the elements that Mullah Mustafa affected were.

What are those elements? There are several. A country (or even a region on the verge of nationhood) does not consist of only one thing. Because of that, we can find Mullah Mustafa Barzani's influence in areas as disparate as the basic geographical shape of the area, the role of Erbil within it, the flag, the continuance of Kurdish language and culture, and more. More than that, he had a significant influence in ensuring that the basic idea of Kurdistan was never forgotten in the way that

The Idea of Kurdistan

some nations have. Kurdistan could have gone the way of Sumeria or Byzantium, becoming a nation from the past that has long since ceased to exist, its culture and language reduced to a mere historical oddity. Instead, today we have a vibrant region that is largely independent, with a strong cultural identity and a modern political system. We haven Mullah Mustafa Barzani to thank for a lot of that.

The Shape of Kurdistan

The shape of the modern region of Kurdistan has been influenced by a lot of factors. Several are historical. Without the division of the region following the First World War, we would certainly never have come to think of Kurdistan simply as a region in the north of Iraq. Without the control of the Ottomans, the Persians, and others, Kurdistan would have been free to form into nations according to its own wishes. Without the historical events that spread my people over such a wide area, Kurdistan would look very different. Without the events of recent history, and the no fly zone imposed by the US, Kurdistan might not exist at all.

There are so many ways that Kurdistan could have ended up a different shape. It could have been larger, if European interests had not split it between them in search of a mixture of oil resources and a balancing component for the Arab populations of the surrounding territories. It could have been smaller, or non-existent, if previous Iraqi regimes had succeeded in their efforts to destroy my people. It could have been a series of separate states, or ended up linked to Iran, or any one of a dozen other scenarios, if things had gone differently.

So why is it the shape it is? One key part of the answer is Mullah Mustafa Barzani. His efforts helped to preserve Kurdistan in the north of Iraq. They helped to see Barzani territory as a key component of Kurdistan. They helped to define the idea of the region as an autonomous unit. They also helped to limit ideas of Kurdistan in a couple of ways.

Let's start with the obvious point, which is that without Mullah Mustafa Barzani, it seems unlikely that Kurdistan would exist at all. I will discuss his efforts to preserve the idea of Kurdistan below, but he also played a crucial role in providing physical resistance to attempts to overrun or destroy the area. His revolts were frequently defensive in nature, attempting to prevent the intrusion of government soldiers or police forces into Kurdistan, or attempting to reclaim land from them on those occasions when his actions took on a more aggressive approach. Mullah Mustafa's aim seems to have been at least partly the holding and defence of the specific territory that is now Kurdistan.

Now, we cannot say that he succeeded with any consistency. The pattern for his revolts seems to have been an uprising followed by a retreat. Yet he was always able to delay incoming forces long enough for the people who followed him to retreat safely, and my people were always able to return eventually. In that, we can say that he successfully defended the most important part of Kurdistan: its people. We can also say that to some extent the act of defence was a necessary one in protecting the idea of Kurdistan as something separate from Iraq. Every time Mullah Mustafa's peshmerga attempted to prevent the advance of British, Iraqi or other forces into Kurdistan, they effectively said that it was *not* just another part of Iraq for them to move into as they wished, but a separate place, that they could only enter by invasion.

More than that, these attempts at defence and revolt were very clear about the area that they were working within. Mullah Mustafa Barzani's revolts were both wider and narrower than those that had gone before. They were wider in that they were not just the small revolts of a single tribe. They were not Sheikh Ahmad's revolt following the First World War, which was in many ways still just a Barzani revolt. They were, instead, revolts

The Idea of Kurdistan

for the whole of Kurdistan, which involved, at least temporarily, people from across the north of Iraq. Yes, Mullah Mustafa's revolt in the 1940s failed partly from a loss of support from other tribes, but the point is that he had the support to lose. He created something broader than a tribal revolt. He created what was, very briefly, a national revolt. And to have a national revolt, you need at least the idea of a nation.

In that sense, Mullah Mustafa's revolts were wider than those that went before. But they were also narrower, because they mostly worked within the confines of Iraq. Indeed, although Mullah Mustafa sought refuge in Iran and the Soviet Union, he mostly seems to have thought in terms of Iraqi Kurdistan rather than the much broader region of Kurdistan, which covers parts of several countries. When his people were offered agricultural land in Iran at the fall of the Mahabad Republic, he rejected it, and thought instead of a return to Iraq. When he encountered the PDK(Iran), he didn't seek to expand it to cover Iraqi Kurdistan, but instead sought to create a separate party to work there. When his revolts failed and he was forced to leave Iraqi Kurdistan, he always seems to have thought in terms of a return there rather than of settling in the place he was forced to flee to.

It is this combination of the expansion and contraction of the idea of Kurdistan that is important for today's region. Mullah Mustafa seems to have been thinking primarily in terms of the region that is now Kurdistan; of freeing those areas of Kurdistan that fell within Iraq. But he also seems to have been one of the first to see it in terms of a modern nation state, rather than in tribal terms or in terms of general ethnicity. In that he seems to have understood that there was more of a chance of succeeding in bringing about a small, focused state than some kind of large, sprawling, super-Kurdistan.

It is an understanding that seems to have informed the whole process of achieving a degree of autonomy. Kurdistan as it stands today is, in terms of the area it covers, essentially what Mullah Mustafa Barzani envisioned for it. It is not the giant region that covers multiple countries, but nor is it the kind of limited area that a single tribe would have covered in the past. In that, the shape of modern Kurdistan is very much down to Mullah Mustafa.

Erbil's Importance

One key point when it comes to modern Kurdistan is the importance of Erbil. Although there are several major cities in the region, each with its own history and place within its district, Erbil has risen to be the most politically and culturally important of them. It is Kurdistan's capital, and consequently the heart of its political system. Its parliament is there. Its presidential residence is there. Much of the region's civil service, military and ambassadorial services are based there.

Where does this sense of Erbil's importance come from? Part of the reason is practical, part of the reason is political, part is historical, and at least some of it is to do with Mullah Mustafa Barzani. Politically, we must remember that the modern Kurdish political system was originally a compromise between the PDK and PUK, designed to allow Kurdistan to move forward peacefully and with stability. Erbil has been one of the political heartlands of the PDK for many years, and they provided the first president of Kurdistan in Massoud Barzani. In those terms, perhaps it is not surprising that the political system should find itself focused on the city initially. Yet those political necessities do not fully explain things. Another of Kurdistan's cities could have been picked, because there are strong political presences in its other cities as well.

Practical considerations may have had something to do with it. Erbil is at the heart of Kurdistan geographically, making for more effective links with its other cities. Today, it provides good links to the outside world with its international airport and

The Idea of Kurdistan

strong land transport links both to the rest of Kurdistan and to Iran further north. Defensively, it is in a good position to ensure the security of Kurdistan's political system, being comparatively easy for the peshmerga to protect in case of any threat, while being easy to evacuate if necessary. In light of Kurdistan's often turbulent history, those considerations are more important than they might seem in other nations.

Yet are these considerations sufficient to decide the whole political heart of Kurdistan? Many of Erbil's infrastructure links are relatively recent, and are mirrored in other cities. Defensively, I would like to think that the peshmerga are capable of defending the whole of Kurdistan, while even geographically, Kurdistan is small enough that none of its cities counts as truly unreachable. Yes, there are minor advantages to having Erbil as a capital city, but these are not enough in themselves to explain why it is so crucial within Kurdistan.

History, both modern and more ancient, probably explains slightly more of it. Erbil is the oldest city within Kurdistan, and indeed has a claim to being the oldest continuously inhabited city in the world. It has historically been at the heart of its district, and has played a major role within the history of the wider Kurdistan. In terms of more recent history, Erbil was an important location in the fight for independence, and was an important place for the PDK in Kurdistan's civil wars.

So practically, politically and historically, there are reasons why Erbil is the political heart of Kurdistan. Yet none of them seems like quite enough on its own to fully explain Erbil's importance within the region. What is the missing element? For me, it is the influence of Mullah Mustafa Barzani. His influence made Erbil a crucial part of the idea of Kurdistan. It did so because of the city's connection to him, because of his limitation of the idea of Kurdistan to something smaller, because of his emphasis on Kurdistan as a region with its own history, and because of the practical connections he forged to the city with the PDK, with defence, and more.

We have the basic connection to Erbil that comes from it being the closest city to Barzani lands. It is perhaps not the city that Mullah Mustafa Barzani would have known best, both because he spent time in exile in Sulaymaniyah and because he spent considerable time out of the country, but of all Kurdistan's cities, it is probably the one that was closest to being his home.

Certainly, when it came to politics and defence, Erbil was the place that many of Mullah Mustafa's efforts were focused on. Certainly in the latter half of his life, when he seems to have moved from an essentially rural strategy to something aimed more at the mass politicisation of urban centres. His later revolts seem to have been focused on the control of Erbil and its environs in a way that his earliest attempts could not be. That transition helped to emphasise Erbil's strategic importance in the region.

Politically, he was the one who made Erbil the most important city to the PDK. Political parties need cities. They provide hubs of communication, large bases of supporters, and often a more educated populace prepared to get involved in political debate. Although he was personally focused on the often more militarily defensible mountains and rural areas, Mullah Mustafa certainly came to see the value of the region's cities in a way that some of his predecessors perhaps did not.

Finally, we have the idea that I advanced in the previous section, which is that Mullah Mustafa Barzani played an important role in committing Kurdistan to its current shape. He did so partly because that was what he found himself faced with, and partly because it allowed for a much stronger idea of Kurdistan as a country, but he did help to focus Kurdistan within Iraq. That was important for the role of Erbil. In a much wider conception of Kurdistan, taking in parts of Turkey, Iran and Syria, it might have been possible for Erbil's importance to be lost. It would, along with the rest of Iraqi Kurdistan's cities, have been off to the side somewhere, well away from the rest of the region. By focusing on a smaller, more achievable concept of Kurdistan, Mullah Mustafa also created the side effect of placing Erbil at the heart of the political unit for which he was fighting. He created Erbil's importance in the new Kurdistan effectively by focusing on a new Kurdistan in which it *could* be important.

Kirkuk

Kirkuk is another of the key cities of modern Kurdistan. It is one of the most important economic centres for the region, with crucial oil resources that help Kurdistan to maintain its independence financially. Those oil resources, however, coupled with a relatively southerly location within Kurdistan, have often made Kirkuk a contentious issue in the past. There have been those who have tried to claim Kirkuk as a part of the main body of Iraq, taking often extreme measures to try to claim it.

The city was, for example, one of the major targets for Saddam Hussein's policy of Arabisation. His government attempted to drastically alter the ethnic balance of the city to ensure that it maintained a sense of connection to his entirely Arab central government. In doing so, he created significant long term difficulties and tensions within the city, which have required much work to stabilise.

So where does Mullah Mustafa Barzani's idea of Kurdistan fit into the history of Kirkuk? The first point that I wish to make is that it was an idea of Kurdistan that *included* Kirkuk. Mullah Mustafa Barzani was very consistent in stating that the Kurdistan he was fighting for was one that had Kirkuk within it. How do we know this? Because he had the opportunity to effectively give Kirkuk away on at least one occasion, and he did not take it. In the 1970s, when the central government attempted to broker a peace with my people, they offered many of the things that Kurdistan has today. They offered it a level

The Idea of Kurdistan

of autonomy that included its own government, its own recognised region in the north, and more.

There are many reasons why Mullah Mustafa ultimately could not accept the deal, ranging from a lack of trust in those involved to the refusal to go that extra step and recognise Kurdistan's independence. Yet one of the most crucial points was that the deal on the table did not include Kirkuk or the area around it. It would have been easy for another leader to view that as an acceptable loss. As simply the price for getting to the position of a largely autonomous Kurdistan. Another leader might have believed that Kurdistan would have been able to expand in the future to take in the city after achieving that initial position of semi-independence. They might even have believed that Kurdistan would be better off without Kirkuk, since its loss would have taken away one of the main things (the oil resources) that so many of those who sought to control Kurdistan over the years actually wanted. They might have seen it as giving away the one reason so many nations had for wanting to keep a tight grip on Kurdistan, and so as increasing its odds of independence.

Mullah Mustafa Barzani did not see it like that, because he had a clear idea of the Kurdistan he wanted to achieve. He understood that if Kurdistan gave away Kirkuk, it would be unlikely to get it back again, because such a move would have helped to produce a worldwide perception of Kurdistan that did not include it. More than that, Mullah Mustafa saw the importance of Kurdish culture, language and people to Kurdistan. He was not about to give up on a predominantly Kurdish city, even if that meant delaying the project he had worked towards his whole life. To do so would have significantly harmed that wider project, because it would have said that it was all right for areas of Kurdistan to remain under direct central government control, which would have set a dangerous precedent for the future.

The Idea of Kurdistan

The later policies of Arabisation demonstrate the importance of this quite clearly. What Mullah Mustafa understood instinctively, later Baghdad governments came to understand too: that ownership of a place on a map is less important than how people perceive it. That changing people's perception of Kirkuk from a Kurdish city to an Arab one meant more than simple military force. Mullah Mustafa understood that the cultural heart of a city was crucial, and refused to let Kirkuk slip from his image of how Kurdistan should be.

Then there is the question of what Mullah Mustafa Barzani's vision of Kurdistan was. It was not just of a small territory eking out an existence. It was of a country that my people could be proud to call their home. One that was secure economically as well as militarily, because so often in these days of modern, high cost warfare, those are the same things. He understood how necessary Kirkuk was to the long term success of Kurdistan, and he wasn't prepared to give up on that vision of Kurdistan as a successful nation.

It is almost directly because of Mullah Mustafa Barzani's image of Kurdistan that Kirkuk remains within it. It would have been so easy to let it go, to suggest that it was not necessary to the finished Kurdistan, or that it would be easier to let it slip away in order to get to the goal of independence quicker. Even today, we can see that the desire to hold onto Kirkuk can cause friction between the KRG and the Baghdad government. Part of Mullah Mustafa Barzani's importance to Kurdistan is the strength of his vision of it. He had a clear vision of the country that he wanted to help bring about, and that is a vision that seems to have become widespread. When people talk about Kurdistan today, it is in the terms that Mullah Mustafa envisaged. Terms that, for Kirkuk, mean its inclusion within the Kurdistan of which it is culturally a part, rather than being abandoned even if it might be more politically convenient to do so.

Symbols of Kurdistan

Today, Kurdistan has many elements of a country that are as much symbolic as practical. A flag, a national anthem. Even elements such as ambassadors exist at least as much to proclaim Kurdistan's existence as a meaningful political entity as to conduct relations with the outside world.

Where do these symbolic elements come from? To what extent, if any, can Mullah Mustafa Barzani be said to be connected to them? In the case of the Kurdish flag, it combines a rich history with a relatively modern full development. A flag very similar to the current one has been used several times in more recent Kurdish history, being one of the symbols used when attempting to claim independence from the Ottoman Turks. It was also used, with only slight variations, as the flag of the Mahabad Republic. Its more recent use began in the late 1980s, as a symbol of renewed commitment to the idea of Kurdistan as a separate country, with particular backing from the PDK.

In that much, we can say that Mullah Mustafa's descendants have had more of an impact on this particular symbol of Kurdistan than he did. Massoud Barzani has, for example, stated that he intends that having been born under the Kurdish flag (in Mahabad in 1946) it will also be flying at the end of his life. The Barzanis have also had a role to play in promoting the idea of the flag's internal symbolism, with red for the struggle for independence, green for the beauty of the region, and white for the peace that holds sway there now.

Yet this is not to say that Mullah Mustafa Barzani was entirely absent from the story of this symbol of Kurdistan. His presence in Mahabad points to an obvious connection, and indeed, the story is that he received the flag from Qazi Muhammad when the republic was about to fall, with an injunction to keep the fight for Kurdish freedom going, as he was the best man to protect the flag. If this story is true, then it seems obvious that

The Idea of Kurdistan

Mullah Mustafa Barzani had a role to play in keeping the idea of the Kurdish flag alive. Certainly, it seems like it points to what the flag was doing in the period between its use in Mahabad and its resurgence in the late twentieth century.

Yet there are questions that we must ask of this story if we are to treat it reasonably. Questions such as what Mullah Mustafa did with the flag in the intervening period, and why he did not promote it more consistently. History does not associate him with the flag in the same way that it does others, and it seems odd that such a thing would be the case if the story were true. We would expect references to it throughout the 1960s and 1970s in particular, where he was working for a degree of autonomy for Kurdistan in the context of the overthrow of the monarchy and the Ba'athist revolution. Yet it doesn't appear. Why not?

There are two potential answers to this, and I can't say with certainty which is true. The first possibility is that Mullah Mustafa Barzani had the flag, but felt for some reason that he could not fly it openly. Perhaps he felt that it was a sufficiently powerful symbol that it would have been a provocation in periods when he was attempting to achieve his ends through political negotiation and careful interaction with outside groups such as the Soviet Union. Flying the flag would have been a fairly strong declaration about the autonomous, even independent, status of Kurdistan, and might have invited the kind of retribution he was not prepared to contemplate. He might also have felt that it wasn't appropriate to use the flag before some measure of independence worthy of it had been achieved.

That is one possibility. The other possibility is that the story, although often repeated, is made up. It does sound in many ways too good to be true. It's the kind of symbolic handing over of the reins of authority that makes for a very good story, and the kind of story that people want to be true on a lot of levels. Perhaps it makes for such a good story that people have simply repeated it again and again, not caring too much whether it was actually likely that Qazi Muhammad, who didn't get on that well with Mullah Mustafa in most other aspects of the Mahabad Republic, would treat him as its natural successor. Perhaps it doesn't even *matter* whether the story was true or not. What is important is what it tells us about the way people felt about Mullah Mustafa, and his role in the process of independence.

The story of the national anthem is essentially the same as that of the flag. It existed before the Mahabad Republic, but it was there that it became a key symbol of Kurdish nationhood, and it is presumably through there that any connection to Mullah Mustafa Barzani came about. Again though, there isn't the kind of clear connection that we would perhaps like, suggesting that if Mullah Mustafa Barzani did have a role to play in connecting the present with the past, it was a relatively subtle one.

Instead, we can say that for both the anthem and the flag, their present adoption has less to do with Mullah Mustafa than with the desire to connect to the Mahabad Republic's brief spell of independence. That is not to say that there is no connection. Almost certainly, for President Massoud Barzani, his and his father's personal connections to the Mahabad Republic provided an additional reason to forge that connection between the past and the present. We can also say that Mullah Mustafa may have played a role in ensuring that the symbols of the Mahabad Republic were not forgotten, and that he helped to teach those around him the importance of the idea of Kurdistan, but his direct influence on those current symbols of the region is quite limited.

Kurdish Language and Culture

Flags and anthems aren't the only symbols of a nation, or of an ethnic group. Language and culture have hugely important symbolic roles to play when it comes to the identity of an ethnic

The Idea of Kurdistan

group. They also have roles to play in making the case for such a group being distinctive enough and dominant enough in a region to warrant its independence from a larger political unit. In some cases, the survival of a language is purely about that sense of identity rather than any practical use as a means of communication, as in the case of the Welsh language spoken in that region of the UK. There, Welsh speakers are almost certain to speak English as well, but it is such a crucial statement of the region's partly separate identity that even road signs feature instructions in both languages.

Kurdish language and culture have always been crucial in preserving the idea of Kurdistan. It is no coincidence that nations throughout history that have sought to repress their Kurdish populations have sought to do so by targeting their language, diluting their sense of cultural cohesion, and trying to impose their own cultural values. In Iraq, forcing education to take place in Arabic was a key plank of a programme of Arabisation designed at creating such a strong Iraqi identity that it would override any sense of Kurdishness amongst my people. In Turkey, there was, for decades, an official denial that Kurds even existed as a people.

Attempts to preserve Kurdish culture and language were, therefore, crucial in bringing about Kurdistan as it exists today. That was a massive job, undertaken by every parent teaching their children one of the dialects of the Kurdish language, everyone who preserved an old song or story. Efforts such as the hundreds of volunteers who helped to create Dohuk's university helped to bring back Kurdish culture and rebuild Kurdistan.

But Mullah Mustafa Barzani had a key role to play too. In his revolts, he emphasised the idea that they were *Kurdish* revolts, and not just Barzani ones. His stated aims in his revolts invariably included the use of Kurdish as the primary language of education and public life in the region, as well as the adoption

The Idea of Kurdistan

of Kurdish officials in important posts. Indeed, the earliest revolts in which he was involved seem to have been aimed squarely at combating specific intrusions of Iraqi Arab culture and officialdom into the region that contained his supporters.

Even in his dealings with the Soviets, we can see Mullah Mustafa Barzani's determination to preserve a clear sense of Kurdish culture and identity. He refused repeatedly to allow his efforts to be absorbed into those of Azerbaijan, knowing that once they had been, all hopes of Kurdish independence would be gone. He insisted on the cultural identity of his followers, even in the face of the homogenising influence of the Communism that surrounded them.

Preserving the Idea

Perhaps that is Mullah Mustafa Barzani's biggest contribution to the idea of Kurdistan. He did not create the idea, because that had been around for centuries before his birth. Other figures played key roles in the birth of nationalism there. Culturally, Kurdish identity owes a lot to everyone who worked to pass on a sense of it to their children. Geographically, Kurdistan's present shape is down at least partly to historical factors beyond Mullah Mustafa's control, even if he did help to create the focus on Kurdistan in its current form that has been at the heart of his party's efforts since.

But there was one thing that Mullah Mustafa Barzani seems to have done better than anyone else. He was very good at saying no to those who wanted to absorb, assimilate, or re-design the Kurdish people. He rose up when the British attempted to impose their authority over traditional tribal life. He rose up again when the Iraqi government tried to impose its officials on the area. He refused to let the Soviets relegate his followers to just a branch of the Azerbaijani movement. Later, he refused to accept settlement terms that didn't preserve the cultural and political integrity of his people.

The Idea of Kurdistan

Mullah Mustafa Barzani wasn't responsible for creating the idea of Kurdistan, but on some level, he understood how important that idea was. He also understood that it was potentially fragile. That if it wasn't protected and reinforced, it could shift and change as people's attitudes changed. That if he gave in on issues such as the preservation of the Kurdish language, or on self-determination, then the opportunity to argue Kurdistan's case on those issues might be gone forever.

In that sense, we can see Mullah Mustafa Barzani as a preserving force for the idea of Kurdish independence, and for the image of Kurdistan that he held. His revolts weren't successful in bringing about the Kurdistan that he wanted, but each one served to remind the people in the region of the image of Kurdistan that the revolt was about. Each time that he sought sanctuary beyond Kurdistan, Mullah Mustafa took that idea with him, beyond the reach of those who might try to change things and force my people to forget about it back home.

As I suggested at the start of this chapter, countries are essentially ideas. Symbols powerful enough that everyone agrees on them. Mullah Mustafa Barzani is typically remembered as an expert in the arts of war. As someone who spent his whole life fighting, and whose contribution to Kurdistan was essentially military. I would like to suggest here that his biggest contribution was essentially symbolic. It lay in the preservation of Kurdistan, not as the functioning, unconquered region that he never quite managed to sustain, but as an image in the minds of both my people and Iraq's rulers. Thanks to Mullah Mustafa Barzani, there was never a moment in his lifetime when Iraq managed to do what Turkey had done and pretend that my people did not exist. There was never a moment, moreover, when you could have said 'Kurdistan' in Iraq and not have people know what you were talking about. Without that strong sense of what Kurdistan was, without that image of it, can we really say that it would exist today in its current form?

Chapter Twelve: The Wider World

Inevitably, history has to focus in. It has to pick out moments, or areas, or individuals. It cannot take in the whole sweep of human history without losing too much in the process. In the case of this work, my focus has been on Mullah Mustafa Barzani and what is today Iraqi Kurdistan. But in order to fully understand those subjects, we have to understand the way they fit into the wider world. We know that Mullah Mustafa Barzani is considered to be highly important in Kurdistan. We know the importance of the Kurdish cause to Kurdistan's people, and how seriously my people take ideas relating to their identity. But how are these things perceived by the outside world? How important are they outside Kurdistan? Have people even heard of Mullah Mustafa Barzani in corners of the globe that do not have large Kurdish populations?

To answer these questions, I intend to explore several things in this chapter. First, I want to explore Kurdistan's place in the wider world, both historically and today. I want to look at how Kurdistan is perceived, and where it fits into the broader web of international relations. Then I want to revisit the idea of Kurdish identity, and explore how that identity is perceived outside Kurdistan. Finally, I want to explore perception of Mullah Mustafa Barzani outside the region. In Kurdistan, he

The Wider World

is a national hero, but what do people think of him in America or Europe? Have they even heard of him?

Kurdistan and the World

Kurdistan's position in the world has varied tremendously over the course of history. It has had highs and lows in its relationships with the countries around it, and with those further afield. Today, that history has led to a complex place in the wider region, and some interesting perceptions within the wider world.

Kurdistan in the Past

Perceptions of Kurdistan in the past have tended to be surprisingly consistent. Certainly for the last few hundred years. Consistently, over that period, observers ascribed particular traits to Kurdistan and its people. Traits that had implications for the period that I have covered in this work, because they affected the way people, and even states, interacted with my people.

One of the most consistent traits ascribed to the Kurdish people was that of being warlike. Perhaps this is because the earliest references to Kurds seem to be in relation to their use as soldiers in the ancient Persian military. Perhaps it is also because it has been, for a long time, a heritage that my people have celebrated. Some of the Kurds given the most historical attention, such as Saladin, are primarily known for their military exploits.

This is a perception that has some basis in fact. Kurds have been used in the armies of many of the empires they have lived within, and our history has often called on us to fight against would-be conquerors. Yet I feel like it is an aspect of our heritage that is often overstated. Not only is there far more to Kurdistan than its fighters, but it also ignores the fact that most nations have military aspects to their history.

Why is this important? Because it played a key role in the

The Idea of Kurdistan

position Kurdistan found itself in after the First World War. The use of Kurdistan and its fighters by the Ottoman Empire to protect its borders was long established, and based on Kurdistan's military reputation. More importantly though, there is some of the language of the Great Powers in talking about Kurdistan and the possibility of granting it independence. Even the Treaty of Sèvres talked about granting independence if Kurdistan was deemed to be ready, and seemed to imply that it was somehow too warlike for independence. Certainly, the act of fragmenting Kurdistan seems to have been designed at least in part to spread that perceived tendency across several countries, where it could be controlled.

Historically, Kurdistan was also seen as tribal and rural, consisting of separate tribes living in the mountains and making use of pasture land on a seasonal basis. Although this was true at the start of the period of this work, further back in history, Kurdistan was actually comparatively urban in nature, with what seem to have been city based allegiances.

Does this matter? I would argue that it does, because the combination of this with the label of 'warlike' paints a pretty clear picture of how the wider, and particularly Western, world perceived Kurdistan historically. It is a combination of traits that people tended at the time to view as 'uncivilised', even though that has never been a word that could accurately be applied to Kurdistan. That is an important characterisation, because it helps to explain many of the ways the outside world tried to treat Kurdistan, even into the period under discussion in this book.

Yet has that characterisation changed? How does the world see Kurdistan today?

Kurdistan's Position Today

How is Kurdistan perceived today in the world? To a great extent, the answer to that depends on where in the world the

The Wider World

person answering that question is. There are also distinctions to be made between the perceptions of ordinary people and those of their governments.

Iraq perceives Kurdistan as a part of its territories, thanks to the after effects of the Treaty of Sèvres, and close to a hundred years of being joined together as a result. Its government has consistently tried to extend its power into the region, and constitutionally, Iraq and Kurdistan have affirmed their links to one another. It is important to understand this, because it helps to explain some of why Iraq has been so reluctant to let Kurdistan go fully, and why it might be reluctant to do so in the future. It views Kurdistan as its territory on the basis of a history of nearly a century of control, creating the classic problem with an area where there is historical weight behind the claims of both sides, making it harder to persuade one to let go of those claims. I am not saying that Iraq is in any way right in its claims to Kurdistan, merely that we must recognise how entrenched those claims have become over the years.

At the same time though, there are clearly elements in Iraq who see Kurdistan as something separate. There is its current nearly autonomous status, so that Kurdistan and Iraq talk to one another more like two neighbouring countries than a country and a region within it. There is the slow disconnection of Kurdish interests from the politics of Baghdad, at least partly through the efforts of Iraq's government. And then there is the fact that Iraq has been seeking to extend its power in Kurdistan for much of the hundred years it has laid claim to it. From police stations and public buildings to full military invasions, again and again, the Baghdad government has sought to stamp its ownership of Kurdistan on the region. One does not seek to build connections in a place that is already connected. The very fact that it feels the need to keep doing these things shows that there have always been those in Iraq who have

The Idea of Kurdistan

recognised that Kurdistan has never been fully integrated with the main body of the country.

Perceptions of Kurdistan among its other neighbours obviously vary somewhat according to the individual politics of the regions concerned. Turkey, Iran and Syria do not react in exactly the same ways to issues around Kurdistan. Yet in many ways, the differences are about their reactions to the idea of Kurdish identity, rather than Kurdistan as a region or potential country.

In terms of perceptions of Kurdistan as a country, its immediate neighbours are in a complex position. On the one hand, Kurdistan is a potential trading partner as one of the most stable zones in the wider area and as a resource rich region. The oil pipeline between Kurdistan and Turkey proves the value of those links. Yet there is also a clear sense of hostility of many of the governments involved, because they fear trouble with their own Kurdish populations, or are at war with them, or they fear the potential for expansion of any Kurdish state.

The result of this is that Kurdistan finds itself essentially surrounded by Arab states that do not fully trust or like it. There are old grudges being continued and old attitudes towards Kurdistan that need to be overcome for a stable region. The process of building that trust is an ongoing one, but it has complicated Kurdistan's cross border relationships for decades.

In the much wider world, the first question is the extent to which people have heard of Kurdistan. Often in the case of the general public in places like the United States or UK, they could not locate Kurdistan on a map. Many of them would never have heard of the region. Even a quick, relatively unscientific sampling of people suggests that there is only a limited popular awareness of Kurdistan in countries outside the Middle East. Even among those who have vaguely heard of the region, there is some confusion. There are those who seem to confuse it with the Central Asian country of Kyrgyzstan, between Kazakhstan and China. There are those who are aware

The Wider World

of it only in terms of Iraq and perhaps Saddam's atrocities against my people. Certainly, most people seem to be unaware of its complex issues over sovereignty, either ignoring it completely or assuming that it must be a country and that therefore there is no problem.

These issues are almost as pronounced among many governments around the globe. Kurdistan maintains a continuous programme of contact with other nations; of ambassadorial visits and talks with senior figures. It does so because it has to in order to ensure that Kurdistan is not forgotten as an international priority. The prevailing mood among those nations further from Kurdistan seems to be one of almost wanting to forget about its existence.

Where it is remembered, it is often a struggle to persuade people to see the region in the way it wants to be perceived. The United States has, for years, had Kurdistan's main political parties on a list of groups supplying money to terrorists or groups conducting armed struggles against their governments. Why? Because those parties did indeed engage in such struggles: against Saddam Hussein. Many countries refused, or continue to refuse, to acknowledge the genocide of the Anfal there. They see Kurdistan's desire for independence as none of their business, or as a symptom of a wider breakdown in stability across Iraq, Syria and beyond, and thus as something to be resisted.

These are attitudes that need to be changed if Kurdistan is to become, and stay, an independent country. It needs international partners, which means that it needs international perception of it to be on its side. It needs other countries to go from either ignoring it or seeing it as a part of the problems of the wider region to seeing it as a part of the solution. That shift in perceptions can only be achieved through an ongoing programme of education and engagement designed to show the wider world what Kurdistan is actually like.

The Idea of Kurdistan

Kurdish Identity and the World

Questions about Kurdistan and questions about Kurdish identity are two slightly different things. Although Kurdistan exists as a homeland for my people, there are obviously many Kurds who live outside the borders of Kurdistan. I have discussed Kurdish identity and the role Mullah Mustafa Barzani played in it elsewhere, so for now, I want to look at the ways it is perceived outside Kurdistan.

First, how is Kurdish identity perceived by Kurds outside of Kurdistan? Is it a strong identity? By that, I mean, would people often describe themselves as Kurdish first, before any national or other identity? The evidence seems to be fairly clear that it is, and that many people do exactly that. The existence of Kurdish independence movements in a number of neighbouring countries seems to point to that. More than that though, we have the existence of strong Kurdish communities in many other countries. Communities, rather than just individuals, complete with the preservation of traditional cultural elements including songs, stories, language and norms.

If anything, Kurdish identity is probably perceived as more important today than it was in the past. The existence of Kurdistan as an autonomous region probably has something to do with that, but so do the growth of mass communications within Kurdistan and its rapid modernisation. Those have tended to mean that a general sense of Kurdish identity has started to take over from the individual tribal or regional identities that played such strong roles before. While I'm sure no one wants those important elements of our culture to die out completely, that growth of a more general Kurdish identity is probably a good thing, and is almost certainly one of the things fuelling Kurdistan's moves in the direction of independence.

Kurdish identity has been actively suppressed in the past by at least one of Kurdistan's neighbours, in the form of Turkey, which denied that there were any Kurds living in its territory

The Wider World

for many years. Today, that is not a stance that it adopts, but it, Syria and Iran all tend to react poorly to significant declarations of a Kurdish identity, seeing them as connected to Kurdish nationalist movements within their countries and thus as increasing the risk of them losing territory. In Iran, the 1979 fatwa against my people was one of the most violent expressions of this attitude, while in the currently ongoing Syrian conflict, many of those involved seem to view Kurds as something separate, to be attacked.

Beyond Iraq's immediate neighbours, some of the surrounding countries seem to have been more willing to accept the Kurds who live there. Jordan has had a population of my people for many years and seems willing to accept expressions of Kurdish culture, while figures from countries such as Egypt have expressed support for Kurdistan. Perhaps they are less worried by the idea of Kurdishness when their countries do not have long standing conflicts with Kurdish populations over the occupation of traditional lands.

Outside the wider region of the Middle East though, the attitude towards the Kurds seems to be one of either general indifference, worry or pity, none of which is the attitude that my people would desire. For many people in the wider world, the Kurds are effectively none of their business. My people's struggle for a homeland, and for a degree of control over their own lives, is to many people just one more struggle in a world full of them, happening somewhere a long way away. Many people don't even know that my people exist as a separate ethnic group.

Many of those who do probably still don't know many details about them. They wouldn't know for example that my people speak several versions of the Kurdish language, or about the ways in which they are spread over several countries. The tendency is to view us as a homogeneous group, and probably to wrongly assume that we already have a country of our own.

The Idea of Kurdistan

Those who do know anything about my people tend to know them either in terms of the warlike stories of the past and multiple rebellions or purely in terms of what was done to us by Saddam. The first view essentially sees all the times my people have rebelled without any of the context that forced those rebellions, combines it with the Kurds' ancient reputation as warrior tribes and comes to the conclusion that we are somehow only interested in violence and expansionism.

It is a view that is ill informed, not knowing enough about the circumstances of Kurdish history to fully understand the situations my people found themselves in. It also ignores the fact that for almost any people or country, history is littered with battles and wars. Does that make them all some caricature of aggression? Obviously not. No more than it does so in my people's case.

The other attitude, pity, comes from those people for whom the Kurds are simply 'those people Saddam used chemical weapons on'. While it is important that the evils of the Anfal should never be forgotten, this attitude makes two mistakes. It misunderstands the nature of the genocide undertaken in Kurdistan, attributing it purely to the evils of one man rather than to an entire system and history. In doing so, it ignores the fact that many of the conflicts involved have yet to be resolved.

Secondly, it reduces my people to simply the victims of an evil man, rather than seeing them as people in their own right. While it is appropriate that Saddam should be reviled for what he did, my people's history and culture amounts to far more than just the period of the Anfal, as I would hope this work has shown.

Mullah Mustafa and the World

We have seen throughout this book just how important Mullah Mustafa Barzani is to Kurdistan. His name is one that is instantly

The Wider World

recognisable in the region. Indeed, I have argued that in many ways he has become a symbol as much as a historical figure, with his name used in a variety of contexts to imply a particular combination of qualities and political views. In Kurdistan, Mullah Mustafa Barzani's name stands for independence, for a particular kind of stoicism in the face of a continuing struggle, and perhaps for a set of military qualities that always formed the heart of his rebellions.

Outside Kurdistan, it is harder to see the impact Mullah Mustafa has had. Just as many people in the world have not heard of Kurdistan, so too, many of those outside Kurdistan have not heard of Mullah Mustafa Barzani. They do not know about his long and complex history with the cause of Kurdish independence. This creates a kind of disconnection, because here we have a man whose life stands as one of the primary symbols of Kurdistan, but it is a symbolism that the rest of the world does not understand. They are left behind when it comes to the idea of Kurdish independence as a result.

Those in the outside world who have heard of Mullah Mustafa have generally done so in one of two contexts: either as the man who engaged in repeated revolts against Iraq, or as Massoud Barzani's father. Both are legitimate contexts in which to have heard about Mullah Mustafa, but each feels like it tells only part of the story. It is a summary without detail, taking us only part of the way towards understanding. Yet the interaction of those approaches tells us something interesting. Today, Mullah Mustafa is as likely to be cited as Massoud Barzani's father as Massoud Barzani is as his son. It says something about the importance of Kurdistan's president that things have gotten to that stage. Yet it also says something about the enduring appeal of Mullah Mustafa's story that his son's achievements have never totally eclipsed his memory. Indeed, Massoud Barzani has been instrumental in promoting his father's memory both in Kurdistan and beyond.

The Idea of Kurdistan

What can we say about attitudes to Mullah Mustafa Barzani outside Kurdistan through his life? Again, we cannot say that he was known by everyone in the world, certainly not with the level of recognition that he had in Kurdistan. Yet there were key figures who knew about him in the Soviet Union, the USA and beyond, and he did receive media attention in the USA.

In the Soviet Union, Mullah Mustafa seems to have been seen as a potentially useful ally, but not necessarily as someone who shared all their ideals. Certainly, the treatment of his men there seemed to be closer to the treatment of potential threats than friends. Yet he was able to maintain his image and position as a leader, getting Stalin and Khrushchev to accept that he was important enough to listen to when they met face to face.

Others, such as the Shah of Iran, seem to have seen Mullah Mustafa as a tool to employ in their own conflicts, but a potentially dangerous one. After all Mullah Mustafa had been involved in the Mahabad Republic, and Iran had its own Kurdish independence movement.

American attitudes to Mullah Mustafa seem to have been shaped by four things: first his time in the Soviet Union. Then, the attitudes of the Shah of Iran. Then, by the effects of media exposure late in his life. Finally, we have the effects of American involvement in Iraq from the 1990s on.

Initial American attitudes to Mullah Mustafa were not always friendly. A few early reports described him as the kind of plucky independence fighter they could respect, but that seems to have changed the moment he was forced to flee to the Soviet Union. The American press assumed that he was a 'Red' and therefore not to be trusted. They helped to circulate the made up stories of him driving around the northern borders of Iran, commanding a tank squadron. Certainly, by the time Mullah Mustafa was back in Iraq in the 1960s, America was so terrified of any hint of Communism that they were exceptionally wary of him.

Which was probably why they came to rely on the attitudes

The Wider World

of the Shah of Iran. He was their major ally in the region, and it was inevitable that the Americans would go along with his assessments of Mullah Mustafa and Kurdistan in general. Yet Iran was hardly willing to allow an independent Kurdistan to come into being, in case that meant the entire southern portion of its territories disappearing overnight. The mistrust the Shah helped to foster was part of the attitudes behind the withdrawal of US support in 1975, and behind the reluctance to allow Mullah Mustafa to visit the USA for medical treatment.

Yet he did make it there, and he was able to do something to change attitudes towards him. Certainly, he was able to raise public awareness regarding Kurdistan through the press attention he received towards the end of his life. Yet it is debatable whether that really did anything to change the minds of those in power at the time.

The final phase of his reputation in the USA came after the beginning of the US involvement in Iraq in the 1990s. Mullah Mustafa, engaged as he had been in his life in a fight that had ultimately ended up being against Saddam, suddenly came to be a much more acceptable figure for the Americans. One about whom awareness continues to grow.

This shift of attitudes is interesting, because it shows how views about a person can continue to adapt to circumstances even after their death. It also suggests the importance of Mullah Mustafa's perception, and why it will continue to be important to project the right image of him to the world in the years to come.

The World, The Message, The Problem

A problem should be obvious by now when it comes to the images of Kurdistan, Kurdish identity, and Mullah Mustafa Barzani. A problem that has potentially serious implications for the future of Kurdistan, and that cannot be ignored. The problem is simply the local nature of awareness about Kurdistan

The Idea of Kurdistan

and its issues. Those within the country almost certainly know all about Kurdistan, have a strong sense of Kurdish identity, and probably know about Mullah Mustafa Barzani. Those in Kurdistan's neighbours may well know these things, as will Kurds spread more widely around the globe.

Yet people around the world more generally often don't know about Mullah Mustafa Barzani, often can't locate Kurdistan on a map, and often know my people only in terms of Saddam's atrocities, if they know about them at all. This is a problematic situation. Why? Because a people who are not in the forefront of the world's attention are easier to attack. Because they are easier to ignore when it comes even to legitimate desires like independence.

Our history has shown that again and again. It has shown allies pulling away from us and enemies attacking us. It has shown broken promises about independence and the implementation of less restrictive modes of governance. It has shown people clearly willing to prioritise Kurdistan's neighbours over its people. Why? Because no one was watching. Because the international community, and the general public in other countries, did not know enough about Kurdistan, or they did not view it as important. Because of that lack of attention, it becomes easy for international leaders to prioritise Iraq, or one of Kurdistan's other neighbours, over its needs.

The only way we will be able to change this situation is through education. My people need to educate the world in their circumstances and culture. They need to continue to shout out their existence, so that it is impossible to ignore them. It is something that Mullah Mustafa Barzani sought to do throughout his life. If he was prepared to walk into the office of Khrushchev and demand to see him, surely we should be able to tell ordinary people about our homeland and who we are?

It is easy to overlook the importance of gaining wider

The Wider World

recognition. Easy to suggest that perhaps we should just get on with living our lives rather than trying to share those lives with the world. Yet the dangers that come from being ignored as a people are too great to leave to hope. We need to live our lives today, yes, but we also need to make sure that people know that we exist so that we will still have them tomorrow.

Chapter Thirteen: Kurdish Democracy

Kurdistan is not yet a country, but it is a functioning state in all but name. It has its own armed forces and police, its own language and culture, its own symbols and its own political system. Mullah Mustafa Barzani, or the idea of Mullah Mustafa Barzani, had a role to play in shaping each of these elements. Certainly, there are key elements of Kurdistan's current democracy that would be very different if he had not been involved in its story.

The Elements of Kurdistan's Democracy

Before discussing Mullah Mustafa Barzani's influence on the democratic structures and elements of Kurdistan, it seems sensible to explore the nature of Kurdistan's democracy. How does it function? What makes it unique? Without first understanding how Kurdistan's political system works, it is hard to talk seriously about the extent to which Mullah Mustafa might have influenced it.

At its most basic, Kurdistan is currently a federal region of Iraq, having representation within the broader Iraqi political system, but also having its own political structures. Internally, it functions essentially as a country would in all but name. Its political system is centred on the city of Erbil, which, as the

Kurdish Democracy

region's oldest city serves as its seat of government. It is a presidential democracy, with a president as well as a prime minister and parliament. The parliament is quite interesting, in that it consists of a single parliamentary chamber, rather than the dual chamber systems favoured in some other countries. That chamber consists of 111 members, elected every four years. The system is designed to create a clear separation between the legislative and executive branches of government, while still providing Kurdistan with the leadership it needs to interact with the world and respond quickly in times of emergency.

It is also designed to ensure representation for all of the people of Kurdistan, not just a few, or even the majority. The electoral system uses a form of closed list proportional representation, where parties get proportions of the seats available depending on their share of the vote, and those seats go to candidates on party lists in the order decided by the party. There have been some discussions recently over whether to move to a system that allows more direct selection of particular candidates by voters, which it is argued might increase the connection between voters and their candidates, but that proposal has not been accepted at the time of writing.

That is one of the most interesting things about Kurdistan's political system, though. Because it is new, because it doesn't have hundreds of years of tradition tying it to particular constitutional forms, it is in a position to think practically about what works. To design and redesign itself from the ground up. To undertake political experiments that other places are not in a position to attempt in order to get the best possible system. Many of the structures outlined above represent thinking that has been suggested elsewhere by political theorists and commentators, but then rejected for reasons of tradition or inertia. Kurdistan is in a position to implement the most modern political thinking in ways that some other areas are not.

It is willing to apply modern thinking in other ways, too.

The Idea of Kurdistan

Perhaps because my people understand what it is to be repressed by others, there is a commitment to equality in Kurdistan's political system that is often not found in other places internationally, let alone amongst its neighbours. Although there is a formal recognition of Islam as Kurdistan's dominant religion in its constitution, there is also a commitment to religious freedom for other groups. There are guaranteed seats in the Kurdish parliament for minority groups, ensuring that they have a voice in national affairs, while the law currently requires that at least 30 per cent of MPs must be women.

Kurdistan's commitment to equality can be found throughout its constitution. The marks of the past are clear in it, in clauses preventing such things as forced movement and entitling children to education in their native language. There is also a broad commitment to equality, banning discrimination on a wide variety of grounds. The core political system is backed up by many elements that would more commonly be found in a country than simply a region. Kurdistan has its own flag, its own anthem, its own ambassadors and its own foreign policy. Its representatives have met with a number of foreign powers to discuss issues including oil rights and joint responses to international humanitarian issues.

The political system is supported financially partly through taxation, but mostly through revenue from Kurdistan's oil resources, which are large enough to allow the region to undertake important infrastructure work without burdening the region's population excessively. While such financial resources might not seem like an element of the political system, they are important in helping to determine its shape and scope. They provide Kurdistan with a measure of financial security that allows its government to provide a quality of life above that of many equivalent sized regions.

Another key supporting element of Kurdistan's political system is its armed forces: the peshmerga. Kurdistan is unique in Iraqi regions in having its own armed forces, separate from those of the central government. The peshmerga forces currently number in excess of 300,000, and have transitioned from the lightly equipped fighters of Mullah Mustafa's day to include armoured regiments and helicopter support. Their presence is important to the political system in Kurdistan because of the element of security they represent, both ensuring stability at the heart of an often turbulent wider region and remaining as a guarantee of Kurdistan's autonomy.

In terms of political parties, Kurdistan is essentially pluralist, welcoming a wide variety of political viewpoints and allowing all parties to campaign freely. The only exceptions are to prevent puppet parties controlled from outside the region, or parties whose aims and methods focus on political violence or sectarian hatred. Kurdistan is trying to move on from its often violent past, and believes that a system in which people are able to speak freely and act politically for whatever they believe in represents a far stronger political situation than the alternatives. Currently, the largest party is the PDK, or Kurdistan Democratic Party, while the president is Massoud Barzani, and the prime minister is Nechervan Idris Barzani.

The Political System

Let's be clear, no one is going to claim that Kurdistan is currently a perfect democracy, with an ideal political system. There are elements of it that attract regular complaints, both outside the region and within it. Yet I would point out that, after the disruptions of the past, Kurdistan's political system is now far more stable than many of those around it. It is far more democratic than others in the region, with people free to express exactly the kind of range of views that they currently do. More than that, it is a system that knows it is on an ongoing journey. One that has not reached any kind of perfection, but that continues to strive towards it step by step.

The Idea of Kurdistan

Can we reasonably say that Mullah Mustafa Barzani influenced that political system? Yes, we can see the significant involvement of his family in the politics of the region today. Yes, we can see that the party he helped to found, the PDK, remains one of the key forces in Kurdish politics, and yes, there is the role he played in shaping many wider elements, such as the peshmerga, that help to shape the wider culture of Kurdistan and so influence politics indirectly. Yet can we say that a man who died before Kurdistan became a modern reality can possibly have influenced the shape of the modern political system?

There are two elements to this. One is that those points I have just mentioned, from the influence of Mullah Mustafa's family to the indirect influence of the peshmerga and the setting up of the PDK, are *not* minor points. Even today, they represent keystones of Kurdish society and politics. Without any one of them, Kurdistan would be a very different place indeed. We cannot simply set those elements aside to look at structural elements of Kurdish politics, partly because of their simple importance, and partly because those elements have had knock-on effects on the shape of the Kurdish political system. Is it possible, for example, that the political system in Kurdistan would have been the same without the existence of the PDK? Without the balance that existed between them and their political rivals from the 1990s on, it seems unlikely that Kurdistan would have had the same political system, or one as open to new influences.

The second point here is, as always, the importance of the idea of Mullah Mustafa Barzani. Yes, he died too soon to have much direct input into the political system of Kurdistan, but it seems impossible that in the years immediately after gaining a measure of autonomy, none of those founding the political system thought about either his values or his influence. Is it a coincidence that Kurdistan acquired an essentially presidential system, where a single figure is expected to stand above the

Kurdish Democracy

regional and local differences reflected in its parliament? Yes, probably some of that is down to its usualness as a mode of democracy around the world, and possibly the influence of the USA in the years when Kurdistan was drawing up its modes of governance, but it seems likely that at least part of it is because Mullah Mustafa's life accustomed policy makers to thinking in terms of heroic political figures.

More than that, we can see more of Mullah Mustafa Barzani's influence if we remember that Kurdistan's current political system was originally a coming together of two separate ones in the wake of gaining autonomy from Iraq and the civil wars that plagued the region in the 1990s. For several years, different areas of the country were effectively under the control of the different political parties of the region, with the PDK being one of the most important. It had direct control at that time of cities including Erbil, and the structures of command and leadership in that period were almost exactly those laid down by Mullah Mustafa Barzani in the 1940s.

Why is that relevant? Because the current political system in Kurdistan was not created in a vacuum. No political system is. The US or UK systems of democracy are sometimes held up as examples, but the US system still has elements that directly reflect the needs of landowners in the late eighteenth century (such as the anomaly of the Electoral College). The British system, meanwhile, is not so much a reflection of conscious design as simple historical accretion, with past solutions to what seemed to be pressing problems forming now unshakable traditions. It is not reasonable to expect, therefore, that the Kurdish system should be a sterile model of perfection, uninfluenced by what went before.

Instead, it is a system that is still in progress, created by the coming together of the spheres of influence of its two main parties and slowly moving towards a more perfect democracy step by step. Even in the region's constitution, we can find

The Idea of Kurdistan

significant evidence of those lingering influences. Its very first page acknowledges the influences and sacrifices of those within the peshmerga and the Kurdish Liberation Movement. Since Mullah Mustafa was at the heart of both, it is hard to see how he cannot have influenced Kurdistan's political systems.

Certainly, some of the values he held seem to have found expression in Kurdistan's modern constitution, albeit in updated form. We can see in his and Sheikh Ahmad's early rebellions that there was a commitment to the preservation of the environment in the states they tried to form. That element is present in the current constitution, in the form of a legal commitment to preserving protected areas. Mullah Mustafa seems also to have been much more interested in the rights of women than many of his contemporaries, and today we find a guarantee in the constitution that at least 30 per cent of parliamentarians will be women. Even the KRG's representative to the UK, Bayan Sami Abdul Rahman, is female. There is a commitment to freedom of religion in the constitution that seems like it must purely be a reflection of modern concerns, yet Mullah Mustafa's history shows that his rebellions were political in tone rather than religious.

In general, we can say that one of Mullah Mustafa's biggest influences on the modern Kurdistan is just how inclusive it is trying to be. While it is undoubtedly intended to be a safe homeland for my people, it also actively strives to be an equal society, where religious and social differences are accepted. I strongly believe that is due at least in part to the nature of Mullah Mustafa's attempted revolutions, which accepted anybody, so long as they were willing to work to help craft the new Kurdistan that he envisaged. While that influence may not be easy to trace directly, it is all too easy to see how things could have turned out under another leader. All too easy to see how the attitudes and values of the Kurdish Liberation Movement could have been shaped in far less accepting or forgiving directions. Imagine that, and it becomes easy to see just how important Mullah Mustafa Barzani's influence was in shaping the current region's political structures.

The PDK

Clearly, there are some areas of the politics of Kurdistan that Mullah Mustafa Barzani has shaped more than others. Yes, there is a case for saying that his values and attitudes have influenced the modern region's constitution, but it is in other core areas that his greatest influence lingers.

Perhaps the most important of these areas is the PDK. The party remains the dominant political force in Kurdistan, polling more than 37 per cent of the votes in the September 2013 elections and providing the region's president, Massoud Barzani. It is crucial to modern Kurdish politics, having been present and victorious in every election the region has had so far. More than that, it has played a crucial role in the construction of Kurdistan as it currently exists, helping to produce the constitution and political system that functions there today.

Mullah Mustafa Barzani is always cited as being directly responsible for the creation of the party. To what extent is that a legitimate assessment of the history? There are other elements that fed into the creation of the party, including the pre-existing political climate and even the creation of the Kurdish Democratic Party of Iran by Qazi Muhammad.

Both elements seem hard to ignore, and it would be wrong to deny their influence on the creation of the modern party. Let's take the political climate first. Mullah Mustafa Barzani was not the first to create a political party dedicated to a free and independent Kurdistan, and that must be acknowledged. While Mullah Mustafa was rising up militarily in the early 1940s, the civilian population of Kurdistan's cities were forming themselves into political associations under the label of the Hiwa Party. Although it is fair to say that the Barzanis were organising themselves against the British and Iraqis who sought to control the region far before the 1940s, that was a tribal, familial and personal organisation rather than a modern political one.

The Hiwa Party, therefore, represents an important precursor to the PDK. So too does the Democratic Party of Kurdistan in Iran, founded by Qazi Muhammad. It seems impossible to believe that it is a coincidence that the PDK for Iraq shares a name with Qazi Muhammad's party, or that it was founded so soon after Mullah Mustafa's arrival in the Mahabad Republic. Instead, it seems far more likely that what he saw there was the inspiration for him to try to emulate things with the creation of the PDK.

It is important to recognise these influences, but it is also important to understand their limits, and the extent to which Mullah Mustafa Barzani's role was still a crucial one, even then. If we take the Hiwa Party, for example, we must still recognise that it was a big step from those local political organisations to a national party like the PDK. We must also recognise that it was Mullah Mustafa who joined the Hiwa Party's efforts with the military ones of the Barzani revolt, forming the Freedom Committee and coordinating the intersection of military and civil power.

We must also remember that ultimately, the Hiwa Party did not last. The PDK probably took at least some inspiration from that early political experiment, and we should be grateful for it, but it is not simply an outgrowth or continuation of the old Hiwa Party. It is a separate political organisation, with its own goals and structures. An easy way to assess this is to simply ask whether the Hiwa Party would ever have morphed into the current PDK if Mullah Mustafa Barzani had not existed. It seems clear that it would not have. It took that extra component of personality and leadership to create, along with the mixture of personal and political connections that Mullah Mustafa Barzani had.

Kurdish Democracy

What about the PDK(Iran)? Again, we must acknowledge the influence there, and probably the connection that Mullah Mustafa Barzani was trying to suggest with the name. However, again the question is whether that translates to a direct, causal connection. Would the PDK always have come into being once Qazi Muhammad's Iranian equivalent had been created?

It is possible that it might have. It is possible that someone in Iraq would have seen the party over the border and decided to use the inherent symbolism of the name. Yet it seems unlikely that the party would have turned out exactly the same way. So much of its construction and structures owes something to the particular situation of its founders that if anyone else but Mullah Mustafa Barzani had founded it, it would have been very different. It is also entirely possible that someone trying to set up a party without direct contact with the PDK(Iran) might not have felt the symbolic link was important, and would have chosen a different name.

Certainly, the existence of the PDK(Iran) would not have been sufficient on its own to produce the PDK. Indeed, there is no suggestion that Qazi Muhammad or his supporters were interested in doing so. They were concerned with the situation in Iran; in setting up a separate homeland there, not in the situation within Iraqi Kurdistan. Which means that Mullah Mustafa Barzani was crucial when it came to the creation of the party. Someone without his contact with the PDK(Iran) in Mahabad would probably have created a very different party, yet most of those involved in Mahabad had no reason or opportunity to create the party at all. Only Mullah Mustafa Barzani and those close to him had that particular combination.

It is a combination that has had a profound impact on Kurdistan as it exists today. Yes, the party is very different today to the one that Mullah Mustafa Barzani founded. It has a whole new political landscape to work within, a situation that is founded on democratic engagement rather than armed struggle, and a society with often very different attitudes. Yes, it is possible that some form of political party dedicated to freedom for the region would have come about without Mullah Mustafa Barzani, yet it seems impossible that the PDK as it currently stands would have come into being without his influence. In that, Mullah Mustafa Barzani and his legacy continue to have a significant influence within Kurdistan.

His Family's Role

One of Mullah Mustafa Barzani's bigger influences on Kurdistan is the continuing role of his family within the region's politics. Mullah Mustafa's son is, at the time of writing, the region's president. Other members of his extended family include the prime minister and the head of the national security council. Barzanis are present in many important positions throughout the country.

Why is that? Obviously, the PDK's political opponents allege that it is simple nepotism, but is it more than that? Is that an allegation that misunderstands both the way the Barzanis work and the long term influence of Mullah Mustafa Barzani on the country? Obviously, I believe that it is, although given that I am Barzani too, I will understand if you don't necessarily believe me. But perhaps if I take a moment to explain, you will see both the influence of historical factors on the current situation and the role of Mullah Mustafa Barzani in bringing it about.

The crucial thing to remember is the nature of the situation when the PDK was being founded. It was in the process of an ongoing rebellion, following the retreat to the Mahabad Republic. That meant a number of things. First, it meant that of course Mullah Mustafa Barzani was going to simply assume the original leadership. It was in an essentially military situation where clearly defined leadership was the most important thing. Where it was, in any case, largely Mullah Mustafa's combination of charisma and leadership holding things together within the newly formed party.

There were dangers in the situation too. The PDK was formed in a situation where Mullah Mustafa and those around him had already been betrayed several times. Where there had been attempts to assassinate him, and good friends of his had been executed. It was a situation where often the only people he could trust were those related to him by either blood or marriage. Dangerous, potentially unstable situations have continued in Iraq and Kurdistan for much of the period since then. Between the struggles against a central administration that often wished to wipe my people out, a damaging civil war, and an occasionally unstable wider environment, it is hardly surprising that senior members of the party continued to take the same approach to the people they could trust. Perhaps now, as Kurdistan is more settled, things will slowly change, but it is not appropriate to judge dangerous past situations by the standards of the present day.

As well as the dangers of the situation in which the PDK was founded, there is the point that for many of the early rebellions against the authorities in Iraq, it was essentially a family or tribal affair. The earliest rebellions seem to have been composed almost entirely of Barzani fighters, the 1940s rebellion being the first that seems to have been truly region wide in character. The consequences from many of those rebellions seem also to have been aimed largely at Barzanis. They were the ones who had to flee for Mahabad. Where other tribes were offered peace terms by the British, they seem to have been the ones who were targeted for arrest and execution. Under Saddam, their men were the ones who were murdered en masse in the early 1980s. To the extent that the PDK began life as an extension of that movement, it is only natural that Barzanis would be involved in it too. Indeed, in the early days of the party, they were often the only ones available.

The Idea of Kurdistan

In this, there is to some extent only the natural political process going on. If someone sees that a party has large numbers of their relatives involved, that seems to take their interests seriously in a way other parties sometimes do not, then it is only natural that they will want to become involved. More than that, there is to some extent a sense of obligation in the decision. A sense that points to the scale of Mullah Mustafa Barzani's continuing influence over the party, and the importance of his memory. There is almost a sense of expectation for those related to him that they should try to live up to the memory of their ancestor by entering public service and dedicating their efforts to Kurdistan. When combined with admittedly large family resources and political connections, it would be very surprising if family members did not succeed in the field.

This is actually the case in many of the world's democracies. Take the USA as an example. It is generally accepted as a beacon of democracy, and yet it seems that statistically, your chances of achieving high office are significantly increased if your family name happens to be Bush, Clinton or Kennedy. No one suggests that this is indicative of anything improper, merely a combination of expectation and opportunity that has helped to create key political dynasties. In India, for example, the family name Gandhi seems to carry with it a magic from its most famous ancestor that holds hopes, expectations and a vastly increased chance of political office. In an attempt to recreate the past, people sometimes latch onto family names, simply because it seems to give them some sense of what they might get.

The same situation applies in Kurdistan. The family name of Barzani is intimately tied up with the fortunes of the PDK, and also with the history of the movement towards a free and independent Kurdistan. It means that it is almost inevitable that it is a political dynasty that will continue. It also means that Mullah Mustafa Barzani's legacy continues to have an effect on Kurdistan, every time its people choose a leader, or its parties select their candidates. His image, and more importantly his name, remains a significant force within Kurdistan, while his family do their best to carry on his legacy in a modern world where so much has changed.

Self-Reliance

Kurdistan interacts with the world, and with the countries around it, in ways that are very different to other regions its size. Its level of independence from Iraq is one unusual element, but there is also a combination of self-reliance and international ties there that is rare in countries/regions of that size. The combination of the two is exceptional, and I would like to suggest that both owe something to Mullah Mustafa Barzani's influence and history.

Kurdistan's level of independence is unusual for a region of a country. It is, in most ways, a country in all but name. It has its own parliament, president, ambassadors and flag. It has its own armed forces and budget, its own language and culture. Yet it presently remains a legal part of a federal Iraq. This situation is not entirely without parallel in the world: each of the USA's states has governmental structures, state police forces, flags and anthems. Quebec in Canada combines several of these elements with distinct linguistic and cultural differences from the rest of the country.

Yet Kurdistan goes further. Federal states elsewhere might have low level militias or armed police forces, but generally, they have nothing so sophisticated as Kurdistan's armed forces. Nor is one of the abiding jobs of that force elsewhere to guard against the possibility of forced closer union by the central government, as the peshmerga's job occasionally has been in Kurdistan. Culturally, even the most pro-independence French-speaking Québecois still has more in common with the rest of Canada than most of Kurdistan has to do with Iraq. Certainly, there is not the history of struggle against the government

The Idea of Kurdistan

there and violence towards the people by that government that has shaped relations in Kurdistan.

Mullah Mustafa Barzani is one of the major factors influencing that sense of independence. On a number of occasions, when it seemed like the independence movement might have been defeated, he was the one who organised its escape to other regions, helping to keep it alive. By doing so, he helped to create a sense in Kurdistan that there was someone working towards freedom who was out there somewhere, even on those occasions when Kurdistan was most oppressed. Without that feeling, it is possible that attempts by successive governments at Arabisation and imposing a broader national culture on the region might have succeeded. Without an awareness that there was a movement out there supporting independence, without a figure to hang that feeling on, it would have been easy for individuals to become disheartened and assume that their desire for that level of independence would never become a reality. Without that sense that there was still a fight going on out there somewhere, it would have been easy, even sensible, to knuckle under and go along with the attempts to change Kurdistan's culture.

More than that, Mullah Mustafa Barzani's memory influences the relations between Kurdistan and the Iraqi central government. While there is no suggestion that Baghdad intends the sort of things towards Kurdistan that previous Iraqi governments attempted, there is a level of caution in relations between the two that directly stems from memories of Mullah Mustafa's life and the events in it. The occasions on which he attempted to deal with the Iraqi government were frequently marked by betrayal and a lack of trust. In that sense, we can say that previous events have scarred current relations, contributing to a desire for independence from control.

That desire translates to some extent into a level of self-reliance that shows itself throughout Kurdistan's relations with

Kurdish Democracy

the outside world. The events of Mullah Mustafa Barzani's life, from the partitioning of Kurdistan when he was a child, all the way to the Iran–Iraq peace at the very end of his life, have shown my people that the international community represents a complex challenge for Kurdistan.

On the one hand, Mullah Mustafa's life has shown just how much international support can do to assist Kurdistan when it is forthcoming. The Mahabad adventure would not have been possible without support from the Soviet Union. Nor would his escape following its failure. Indeed, other countries, most notably Iran, played a key role in allowing Mullah Mustafa Barzani to escape following several failed revolts. In the 1970s, the revolt that took place would again not have been possible without outside support, and the encouragement of the USA.

Yet there is the other side of that. There were incidents in Mullah Mustafa Barzani's life that showed clearly just how quickly that support could be withdrawn. There was the Soviet withdrawal of support from the Mahabad Republic and the US withdrawal of support from the Iran–Iraq war. More than that, there was the British influence throughout his early life, as one of the key forces pressing against the rebellions his people undertook. There were the moments following the two world wars he lived through, first carving up Kurdistan, and then pushing the Soviet Union back from its involvement in the region. All of these incidents have had an impact on Kurdistan, helping to teach its government the dangers of over-reliance on international support.

The result of this combination is an active foreign policy that seeks international support and partners, but that does not seek to make Kurdistan dependent on that support. Kurdistan has occasionally been accused of being excessive in trying to preserve its access to oil reserves, yet that is not about greed. Instead, it is about avoiding two things. First, it seeks to avoid over-dependence on other countries for resources, because it knows from the lessons of Mullah Mustafa's life how quickly that support can evaporate. Second, it seeks to avoid being forgotten about. It is all too apparent from the early history of Mullah Mustafa's life that Kurdistan interested the international community only to the extent to which it could provide oil. Is it surprising that it would wish to maintain those resources now, and thus the international support that helps to maintain Kurdistan's independence?

These key elements of Kurdistan's current political climate may not seem like they have been influenced directly by Mullah Mustafa Barzani, yet it is lessons taken from his life that have helped to produce these attitudes. Because he was so central to so much of Kurdistan's recent history, it is impossible to ignore his impact upon these elements.

The Army and Peshmerga

Kurdistan's peshmerga defence forces are a fundamental part of its democracy. They might not be directly involved in the politics of Kurdistan, but their existence is crucial to guaranteeing the security of the region. They give Kurdistan the freedom and autonomy it needs for its democratic process to function in the way it does. Without them, it is hard to believe that Kurdistan would have either the level of independence that it does or the level of stability that marks it out in the wider region. Their role and strength is also a key political issue; one that is of great importance to Kurdistan and its leaders.

The peshmerga forces are also an area where Mullah Mustafa Barzani's influence is easy to detect. Not just because Barzani fighters were key members of the peshmerga in so many of the revolts in which they fought. No, Mullah Mustafa's influence was crucial in teaching them the tactics that they used for so long, in establishing command structures for them, in giving them a sense of collective purpose larger than simple tribal interests.

That is a crucial element that he brought to the peshmerga. Before Mullah Mustafa Barzani, and even through the early phases of his life, each tribe and family had its fighters, and each would fight essentially separately. Occasionally more than one tribe would come to bear on a particularly important problem, but there was rarely a sense of action on a national level. Mullah Mustafa's revolt in the 1940s changed that. For a while, at least, it was a truly region-wide rebellion in a way that most weren't before. To accommodate that wider scope, Mullah Mustafa gave the peshmerga two things: a set of command structures that led ultimately to him, and a wider feeling of the peshmerga being a part of something bigger than local conflicts.

He brought the same ideas with him to the Mahabad Republic, where those who came with him formed the core of the new republic's armed forces. Although the republic failed, the experience of training peshmerga there has fed into the modern defence forces of Kurdistan, because it was the first opportunity to build a force like that from scratch, and to think about it on a national level. Mullah Mustafa Barzani was solving problems that faced Kurdistan's Regional Government when it came into being in the 1990s.

More than that, he was creating conditions in which the KRG could solve those problems later on. It was Mullah Mustafa Barzani who created the sense of peshmerga being a force for the defence of Kurdistan, rather than just local inhabitants fighting to protect their particular village. He created a sense of national identity in the military, and a sense of discipline that has proved invaluable in maintaining stability in Kurdistan in the face of outside threats.

The Political Agenda

Can we say that Mullah Mustafa Barzani continues to influence the modern political agenda? In one sense, it is impossible. The

The Idea of Kurdistan

political agenda is determined by current events around the world and in Kurdistan, with the events of the past having only limited influence over them.

Yet in another sense, Mullah Mustafa's influence *is* still there. Because the ways in which governments respond to events are determined not just by some cold, emotionless reckoning of the benefits, but also by the broader attitudes of their societies. In Kurdistan, those attitudes were strongly influenced by Mullah Mustafa's life.

Partly that is because of the role he played in preserving a sense of Kurdish identity within Kurdistan. We know that he made efforts to try to preserve the Kurdish language and way of life as well as searching for political autonomy. These are core cultural elements that are entirely relevant to political decisions today, because without Mullah Mustafa's influence, those decisions would be made by people with entirely different cultural values and ways of thinking.

The events of his life almost certainly also had an influence on attitudes more widely. Because his periods of exile took in a wide variety of different regions with different inhabitants, cultures and attitudes, it could be argued that Mullah Mustafa was exposed to the benefits of an essentially plural, tolerant society years before that became the modern norm in the region. Certainly, it seems like the increasingly important role of women in Kurdistan has been influenced by the women who played key roles in the story of the revolts in which Mullah Mustafa was involved.

On one final level, we can see that his influence remains, because large portions of Kurdistan remain committed to its independence. Even while different political parties disagree over many of Kurdistan's other political issues, that one remains fundamental to many of them. In that sense, they are continuing the mission that Mullah Mustafa devoted his life to.

So no, Mullah Mustafa Barzani probably does not directly

influence the smaller issues of the modern Kurdish political agenda. But his core concerns still gel with those of Kurdistan, and his efforts definitely influenced the attitudes in Kurdistan that determine how the region responds to the issues that face it. In that, Mullah Mustafa Barzani's influence is hard to deny.

Mullah Mustafa Barzani's Influence

So overall, how much influence did Mullah Mustafa have over Kurdistan's democracy? I would argue that he had a huge influence. Without his efforts, it probably wouldn't exist at all. Certainly, if it did exist, it would be a very different place politically. Mullah Mustafa Barzani was responsible for Kurdistan's main defence force, for its largest political party, and for many of the political attitudes that exist within the region. He even helped to define some of the broadest parameters of the political debates within the region. While no one will claim that Kurdistan has achieved political perfection yet, it is certainly attempting to do so, and Mullah Mustafa's influence remains a key component of it.

Chapter Fourteen: The Future

What does the future hold for Kurdistan? It is a difficult question to answer. The past does not hold a clear blueprint for the future, but rather a collection of possible pathways. Which ones the region walks down will come from the choices and actions of not just a few, but millions of people. Trying to predict the future is necessarily a game of guesswork and opinion, especially in a region where so few things have been predictable in the past. Even so, I believe that there are general trends that we can consider, along with emerging forces around Kurdistan that suggest at least some of what might happen in the years to come.

Independence

The big question for many people in Kurdistan is whether the future is likely to contain full independence for the region, and if it comes what form that independence will take. Currently, it exists as a semi-autonomous region within a federal Iraq, so does the potential exist for that to change?

On one level, it could be quite difficult. Kurdistan's current constitution identifies it as a federal region, while Iraq's does not allow a mechanism for areas to leave its political orbit. It allows only for the creation of what already exists, which is a

The Future

region with its own government, but still at least nominally under the rule of Baghdad. On a legal level, full secession would require a change in the constitution, and that seems unlikely to come about.

It is possible, of course, that Kurdistan might ignore the Iraqi constitution and simply proclaim independence. To some extent, it seems like the most likely approach to independence, because it seems unlikely that the Baghdad government would ever turn around, grant independence to the region and simply wish Kurdistan good luck. Yet it is a future that potentially creates problems.

For one thing, if history has shown us anything, it is that the Baghdad government is unlikely to let go of the resources and territory that Kurdistan represents willingly. While it is possible that negotiation might prevent outright war, the history of violence in the past under a variety of rulers makes it unlikely. The first reaction of almost any government on being told that Kurdistan is trying to declare independence seems to have been to send in troops.

It is even an understandable reaction, on some levels. Governments cannot generally allow easy secession within their countries, because it is politically damaging for them as the people who 'lost' a region, because of the loss of resources, and because of the risk of further fragmentation it creates. Lose one territory, and a government creates the conditions to potentially lose more. Even the Kurdish Regional Government understands that desire on the part of governments to maintain their territory. The constitution of Kurdistan, after all, contains provisions forbidding the further breaking away of regions or cities within it.

So there is a possibility that a declaration of independence might lead to renewed violence around the region. Indeed, previous moves in that direction have brought militarisation along the Iraq–Kurdistan border in the past. Yet there are

The Idea of Kurdistan

potential differences between such violence and that which has gone on in the past. Previously, Kurdistan had to rely almost entirely on small peshmerga forces. The stories of Mullah Mustafa's rebellions were essentially those of small groups of lightly armed men fighting guerrilla wars, with only occasional additions of artillery or heavy armour. Today, Kurdistan's defence force is a well-armed and well equipped regular force, able to hold its own in a conflict rather than merely trying to delay the inevitable long enough to escape.

More than that, there is the possibility of wider fragmentation to consider. Part of the reason Iraq is so eager to hold on to Kurdistan is the worry that if it were to leave, other regions would also seek independence. At the time of writing, the west of Iraq looks like it might be making moves towards a potential secession. Such fragmentation might potentially make it easier for Kurdistan to leave, by forcing the Baghdad government to make choices about what territory it could realistically hold onto, or by forcing it to try to act in multiple directions at once. As we have seen several times in Kurdistan's modern history, the times when it has enjoyed the greatest measure of freedom have tended to be those when the nations that claimed it were distracted by other events.

Would that work in the longer term? Ultimately, as Mullah Mustafa's life has shown us, attempts at Kurdish independence only tend to work to the extent that they are supported by outside members of the international community. From the failure to achieve independence following the First World War when the Great Powers wanted to take the territory, to the short lived Republic of Mahabad failing when the Soviet Union was forced to withdraw its support, international politics often count for more than the local situation when it comes to the survival of a newly declared country.

In the modern context it comes down to a combination of long term support, strategic usefulness, and formal recognition

The Future

by the UN. That recognition is arguably the most important aspect. With it, what was a breakaway region becomes legally a new country, as with recent examples like South Sudan. That legal status does not make them safe, but it creates a measure of protection by allowing them to request outside aid and legally preventing other nations from attacking them.

Would Kurdistan be likely to get such recognition? To some extent, its time as an autonomous region makes it more likely, because it demonstrates to those nations with vested interests in the region's oil reserves that the region is capable of functioning stably and relatively independently. It also seems likely that Kurdistan's attempts to build up good international relations in the time since its creation as an autonomous region will have helped to build some of the support it needs to gain that recognition. Even amongst those who would probably prefer to see Iraq remain in its present form politically, there have been those who have suggested that a three-state solution is probably the likeliest outcome.

Yet there are also voices against independence in the international community. The nations around Kurdistan are probably worried about the possibility, as they have traditionally tried to avoid it happening. Major international powers, such as Russia, China and the USA, may be concerned over whether it is a move that will add to the general stability of the region or not. Although it seems hard to imagine how a stable, functioning democracy in the middle of the region could do anything except improve its overall safety.

There are probably two or three scenarios that worry the international community. One possibility is that it might spark further fragmentation, not just within Iraq, but within Kurdistan itself. It is, after all, a region that has already experienced one civil war, and which has significant political divisions between its cities. Even its constitution feels that it needs to explicitly forbid the breaking away of areas within the region. Currently,

The Idea of Kurdistan

the desire for independence from Iraq serves as something of a uniting force for Kurdistan, but has there also been sufficient work done to craft Kurdistan's identity and prevent further fragmentation in the future. I would argue that it has, and that, as we have seen, Mullah Mustafa was crucial in crafting Kurdistan's image of itself.

The second worry is to do with the possibilities for further violence that secession might create. International politicians undoubtedly want things to move towards stability in the Middle East, and there are two potential scenarios around any potential independence for Kurdistan that must worry them. The first is the possibility of Kurdistan coming under attack by its Arab neighbours, either in an attempt by Baghdad to take it back or an attempt by another country to seize its resources while it is finding its feet. In answer to that, I can only say that Kurdistan should not be made responsible for the potential actions of others, and that it at least has the resources and means to defend itself if necessary.

The other scenario that worries some commentators is the idea of an expansionist Kurdistan, seeking to take territory from the surrounding nations on the basis either that the population is mostly Kurdish or that the lands are a part of the larger area of Kurdistan. This fear is undoubtedly based on the experience of nationalist movements in other countries, as well as some of the rhetoric from Kurdistan, which has done things such as referring to the largely Kurdish areas of Syria as Western Kurdistan.

There is no simple answer to this, because it would be a lie to suggest that Kurdistan would ignore these areas if they wished to be a part of it. All peoples have the right to self-determination, after all. But Kurdistan has enough experience of being conquered by others that it would never seek to gain these areas by military force, and in any event, it has no current wish to destabilise its situation by engaging in such often dangerous endeavours. Kurdistan has the revenue to be self-sufficient, and a military just big enough for self-defence rather than aggression. It has no need for the kind of expansionist approach some people fear.

These fears though do not have to come to pass. They are scenarios that could potentially happen in the event of independence, but all that means is that we must be vigilant and take steps to ensure that they do not. They are not in themselves barriers to the independence that I believe Kurdistan is likely to achieve at some point in the near future. Independence remains the goal for much of the region, as it was in Mullah Mustafa's time, and it seems like it is a future that my people will continue to work towards until they achieve it.

Politics

A week, we're told, is a long time in politics. Politics reacts to current events to a great extent, meaning that in some ways it is impossible to predict what the political climate will look like in the future. However, it is possible to look at some of the core elements of Kurdistan's political climate and suggest ways in which things might change in the future.

Independence is likely to remain a political issue for the foreseeable future, certainly until it is achieved, and possibly beyond. It is likely to remain a core plank of Kurdish political debate, and is likely to be one of the long term aims of several of the political parties there until such time as it is achieved. With that issue standing over the others in Kurdistan, it seems likely that the PDK, with its dedication to independence, will maintain a level of support for some time to come.

In the longer term, one of two scenarios will have come about: either Kurdistan will have achieved independence, or it will have remained as a part of a larger Iraq. Each scenario brings with it potential consequences for the politics of the region.

The Idea of Kurdistan

If independence is achieved, then it seems likely that there will be an initial upsurge of good feeling politically towards those parties associated with gaining independence. After that though, there is the potential for things to get more complicated. Currently, the question of independence provides almost a focal point for Kurdish politics. Parties' stances on independence are a crucial part of their political identities, yet in a post-independence Kurdistan, that focal point would be gone. Politics would have to shift its emphasis, and the main political parties would have to adapt to that shift. There would probably be an initial phase focused on securing Kurdistan's future as an independent nation, ensuring that it was truly self-sufficient economically and militarily.

After that, the political focus would probably switch to domestic issues. There is a potential for greater plurality in the political system at that point, although only if the existing parties did not succeed in adapting to the new challenges. There is also a greater likelihood of people changing the way they vote from election to election, as smaller, local issues take over from the bigger push towards freedom from outside control. It is a potential problem for those parties, simply because their focus has been on independence for so long, but we can already see signs of them adapting to the need to deal with day to day issues. With that in mind, there is no reason why the broad political landscape would not stay the same following independence.

In the second scenario, where independence is not achieved in the near future, much will depend on the reasons for it. If it is a clear case of outside forces preventing Kurdistan's independence, then it seems likely that the political landscape will look much the same as today, with discussions of regional issues sitting almost beneath an umbrella of feeling focused on independence.

If the reason is that over time the Kurdish public loses some

The Future

of its appetite for continuing that push towards independence, however, that could result in a situation much like the post-independence one outlined above. Regional level issues would start to take precedence, and voters would probably seek to make less of a commitment to a single party, casting their votes according to the issues that affected them at the time. It is likely that power would shift between parties to a greater extent as different issues took precedence, while those parties focused on independence could find themselves facing difficulties if they appeared to do so to the detriment of other policy areas.

There are other ways in which Kurdish politics are likely to change in the future. There is the potential for changes to take place in the political system, although it is hard to guess exactly what those changes will be. It is more the case that Kurdistan still seems to be in the phase where it is tinkering with its political system, trying to get the balance of it right. As evidence for this, we have for example the changes increasing the minimum percentage of women required in Kurdistan's parliament. There is also the possibility that independence might change the shape of Kurdistan, requiring adjustments to its voting system to compensate. Showing a willingness to make such changes is also likely to be a key political move in a climate where the people of Kurdistan seem to expect an almost constant sense of progress from their politicians.

It seems likely that, in the immediate future at least, Mullah Mustafa Barzani's family will continue to play a role in the politics of the region. Massoud Barzani may be coming towards the end of his term as president as I write, but Nechirvan Idris Barzani remains the prime minister, and has the potential to run for president in the future as one of the most senior figures within the PDK. The Barzani family's long involvement with that party also tends to suggest that they will continue to be involved with it, and that they will continue to appear in important positions within Kurdish politics after the fashion of political dynasties elsewhere in the world. This is particularly likely to continue to be the case for the current generation, partly because there are already Barzanis waiting in the wings, having worked their way to political positions below those of immediate power, and partly because the older Barzanis are still of that generation that found out the hard way under Saddam and during the civil war that family members were often the only people who could be trusted.

Over time, of course, that may change. However, at this point, it is the case that members of the Barzani family see politics as a viable career option, rather than the strange and distant thing it must appear to some people. As such, it is likely that even in the longer term, it is a name that will continue to appear in Kurdish politics.

International Relations

As we have seen several times in the purely biographical sections of this work, Kurdistan's fate has often been dependent on its relations with the wider world. Its history has often been about a complex balancing act of international relations. On the one hand, it wants to be independent, and is not prepared to become so dependent on outside powers to achieve that aim that it simply trades one outside ruler for another. On the other, Kurdistan's ability to balance those outside forces that do not wish to see it as an independent country often comes down to its ability to secure international support.

The state of its international relations in the future will to some extent come down to whether it achieves independence and when. Yes, it currently has a thriving foreign policy focused on building relations independently of Iraq, but most of the countries it deals with still do so in the context of it being a part of Iraq.

If Kurdistan were to remain a part of Iraq in the future, then it is likely that its international relations would be limited by

The Future

that factor. It wouldn't be in a position to make treaties that were not compatible with those of Iraq as a whole, and the range of matters that international partners sought to discuss with Kurdistan would probably also be limited. Then there is the question of the level of support they would be prepared to provide for a Kurdistan focused on independence in the future. There is some evidence to suggest that several international powers would prefer that Kurdistan remained a part of Iraq, because of broader fears that the country would fragment in an unstable way. Perhaps they fear that without what is one of the most stable regions in the country, the rest of it will not be able to maintain coherence. At the moment, that feeling is perhaps counterbalanced by a sense that a three-state solution in Iraq may be inevitable, but in the future, the feeling may be harder to overcome.

If Kurdistan does become independent in the future, then it will face an intriguing set of questions and challenges when it comes to international relations. Its current strongest international relations seem to be with countries such as the USA, and it is understandable that they should be. Yet in the event of independence, it will probably be important for Kurdistan to forge the widest range of international connections possible. Indeed, it will probably be important if it is to achieve UN recognition of any move towards independence.

That is important because Kurdistan's location places it close to a number of other important international powers, including China and Russia. That location is part of the reason it and the surrounding region have found themselves as a political battleground through much of the twentieth century. In the event of independence, it will certainly seek outside support from its current partners, but it must also demonstrate to the other major powers in the region that its independence does not pose a threat to their interests, and that it is prepared to work in a balanced way with all those around it.

The Idea of Kurdistan

That is a potential challenge, but it is one that Kurdistan seems like it should be more than equal to. It has demonstrated through its history that it is prepared to work with any outside power that does not seek to dominate or claim it. More than that, there is every reason to suspect that Kurdistan would want to work with multiple international partners in the future. Historically, it has learned the lessons of over-dependence on a single source of international support and goodwill. As such, it makes sense for it to have back-up plans in place, and to seek to ensure that it gains international political support from a number of sources.

Can it do so? Kurdistan's history of connections with several different countries seems to suggest that it can. So do its current attempts to forge economic and trade links with a wide variety of partners, from the USA to Japan and beyond. Its oil and other resources will help to attract international partners for some time to come, and will also give it a reason to engage with international companies. Perhaps the biggest aspect in Kurdistan's favour, however, is its position as a relatively stable, free point in a region that is often quite unstable. It currently provides an opportunity for the international community to engage in the region in the knowledge that their people will be safer than they might be in several of the neighbouring areas. If Kurdistan can retain that level of stability, it will be in a good position to attract international political interest and foreign businesses.

That is a crucial part of Kurdistan's international relations in the future. In today's world, the largest businesses are almost as powerful as some governments, and Kurdistan needs to consider its relations with global enterprises carefully. The same principles that have guided its relationships with foreign powers should apply. It should seek a plurality of interest to prevent any one from becoming excessively dominant, and should be careful not to become over dependent on a particular relationship.

The Future

With those caveats in mind, Kurdistan is probably in a good position to attract relationships with multinational businesses as well as countries. Its stability is a key part of that, but so is a relatively open society, as well as a wealth of natural resources. It provides a society that is considerably less restrictive to do business in than many of the nearby alternatives, and that is potentially more open to the changes that international engagement brings with it.

That combination suggests that Kurdistan's international relations are likely to be successful in the future, particularly if it achieves independence on a level that allows it to fully make its own decisions about those relations. That kind of freedom potentially brings with it new challenges, and the need to preserve Kurdistan's way of life in the face of outside influences, but it also looks set to open up a wide range of new opportunities for the region over time.

Security

Of course, for any country or region, planning for the future isn't all about the things that might go right for it. Security must always be a concern, and it is worth looking at the sort of security challenges Kurdistan might potentially face in the future, along with the sort of planning that will be needed to cope with those challenges.

Some of them are likely to remain the same regardless of whether Kurdistan achieves independence. Pressure from Baghdad will remain, and while that is unlikely to spill over into force in the near future, it must be balanced by at least a military readiness on Kurdistan's part.

Internal security will also remain a key issue for Kurdistan whatever its status in the future. Much of its position in the wider region is founded on its current stability, and it must make an effort to maintain that stability in the face of those forces that might seek to pull it apart. That does not mean pushing in the direction of repression or authoritarianism. Both of those would represent a failure as great as substantial civil unrest. They would help to make Kurdistan less like the place it wants to be, and less like the place it needs to be to attract attention from the outside world. Instead, the Kurdistan of the future must continue to recognise that public consent and a relatively high level of freedom compared to its neighbours are crucial to both its stability and identity.

Internal threats could come from a number of sources, although currently, none seems organised enough to represent a real issue for the region. There are groups that have been banned in the region because of the disruption and damage to public order they have caused in the past, and it is possible that remnants of them could continue to be problematic in the future. It is interesting for Kurdistan that those potential internal challenges come from the extremes of a number of political directions, rather than the single but more powerful threats faced by the countries around it. Perhaps that is a reflection of the greater political plurality that is one of Kurdistan's great strengths, and certainly, it is that plurality that will allow it to overcome any potential challenges. It is when people do not feel that the political process adequately represents their views that they turn to other methods, so the Kurdistan of the future must continue to ensure that it is for everyone there.

Its police force is obviously a major component of future security, and Kurdistan is putting a lot of effort into ensuring that it has a modern, well trained police force that is there to serve the country as a whole and is not political in nature. It is crucial that it continues to work in that direction, because the effective training of any police force is always an ongoing project.

Militarily, Kurdistan already has significant armed forces of its own, having had to protect itself from outside threats since the 1990s. It is also the only one of Iraq's regions with an

The Future

exemption to its constitutional injunction against the raising of militias. Kurdistan must be careful of that word in the future, however. A militia seems to imply a relatively lightly armed, almost part-time force. Since Kurdistan is effectively entirely responsible for its own defence, however, it is important that it maintains a full military capability.

The experience of small countries in troubled areas suggests that Kurdistan's military will, in future, have to be founded largely on the acquisition of advanced technology. Although its armed forces have a history of using the terrain and guerrilla tactics, that history has also demonstrated that Kurdistan has been vulnerable to forces using aerial attacks, and to armour light weaponry could not damage. Since it is unlikely that Kurdistan will ever have the population to compete against a larger attacker through sheer numbers, it seems likely that in the future it will have to focus on producing a smarter, better equipped, more mobile force wherever possible. Yet in many ways, isn't that what it has always focused on?

That will be particularly important in the event that it becomes independent, because that will change the nature of the security threats Kurdistan faces a little. Although it already undertakes most of the security operations of a small country: securing its borders, dealing with internal threats and showing that it is not a vulnerable target to be attacked, independence would bring new challenges. Currently, its position is guaranteed at least in part by its connections to wider security operations.

If it became independent, then it would need to show that it was not suddenly a target for the other countries around it. Kurdistan would also have to make sure that the infrastructure connecting it to the outside world remained secure. At the same time, however, it would have to avoid giving the appearance of being militarist or aggressive in its approach. That is vital in order to continue attracting international support, and to avoid the danger of attacks on it to deal with the 'threat' it poses.

In general though, the security situation in Kurdistan's future looks set to be a stable one. In terms of security and military matters, it is already effectively working the way a country would. It has been securing its own defence for almost two decades at the time of writing, and is currently internally stable with the capacity to stay that way. In other areas, sudden independence can be the catalyst for internal upheaval or outside aggression, but in Kurdistan, it seems likely that independence would not destabilise the region's security situation.

Economics and Culture

The economics of Kurdistan are to a great extent what have made it a target for others looking to control it. The oil resources that lie beneath it make it too valuable for many others to allow it to go its own way. Yet what about its economic future, and what about the future of Kurdistan in cultural terms?

Economically, Kurdistan's reliance on oil revenue makes it relatively self-sufficient. It gives it the resources it needs for building and infrastructure projects without having to resort to the high levels of taxation seen in other countries. Those oil revenues are important enough to the region that the whole shape of Kurdistan has been dictated by them in the past, and control of its oil resources has been a key political issue within the region for as long as it has been in existence.

In the short to medium term, that oil revenue will probably continue to make Kurdistan economically vibrant. In the much longer term, since oil is a finite resource, sustainability becomes a potential issue. Kurdistan will need to come up with ways to use the early economic advantage oil has given it to produce an economy that will continue to succeed even after its oil reserves are eventually exhausted. In many ways, it is already on the path to this, however, given its high level of reinvestment in infrastructure, education and public works. If and when the oil eventually does run out, Kurdistan is unlikely to revert back

The Future

to being the minor agrarian economy that it was before its discovery, but should hopefully have placed itself in a position to take advantage of other emerging economic trends.

Even today, we can see that it is starting to place its economy on a somewhat wider base, with more high tech development and the building of economic links with international partners. Kurdistan has started to attract international investment, which will hopefully help it to build an important corner of the economic life of the wider region in the future. Even more importantly, many of those within it have started to invest beyond Kurdistan's borders, using the newfound wealth of the region to start to build up the sort of businesses that will be sustainable for decades to come.

It is likely that this back and forth investment beyond Kurdistan's boundaries will continue into the future and even increase. Kurdistan's natural resources will continue to draw in businesses for a considerable period to come, but so will its relative stability. In terms of the countries surrounding it, Kurdistan represents one of the most stable, open and democratic options in which to work, which is likely to continue to be of interest to companies around the globe. If it should achieve independence, that attractiveness is only likely to increase, both because it would mean that Kurdistan would have complete control over its own economic life, and because it would reduce the sense of it being tangentially connected to a much less stable political situation in Iraq.

Culturally, it seems likely that the future holds a combination of change and stability for Kurdistan. The Kurdistan of today is not one that Mullah Mustafa would recognise. Its constitution today enshrines freedoms for women, and of religious and cultural choice, that were just not the norm around much of the world when he was first born. Things have changed to get to this point, and it is inevitable that the Kurdistan of tomorrow will change over time, becoming something new with each generation. Ideas, values and cultural norms all evolve over time, and it is entirely normal that they should. It is important that Kurdistan holds that room for slow cultural change within it, in a way that many of its neighbours seem unwilling to.

What are the forces that are likely to act on Kurdistan's culture as time goes on? One part of it is Kurdistan's international focus. Economically and politically, it is looking beyond its borders to find partners capable of supporting its occasionally stated dream of being a second Dubai, an oasis of calm in a turbulent region and an economic centre thanks to its natural resources. It seems inevitable that those economic and political connections will bring with them cultural influences, exposing Kurdistan to trends and global ideas that are not already present within it.

That exposure will come in other ways too. As its international transport links have improved, it has become possible for more of Kurdistan's inhabitants to travel the world, and for more people to visit the region. In particular, Kurds from many different areas of the globe have been prepared to travel to Kurdistan to see the closest thing to a Kurdish homeland that exists in the world today. If Kurdistan achieves independence, that trend is likely to continue, and is likely to be accompanied by large numbers of Kurds seeking to settle there. Its relative stability also means that, where once it was the place that people sought refuge from, now it is a region to flee to when faced by humanitarian disasters in the neighbouring countries.

All of these people will bring with them different ideas and ways of thinking. Different concepts of what it means to be Kurdish in the case of those Kurds coming 'home' to Kurdistan, or simply different ways of being a part of Kurdistan for others. It is likely that Kurdistan will, over time, find itself a melting pot for ideas and people from around the world.

And yet it also seems likely that Kurdistan will retain a character in the future that is still distinctly Kurdish. It will

The Future

retain Kurdish as the primary language of public life, and there will be that sense of shared history there that is sometimes not present as strongly in other nations. If it achieves independence, it is likely that many of those it attracts to it in the aftermath will be ethnically Kurdish, looking for a homeland that fits with them culturally and in terms of their aspirations. So while it is likely that Kurdistan will become more 'global' in terms of the influences on it, it is also likely to become in some senses even more distinctly 'Kurdish'.

This is a combination that fits in many ways with Mullah Mustafa Barzani's vision of Kurdistan. It is undeniable, from the ways in which he sought assistance abroad, that he was prepared to accept outside influences on the region up to a point. Yet he was also careful to step back the moment it seemed that those influences were about to compromise a sense of what it meant to be Kurdish. It seems like a combination of approaches that is likely to continue in Kurdistan for a long time to come, creating a region that is both international and local, distinct but still inclusive.

The Legacy of Mullah Mustafa Barzani

Since this book is partly a biography of Mullah Mustafa Barzani and partly a commentary on Kurdistan, we should ask at this point to what extent his influence on Kurdistan is likely to continue in the future. Does Mullah Mustafa have a legacy strong enough that it is likely to continue to affect Kurdistan as it moves towards independence?

It seems almost certain that it will. The most basic point is that Mullah Mustafa's greatest dream, of an independent Kurdistan, is likely to be a reality in Kurdistan's future. If and when Kurdistan becomes independent, that will be the culmination of Mullah Mustafa Barzani's legacy. Indeed, to some extent, anything this Kurdistan undertakes as an independent nation will represent a continuation of that legacy

The Idea of Kurdistan

on some level.

Yet if Kurdistan becomes independent, will Mullah Mustafa's legacy continue to have an influence on the new country? If his aim is achieved, does that effectively bring an end to his role in Kurdish life? I would suggest that it does not.

Instead, aspects of that legacy seem set to continue for the foreseeable future. Yes, Kurdistan's position regarding independence is the most obvious area that he has influenced, but Mullah Mustafa's influence is also likely to be felt long into the future in politics, international relations, security, and Kurdistan's culture.

Politically, his legacy is obvious. His family are present at the highest levels of Kurdish politics, while the party he helped to found is one of the region's most important political forces. In security, the army still owes much to the models he helped to put in place, while culturally, his work in keeping Kurdish culture alive means that culture will be free to continue long into the future.

As I have stated previously, we can't really know what is going to happen in the future in Kurdistan. We can make broad guesses, but it is impossible to know with certainty what will happen in any area. One thing that does seem certain, however, is that Kurdistan will continue to meet the challenges it faces head on, in part thanks to Mullah Mustafa Barzani's legacy.

Chapter Fifteen: Conclusion

Garibaldi and the Problem of Heroism

In 1867, just over a hundred years before Mullah Mustafa Barzani's last uprising in Kurdistan, the Italian nationalist Giuseppe Garibaldi took his famous red shirt wearing soldiers to attack Rome and attempt to bring it into the rest of Italy. He found his forces defeated and himself captured, although he was quickly freed and able to leave for the small island of Caprera. From there, he was able to exert some further influence for another decade and a half, even holding a seat in the Italian parliament while pressing for universal suffrage.

Opinion is divided on Garibaldi. In the minds of many of the Italian people, and those historians with a romantic tendency, he is an Italian national hero. A man who won important victories in the battles for unification and freedom from international interests. Other commentators think that his role in the unification of Italy has been somewhat overstated. They point out, for example, that his impressive victory at Trentino against the Austrians in 1866 was actually far less important to Italian independence than the numerous Prussian victories in the Austro-Prussian War occurring at the same time. They point out his repeated unsuccessful attempts to capture Rome, which were seen as an embarrassment at the time. They point to the

The Idea of Kurdistan

roles of other figures such as Mazzini or Cavour.

Why bring up a figure who died twenty years before Mullah Mustafa Barzani was born and who lived thousands of miles away? Who never had any interest in either the Middle East in general or the cause of Kurdish independence in particular?

Partly, I have mentioned him because of the superficial similarities that can be seen between the two. Both were involved in nationalist causes, seeking freedom from outside elements (largely the Austro-Hungarian Empire in Italy's case, Iraq in Kurdistan's). Both were essentially military figures, with leadership over forces that were irregular or semi-regular in approach. Garibaldi had his 'Hunters of the Mountains', Mullah Mustafa Barzani the peshmerga. Both had famous international adventures (in South America, in Garibaldi's case, rather than the Soviet Union). Crucially, both are still seen as national heroes in their respective homes.

It is that perception as a hero that forms the second reason why I have brought up Garibaldi here. I would like to talk about both the process by which a people decides on its heroes, and what I think of as the 'problem of heroism': the growth of a legend far beyond its originator, to a level where no one could live up to it.

So, how do nations and peoples select particular figures as heroic ones? Why Mullah Mustafa Barzani rather than someone else? Why Garibaldi in the Italian case? The similarities between the two hopefully tell us something about that, and about the elements that go into the decision. We can see, for example, that they were both essentially military figures. That makes sense. Stories of battles and campaigns make for better reading than ones about dull, behind the scenes politics. Both figures connect strongly to the idea of popular uprising, rather than the imposition of a new order from outside. Both demonstrated determination and commitment to their causes; an unwillingness to give up when setbacks would have persuaded other people

Conclusion

to stop. Crucially, both provide embodiments of key historical events, rather than forcing us to envisage historical forces grinding away behind the scenes.

Both make for better stories, in other words. That is both the attraction and the potential problem of heroes: that the story outgrows the man. Then we look back at the man and we miss what he did achieve because we are too busy feeling disappointed that he did not live up to the story.

Yet does that mean I am saying that we should simply see Mullah Mustafa Barzani the way many people see Garibaldi? As a kind of noble failure? As an individual whose only role here is to be turned into a kind of storybook figure? One who could never be everything people want him to be?

There are elements of similarity. It is hard to deny that Mullah Mustafa Barzani's attempts at revolution for Kurdistan did not succeed in bringing about the independent state he wanted. He was forced into exile, and he didn't live to see the establishment of the modern Kurdistan that currently exists. Attempting to deny that would merely be ignoring the facts.

Yet there are other facts that matter, too. It matters that Mullah Mustafa Barzani managed to make himself into a symbol of continued Kurdish defiance. It matters that he carried the Kurdish flag. It matters that he was involved in discussions that brought international support to Kurdistan's cause, and that his adventures abroad raised the profile of the region. So no, Mullah Mustafa Barzani was not just the same kind of figure as Garibaldi.

Yes, he did the noisy, dangerous work of war. Yes, he is loved for what he did in the same sort of way, but he was also responsible for the things that weren't so obvious. For things that helped to lay the groundwork for Kurdistan. He did the dull political work. He helped to craft Kurdistan's image of itself. All those things are important too.

There is a simple test here that shows the difference between the two. A simple 'what if' question. What if Garibaldi had died in South America in his youth? The answer to that question seems to be that Italy would still be Italy, almost exactly the same. If we ask the same question of Mullah Mustafa Barzani's life though, can we really say that Kurdistan would still be what it is today?

Addressing the Key Questions

Which brings us back to the key questions I outlined at the start. There, I asked four things:

- How is Mullah Mustafa Barzani remembered in Kurdistan?
- How much did he shape its political, cultural and geographical forms?
- How much of an impact did he have on the image and identity of Kurdistan?
- How important was Mullah Mustafa Barzani to Kurdistan overall?

I have attempted to find answers to those questions throughout this work, and the answers are necessarily both nuanced and complex ones, open to interpretation in many cases. However, by this point, I believe that we are in a position to provide answers to all four questions.

The Shape of Kurdistan

When it comes to Mullah Mustafa Barzani's impact on the shape of Kurdistan today, we must discuss his impact on a social and political level as well as the ways in which he shaped the debates around Kurdistan. Yet as we have seen at a number of points in this work, he did have an impact on the geography of Kurdistan too.

Why is that? Because the life and rebellions of Mullah Mustafa Barzani forced people to define what they were arguing over

Conclusion

when they talked about Kurdistan. When they fought over it, too. There are three elements of his life that had key roles to play in establishing the shape of Kurdistan as it stands today.

The first is that his rebellions were primarily against the Iraqi government. There were moments when he was involved in rebellions against the British, or where he was attempting to defend the Mahabad Republic, far from Iraq. However, those do not seem to represent the main elements of his rebellions. Indeed, his travels to the Mahabad Republic were themselves the result of a failed rebellion in Iraq.

The result of these rebellions was that they tended to define the fight for Kurdistan as one occurring essentially in Iraq. Although historically, Kurdistan spread over parts of several modern day countries, Mullah Mustafa Barzani's actions helped to define the struggle for independence primarily as one against Iraq. Which meant that Kurdistan, when it came into being as a largely autonomous region in the 1990s, was contained entirely within Iraq.

This geographical focus is maintained by the emphasis on Barzan and the wider region around Erbil through much of Mullah Mustafa Barzani's life. Although this is no more than a natural consequence of where he happened to be brought up and based in Kurdistan, it has helped to contribute to an idea of Erbil as being at the heart of Kurdistan. Again, this has helped to create an essentially Iraq-based vision of Kurdistan, but it also helped to shape political elements such as the location of the parliament.

We also have the failure of the Mahabad Republic. Although it is hardly something that was down to Mullah Mustafa Barzani, it is an experience within his life that was crucial to the shape of Kurdistan today. It taught him and others that attempting to establish a homeland elsewhere was unlikely to succeed, and so brought the focus back onto the region that we now know as Kurdistan.

The Idea of Kurdistan

Finally, and perhaps most importantly, we have Kirkuk. Mullah Mustafa Barzani refused to give up Kirkuk in the 1970s, even though it meant a longer conflict with the Baghdad government. That decision has had a key impact on both the shape and economic viability of Kurdistan today, giving the region a very different shape to the one it would have had without the city but also providing it with the resources to rebuild.

If Mullah Mustafa Barzani may have shaped Kurdistan geographically, he certainly did so politically. He played a key role in the establishment of the PDK, and led it for many years. As the PDK continues to be one of the largest political parties in Kurdistan, and provides its president at the time of writing, it is hard to deny the impact of Mullah Mustafa Barzani on the shape of Kurdistan's political landscape.

Indeed, his impact extends on a more personal level, since his son, Massoud Barzani, is Kurdistan's first president, and other relatives of Mullah Mustafa Barzani are forging important political careers for themselves. Although there may have been those who have questioned so many members of the same family going into politics, it is hard to deny that Mullah Mustafa Barzani's life instilled the desire to enter into that arena in his family.

On a wider level, Mullah Mustafa Barzani had a role to play in bringing about Kurdistan's current party political system, starting a move away from purely tribal politics. Just founding a political party, at a time when it would have been easy to rely purely on personal authority as the son and grandson of Barzani leaders, established Kurdistan's commitment to democracy in the long term. I am not claiming here that Mullah Mustafa Barzani always behaved in a way that was perfectly consistent with democracy, or that Kurdistan's democracy has been perfected yet, but he certainly laid the groundwork for the shape of Kurdish democracy. Groundwork that has helped to define the issues and work that the Kurdish parliamentary system does today.

Conclusion

The Image of Kurdistan

How much of an impact did Mullah Mustafa Barzani have on the image of Kurdistan, both at home and abroad? I hope that the second half of this book has convinced you that many of Mullah Mustafa Barzani's most important achievements came in this field. That he helped to shape Kurdistan's image of itself in ways that later allowed it to function as an autonomous region. That he helped to craft its identity abroad, keeping the idea of Kurdistan alive with a succession of foreign leaders and not allowing Kurdishness to be subsumed into general cultural life, the way it almost was in, for example, Turkey. More than that, he played crucial symbolic roles, both in terms of preserving Kurdistan's symbols and in terms of becoming a symbol of Kurdistan himself.

In terms of Kurdistan's image of itself, Mullah Mustafa Barzani helped to preserve the idea of Kurdistan as something both unified and separate. To some extent, he helped to *create* the idea of Kurdistan, at least as we envision it today. When he was born, remember, Kurdistan was largely a world of separate tribes, spread over a large area that had previously been multiple kingdoms. By the time of his death, Mullah Mustafa Barzani lived in a world where Kurdistan understood itself as a coherent nation, where there was a strong sense of Kurdish identity over and above simple tribal identity, and where there were strong symbols of Kurdish national identity, including its flag. Mullah Mustafa Barzani helped to present an image of Kurdistan to itself, helping to form an image that exists today as something real, a region with its own government, society and culture.

In terms of the wider world, Mullah Mustafa Barzani had contact with numerous officials and government officers beyond Kurdistan. Aside from the direct impact of those connections in terms of foreign assistance for my people, those moments of contact almost certainly helped to shape foreign opinions of

The Idea of Kurdistan

Kurdistan. For those key individuals in the Soviet Union Mullah Mustafa Barzani met, for example, it seems likely that it would have been the first time they met with a representative of my people. Their opinions of Kurdistan were probably formed in the long term by political reports and briefings, but their immediate image of the region came from meeting Mullah Mustafa Barzani.

Whether it was Iran, the Soviet Union, the United States or other countries, Mullah Mustafa Barzani helped to project an image of Kurdistan and its people into the world. He understood the importance of foreign powers to the region, and he attempted to influence their policies towards it by building their perception of Kurdish identity.

Mullah Mustafa Barzani's involvement in the symbolism of Kurdistan was no less important. Whether it was carrying the region's flag with him, maintaining the symbols of the Barzani, or insisting on the preservation of the Kurdish language, he had a key role to play in the maintenance of the symbols of Kurdish identity. He understood the power of symbols, and more than that, he understood that the long term fight for Kurdistan's independence was not just a military one. Even though he is best remembered for his military adventures, Mullah Mustafa Barzani had the vision to realise that constructing a country would take more than that.

More than that, he managed to become one of the symbols that he did so much to promote. Mullah Mustafa Barzani understood the damage that had been done to my people's sense of history and to their sense of their collective identity. He managed to become a kind of living symbol of their cause in life, with elements such as his survival abroad managing to symbolise the continuation of the Kurdish independence movement. For many people, that movement *became* Mullah Mustafa Barzani, to such an extent that it seemed natural to bring his remains home to Kurdistan following his death, and

Conclusion

that people continue to have his image around them through large swathes of Kurdistan.

To a great extent, Mullah Mustafa Barzani came to symbolise what it meant to be Kurdish. He was a man willing to fight for his home and his identity, who for much of his life was not able to live in his home country. He was a part of the old tribal life and a part of the modern world. An international traveller who nevertheless came to be buried in Kurdistan. In a Kurdistan in need of symbols, Mullah Mustafa Barzani's role in shaping its image of itself cannot be underestimated.

Memories

How is Mullah Mustafa Barzani remembered in Kurdistan and the wider world? The answer to that is a complex one, because it varies according to location, feelings about the cause of Kurdish independence, generation and more.

It is hard to ignore the fact that there are large parts of the world where no one has heard of Mullah Mustafa Barzani. That is important, because it is easy to forget, when talking about the history of Kurdistan, that not everyone understands it in the same way that my people do. Not everyone, come to that, has heard of Kurdistan. That is important because it emphasises the link between Mullah Mustafa Barzani and my people. Typically, it is difficult for someone to have heard of one without having heard about the other. Anyone who knows of Kurdistan and its situation will probably have heard about Mullah Mustafa Barzani. Anyone who has heard of him will have done so in the context of Kurdistan and its movement towards independence. Mullah Mustafa Barzani is so bound up with Kurdistan that he cannot be separated from it.

For those outside Kurdistan who have heard of him, that connection remains important. How they feel about Mullah Mustafa Barzani largely depends on their feelings about Kurdistan in general, and about the cause of Kurdish

The Idea of Kurdistan

independence more specifically. Those in favour of my people's cause tend to see Mullah Mustafa Barzani as a key, and even heroic, figure. At the very least, they tend to recognise the representation of key aspects of Kurdish identity in the way he is presented to the world.

Those who are against the idea of Kurdish independence tend to either try to minimise Mullah Mustafa Barzani's importance or remember him in ways that are consistent with qualities that 'prove' to them that Kurdistan cannot be trusted with independence. Perhaps they suggest that his role in Kurdistan was not as great as has been claimed, or try to brand him as a conservative tribalist, too reliant on violence. In countries where my people's very identity has sometimes been ignored, like Turkey, Mullah Mustafa Barzani's memory forms another fragment of the culture they have sometimes tried to deny.

Again though, this emphasises the point about just how intertwined Mullah Mustafa Barzani and Kurdistan are. His memory has become a part of the cultural fabric of the budding nation, to the extent that the nature of that memory has become a point of political argument and continued discourse.

The spread of opinion about Mullah Mustafa Barzani abroad tends to depend somewhat on the country in which one finds oneself, but also on whom one is speaking to. There are of course large Kurdish communities outside Kurdistan, in Iran, Syria, Turkey, and the wider world. In those, Mullah Mustafa Barzani is typically remembered in the same sorts of ways he is remembered within Kurdistan itself.

In the countries around them, it is often a different story. Indeed, it could be suggested that some of the harshest treatment of Mullah Mustafa Barzani's memory has come in those countries, because of the identification of him with movements towards independence for the Kurds of those countries.

Further afield, there is probably less recognition for his name,

Conclusion

but also a less polarised attitude to his memory. Some of the more interesting research into his role in Kurdistan has come from abroad, simply because researchers from abroad are able to stand outside what has been said before long enough to examine it properly.

As we have seen in this work, Mullah Mustafa Barzani's memory, and the *idea* of what he represents, have both been crucial in Kurdistan's interactions with the world. Arguably his most important moments came in those instances of contact with the world outside Kurdistan, creating an impression of Kurdistan, its leaders and its people that continues to be influential even today.

How is Mullah Mustafa Barzani remembered in Kurdistan? We can say that, in general, his memory is respected, even by those political opponents who do not necessarily agree with the things his party stands for. There are perhaps some who would attack it, seeing his image as bound up with that of his party, but in general, this is not the case. His image is a common one in Kurdistan, and his memory seems to have achieved a status that broadly transcends politics.

Partly, this is because of the importance of his role within Kurdistan's past. He was a leader, and one who was clearly committed to Kurdistan and its people. Partly, it is because he is a figure from the past, and not a current political opponent. Mostly though, I suspect it is because Mullah Mustafa Barzani represented something about what it meant to be Kurdish at a time when many people were trying to suggest that it meant nothing at all.

Importance

I would like to think that in this work I have shown that Mullah Mustafa Barzani was extremely important to Kurdistan and its people, and not just on the levels that are commonly attributed to him. Indeed, I would like to suggest that in many ways the

The Idea of Kurdistan

symbolic levels have counted for more than the military achievements.

What did Mullah Mustafa Barzani achieve militarily? Well, he played important roles in a number of Kurdish uprisings. He led them, led troops within them, and fought first against the empire of the Ottoman Turks, and then against the country of Iraq that had been imposed on Kurdistan from outside. I will not try to overstate the extent of his military success here. He never achieved the kind of outright victory needed to produce a truly independent Kurdistan, and indeed on several occasions his uprisings ended in failure. Yet in the circumstances Mullah Mustafa Barzani found himself in, could anyone else have reasonably expected to have achieved more? He was at least able to protect his people on a number of occasions, and also to force successive Iraqi rulers to the negotiating table.

If it is militarily that we tend to remember Mullah Mustafa Barzani, as the leader of peshmerga willing to stand up to governments making claims to Kurdistan, it is perhaps politically where he had his biggest impact. He played a key role in the establishment of the PDK, and led it politically for much of his life. In doing that, he both helped to provide a focus for the Kurdish nationalist movement and also helped to transform the political life of Kurdistan by moving it away from ideas of simple tribal authority and towards the concept of party politics. Even if that concept did not come to full fruition during his life, Mullah Mustafa Barzani must get some of the credit for moving towards it.

Politically, he served as a point of contact. That meant that he was often the one people negotiated with when they sought to negotiate with the people of Kurdistan. He was also a crucial figure in talking to foreign powers that would be crucial to Kurdistan in the years after his death. The connections Mullah Mustafa Barzani made, in the Soviet Union, in Iran, in the United States and beyond, have been crucial to Kurdistan's

Conclusion

place in the world. As that point of contact, he made decisions in the long term interests of my people. He refused, for example, to give up Kirkuk in the 1970s, even though doing so might have given Kurdistan the illusion of independence. He understood that without resources, the region would soon fall prey to its neighbours once more.

Socially, it is perhaps harder to see a direct impact. Kurdistan is still in the process of moving on from the kind of society that Mullah Mustafa Barzani would have grown up in, on a constant journey forward. Yet that probably says more about the pace of change in Kurdistan than about Mullah Mustafa Barzani.

Perhaps his greatest roles though have been symbolic ones. Mullah Mustafa Barzani provided a symbol of continued resistance at a time when it looked like the Kurdish way of life might be destroyed. He played key parts in so many of the most important events for my people, and so his name has managed to become a kind of shorthand for all of those events. More than that though, in a Kurdistan where outside authorities have done much to destroy the history of my people, he has provided people with a key historic figure to look back to, seeing themselves in a different light because of him. In a lot of ways, Mullah Mustafa Barzani's past helped to define what it means to be Kurdish in the present.

In answer to the question I asked at the start then, about how important Mullah Mustafa Barzani was to Kurdistan, we can safely answer that he was crucial to it. He helped to ensure its continued existence. He helped to craft its political structures. He continues to play a crucial role in its sense of identity. Yes, if he had never existed, someone else might have been able to fulfil any one of these roles. Yet can we seriously say that any one other person could have filled them all?

That is the true importance of Mullah Mustafa Barzani, and why I feel that it is crucial he is never forgotten, either by my people, or by the wider world in which they live.

The Idea of Kurdistan

Mullah Mustafa Barzani's Role in Kurdistan

What do the answers to these questions mean about Mullah Mustafa Barzani's role in Kurdistan? Well, they make several key points. First, they show us, as the rest of this work has, just what a remarkable life he had. Relatively few of my people have been to all the places he went and did all the things he did. To do all those while also serving as a leader, carrying the weight of expectation that came with that, is exceptional. Parts of the story in this work have been similar to parts of the lives of Mullah Mustafa's contemporaries, but how many of them can we truly say experienced as many of the key events in Kurdistan's modern history?

They show us that he did achieve a great deal. Not everything that he or the Kurdish people wanted, because he didn't live to see Kurdistan as it is today. Yet he did achieve significant military victories, he did have a role to play in important political changes, and he had a crucial role to play when it came to keeping my people's identity alive.

That is one thing that I hope this book has emphasised more than the rest of it. The importance of Mullah Mustafa when it comes to the *idea* of my people. To their sense of who they are and where they belong. Many people have won battles, and more than a few have achieved a great deal politically. Those things are important. Mullah Mustafa Barzani deserves to be remembered for them, but he also deserves to be remembered for the work he did in preserving my people's sense of themselves, and in finding a version of it that could fit within the world they found themselves living in.

I also hope that this book has emphasised the importance of the idea of Mullah Mustafa Barzani alongside the reality of the man. Because I believe that Mullah Mustafa's life tells us something about the way in which historical figures find a place within a kind of broader national consciousness. In the same way that we might say that some shadow of Winston Churchill

Conclusion

and Queen Victoria has become part of what it means to be British, or the historical ghosts of Lincoln, Washington and Kennedy are crucial to being American, in a lot of ways, the memory of Mullah Mustafa Barzani has become a crucial part of the idea of what it means to be Kurdish today.

Historical figures matter, not just because of who they are and what they did, but because of what they tell us about ourselves. As well as everything they achieved in life, they serve as a kind of shorthand for particular ideas. This is particularly the case for those figures who have become national heroes. Mullah Mustafa Barzani set out to create an independent Kurdistan. Now, in the minds of so many people, he stands for it.

The Future

Will the conclusions we draw here always be true? Of course not. It is in the nature of historical research that it is reassessed by future generations. This is normal, and is simply a consequence of the ways in which history tends to reflect the needs and interests of those telling it.

So, can I envisage a future where Kurdistan will not be interested in the history of Mullah Mustafa Barzani? It is possible, of course. None of us can predict the future. Yet the same things that make his story so important now – his connection to Kurdistan, his symbolic role – make it hard to envision how Kurdistan *as it currently sees itself*, could do without the idea of him.

That is how important Mullah Mustafa was to my people.

In Summary

The story of the war stopping in 1993 while Mullah Mustafa Barzani's remains were returned to Kurdistan is a well-known one. Of my people standing back from a time of desperate fighting while his bones were taken back to Barzan. Yet it is a

The Idea of Kurdistan

story that is told and retold for a reason. Whatever else he was, whoever else he was, Mullah Mustafa Barzani was a part of Kurdistan. I hope that in this book, I have helped to show just how much of a part.

When Mullah Mustafa Barzani died, I was not old enough to have seen him in the flesh. I was still a young child, too young to have any real idea about him. Any image I do have of him has been gleaned from pictures and brief fragments of description, brought to life by a combination of what I know about his past and the things others have told me about him.

Yet I do have an idea of him in my head, as surely as I do for the people I have met. It is an idea formed of scraps and shavings of fact, hints of stories, things told to me by those who did meet him. Taken together, these have helped to form an idea for me of what Mullah Mustafa Barzani must have been like.

I am not unique in this. I am very far from unique. Perhaps being Barzani has given me access to more information about Mullah Mustafa than most people have, and perhaps it has meant I grew up in a family that was very aware of him. Even so, I think that the vast majority of my people have some sort of idea of who Mullah Mustafa Barzani was.

Think about that for a moment. Think about how many millions of Kurds there are in the world. Even if we say that only a percentage of them has some image or idea of how they see Mullah Mustafa Barzani, that is still millions of such ideas. Millions of versions of the life of one man, and how he connected to Kurdistan.

You have been reading my version. Just mine. I have tried for factual accuracy, and even for what objectivity is possible, but I make no claim for it to represent the views of millions of my people around the world, or even that it will be a perfect representation of a man I never met. I would like to think that this version captures some of the essence of who Mullah Mustafa

Conclusion

was, and I would like to think that I have been able to shed some light on issues that have been seen as the key ones of his life.

I would also like to think that, in emphasising the ways in which Mullah Mustafa Barzani was seen in his time and is remembered now, I have been able to show the importance of that side of his life. The importance of his role, not just as a leader, but as a symbol, and as someone who had a crucial role in pushing forward Kurdistan's identity.

This point is further illustrated in the very recent and ongoing events in Iraq as I pen the last draft of this manuscript. Kurdistan is acknowledged globally as a relatively peaceful region of Iraq and our current leader, President Masoud Barzani, stood shoulder-to-shoulder with the British Foreign Minister, William Hague, at an emergency meeting in Erbil to address the current threat within and future of Iraq. It is thanks to the legacy of the Barzani family that this is possible and now, the idea of Kurdistan as an independent country, not just an autonomous region, is closer to being realised than ever before.

Bibliography/Further Reading

Arburish, Said K, *Saddam Hussein: The Politics of Revenge* (Bloomsbury, New York, 2000)

Barzani, Massoud, *Mustafa Barzani and the Kurdish Liberation Movement* (Palgrave, New York, 2003)

Bengio, Ofra, 'The Iraqi Kurds: The Struggle for Autonomy in the Shadow of the Iran–Iraqi Conflict', *Immigrants and Minorities*, vol. 9, no. 3 (November 1990) pp249–68

Bird, Christiane, *A Thousand Sighs, A Thousand Revolts* (Random House, New York, 2005)

Bullock, John and Harvey Morris, *No Friends but the Mountains: The Tragic History of the Kurds* (Oxford University Press, 1992)

Bruinessen, Martin van, *Kurdish Ethno-Nationalism Versus Nation-Building States* (Isis Press, Istanbul, 2000)

Chaliand, Gerard (ed), *A People Without a Country: The Kurds and Kurdistan* (Olive Branch Press, New York, 1993)

Dodge, Toby, *Inventing Iraq: The Failure of Nation Building and a History Denied* (Columbia Press, New York, 2003)

Fromkin, David, *A Peace to End All Peace: The Fall of the Ottoman Empire and the Creation of the Modern Middle East* (Henry Holt and Co, New York, 1989)

Hiltermann, Joost R, *A Poisonous Affair* (Cambridge University Press, 2007)

Bibliography/Further Reading

Hiltermann, Joost R, 'Of Blood, Oil and Kurdistan' (International Crisis Group, 2011)

Human Rights Watch, *Genocide in Iraq: The Anfal Campaign Against the Kurds* (Human Rights Watch, New York, 1993, 2006)

Human Rights Watch, *Syria: The Silenced Kurds* (Human Rights Watch, New York, 1996)

Korn, David A., 'The Last Years of Mullah Mustafa Barzani', *Middle East Quarterly*, vol. 1, no. 2 (June 1994)

Kreyenbroek, Philip G, and Stefan Sperl (eds), *The Kurds: A Contemporary Overview* (Routledge, London, 1992)

Laizer, Sheri, *Martyrs, Traitors and Patriots: Kurdistan After the Gulf War* (Zed Books, New Jersey, 1996)

Lawrence, Quil, *Invisible Nation* (Walker and Company, New York, 2008)

Lennox, Gina (ed), *Snow and Honey: Voices from Kurdistan* (Halstead Press, New South Wales, 2001)

Makiya, Kanan, *The Republic of Fear: The Politics of Modern Iraq* (University of California Press, 1998)

McDowall, David, *The Kurds: A Nation Denied* (Minority Rights Publications, London, 1992)

Meiselas, Susan, *Kurdistan: In the Shadow of History* (Random House, New York, 1997)

Middle East Watch, *Human Rights in Iraq* (Yale University Press, 1990)

Winds of Death: Iraq's Use of Poison Gas against its Kurdish Population (Physicians for Human Rights, 1989)

Randal, Jonathan C, *After Such Knowledge, What Forgiveness: My Encounters with Kurdistan* (Farrar, Straus and Giroux, New York, 1997)

Schuurman, Susan J, *An Inconvenient Atrocity* (University of New Mexico, 2007)

Talabany, Nouri, *Arabization of the Kirkuk Region* (Khak Press, London, 1999)

Barzanihistory.com (various)

Glossary

Algiers Accords – The 1975 agreement between Iraq and Iran promising the cessation of hostilities, and particularly the use of peshmerga fighters. The agreement cleared the way for many of the attacks on the Kurds in the late 1970s.

Anfal – Or the 'spoils of war'. The 1987–88 campaign by the Iraqi military aimed at the extermination of the Kurds in numerous, mostly rural, areas of Kurdistan. It featured the extensive use of chemical weapons, notably at Halabja, but also the systematic destruction of villages and the imprisonment or murder of all Kurds found.

Arabisation – The policy of introducing Arabs and Arab culture to Kurdistan to strengthen the Baghdad regime's control over the region. It included Arabic teaching in schools, the giving of land to Arabs who were persuaded to resettle, and an emphasis on Arabic culture as the default throughout Iraq.

Ba'ath – The ruling party of Iraq from 1968 to 2003, and currently the ruling party in Syria. Socialist and Pan Arabic in its doctrines. Officially headed by Saddam Hussein in Iraq from 1979, although he had de facto control from 1976.

Barzani – The tribe within the Kurds to which I belong, and which has traditionally been strongly in favour Kurdish autonomy. Barzani men and boys were targeted in the 1983

Glossary

mass murders, while Barzani leaders such as General Mullah Mustafa Barzani have been key figures in the resistance to rule from Baghdad. Traditionally, Barzani men are identifiable by red and white scarves, worn in pairs by Barzani family members.

Massoud Barzani – General Mullah Mustafa Barzani's son, responsible for maintaining a government in exile during much of the persecution of my people and for leading the defence of the freed Kurds in the 1990s. The president of the Kurdistan Regional Government at the time of writing.

General Mullah Mustafa Barzani – Arguably the most important figure in the struggle for Kurdish independence and highly revered by my people. He led numerous revolts against outside rule, including those of 1945, 1963–66 and 1968. He was involved in the establishment of the Republic of Mahabad in 1945–46, and spent time exiled in the Soviet Union after that country withdrew its support a year later. The peace accords of 1971 that he helped to negotiate ultimately failed, but the principles of separate governance for the region that they contained helped to pave the way for the current region of Kurdistan.

British Occupation – The British first occupied Kurdistan towards the end of the First World War. They maintained a presence there until the end of the mandate given to them in the Treaty of Lausanne, and re-invaded during the Second World War to prevent German control of oil resources.

Civil War – The Kurdish Civil War took place between 1994 and 1998, as outside restrictions forced the political groups of the region to fight over the control of resources. Today, it serves as a warning of what can happen when the political process fails.

Dohuk – One of Kurdistan's main cities, in the north-west of the region, and capital of an administrative area centred on the city. Also spelled Duhok. Its university, originally opened

The Idea of Kurdistan

by volunteers using former regime facilities, is often seen as symbolic of the spirit of rebuilding in Kurdistan.

Erbil – Sometimes known as Arbil or Hawler (in reference to the city's ancient name), this city stands roughly in the centre of Kurdistan and is home to the KRG as well as being at the heart of its own administrative unit. One of the largest cities in Kurdistan, it is also home to Erbil International Airport, Kurdistan's first international airport and one of many key infrastructure projects undertaken in the region.

Halabja – A city close to the Iran–Iraq border. Targeted by the regime with chemical weapons on the 16th March 1988 as part of the Anfal. One of the only attacks on a city during this campaign, with around 3,000–5,000 civilian deaths.

Saddam Hussein Former dictator of Iraq. Had de facto control of the country from 1976, and official control from 1979. The driving force behind the genocide of the Kurds. Despite that, his execution was for a number of earlier murders, and he never faced trial for genocide.

Iraqi Kurdistan – Northern, largely autonomous region of Iraq, taking in cities including Erbil, Sulaymaniyah, Dohuk and Kirkuk. With an independent government, its own flag, anthem and ambassadors, it is a country in all but name. Not to be confused with the wider area of Kurdistan, spread across several countries, where the population is predominantly Kurdish but divided by national borders.

Kirkuk – A city in the south of Kurdistan, noted for its oil reserves. Those reserves have made it the object of numerous disputes, and the target for extensive policies of Arabisation.

Nikita Khrushchev – Communist leader who succeeded Stalin. Generally regarded as more moderate, despite being involved in major incidents of the Cold War, including the Cuban Missile Crisis.

KRG – The Kurdistan Regional Government. The democratically elected government of the region, currently based in Erbil.

Glossary

Mahabad Republic – The short lived Kurdish homeland created in an early form in 1941 in northern Iran, under Qazi Muhammed. Declared independence from Iran in 1945. It failed in 1946 when the Soviet Union withdrew military support, leaving it open to attack from those who did not wish it to exist. Many of those involved in the republic were subsequently executed, but General Mullah Mustafa Barzani and 300 followers were able to escape to the Soviet Union.

Monarchy – Iraq's monarchy consisted of just a single ruler, King Faisal. He was put in place by the British in 1921, and remained in power until his overthrow in 1958.

OPEC – Organisation of Petroleum Exporting Countries. A trans-national organisation composed of those countries engaged in the export of oil. Since Iran and Iraq are both members, several important negotiations have taken place during OPEC summits.

Peshmerga – Kurdish freedom fighters/irregular soldiers, often forced to use guerrilla tactics due to the heavier weaponry, artillery and air superiority of the regime's forces. They were key in helping Kurdistan break free of Saddam's control.

PDK – The Kurdistan Democracy Party. Kurdistan's main political party during the period covered by this book, founded by General Mullah Mustafa Barzani. His son, Massoud Barzani, is the party's current leader, as well as the president of the Kurdistan Regional Government.

PUK – The Patriotic Union Kurdistan. Another of Kurdistan's major political parties.

Joseph Stalin – Communist leader of the USSR from the 1920s until 1953. Notorious for the violence and mass murder of his regime. Met with Mullah Mustafa Barzani.

Sulaymaniyah – One of Kurdistan's main cities, in the East of the region. Controls the administrative district of the same name, and has more than 1.5 million inhabitants. It is often seen as one of the most important cultural centres in

Kurdistan. As with the region's other major cities, it has undergone extensive rebuilding in recent years.

Treaty of Lausanne – A treaty signed in Switzerland in 1923. It effectively overturned the promises of the Treaty of Sèvres, creating modern Iraq and failing to provide land for an independent Kurdish state.

Treaty of Sèvres – A treaty of 1920, between the Ottoman Empire and the Allies of World War One. Its terms included provisions for the later creation of a Kurdish homeland, but those were never put into practice.

Yalta Agreement – Agreement for the dividing up of the world in the wake of World War Two. It set the limits for Soviet expansion, but in so doing, effectively undermined the Mahabad Republic.

Yezidism – A religion rarely found outside Kurdistan, related to Kurdistan's pre-Muslim beliefs.

Key Dates

14th March 1903 – Birth of Mullah Mustafa Barzani.

1907 – Sheikh Abdul Salam Barzani's telegram to the Ottoman Turks begins his rebellion against them. Many Barzanis, including Mullah Mustafa, are imprisoned.

1908 – Successful ambushes of government forces bring the Ottomans to the negotiating table. Concessions include the release of prisoners.

1914 – Outbreak of World War One.

14th December 1914 – Execution of Sheikh Abdul Salam Barzani by the Ottoman Empire.

1915 – Armenian Massacres. Treaty of London establishes principle of redistributing Ottoman territories following the war.

1917 – British occupation of Ottoman territories that are now Iraq.

1919 – Kurdish rebellion under Sheikh Mahmud and Sheikh Ahmad as the British sought to extend their authority into Kurdistan. Capture and imprisonment of Sheikh Mahmud.

1920 – Creation of Iraq by the British with the backing of the League of Nations.

10th August 1920 – Signing of the Treaty of Sèvres, which included the promise of an independent state for the Kurds.

The Idea of Kurdistan

1921 – Imposition of King Faisal on Iraq as a ruler with British 'support'.

24th July 1923 – Signing of the Treaty of Lausanne overturned many of the promises made in the Treaty of Sèvres. Upsurge in violence in Kurdistan.

1925 – RAF bombing of Sulaymaniyah.

1926 – Entry of Iraq into the League of Nations.

1929–30 (approximate) Request by Mullah Mustafa Barzani that the Governor of Mosul replace British forces in Kurdistan with Iraqi ones.

1930–31 Arrahat Rebellion in Turkey. Sheikh Ahmad offers sanctuary to those driven out of Turkey, and general support for the revolt.

1932 – Barzani revolt in response to military action by the Iraqi government.

1933 – Withdrawal into Turkey by Barzanis. Sheikh Ahmad is handed back to the Iraqi authorities by the Turks. He persuades Mullah Mustafa Barzani to go to Mosul, where he is arrested.

1935 – Trials and executions of many of those captured by the Iraqi government.

1936 – Attempt to poison Mullah Mustafa Barzani. He and his family are moved to Baghdad.

1939 – Movement of Mullah Mustafa Barzani and his family to Sulaymaniyah.

1939 – Outbreak of World War Two.

1941 – Direct occupation of Iraq by the British to prevent incursion by German forces. In Iran Qazi Muhammad and his followers gain administrative control of Mahabad Province.

1943 – Mullah Mustafa Barzani escapes Sulaymaniyah and flees to Iran.

1943–45 Mullah Mustafa Barzani returns to Iraqi Kurdistan. Rebellion there, targeting police stations and other public buildings.

Key Dates

1945 – Formation of the Freedom Committee as talks with the British and Iraqi governments failed. Renewal of the revolt, despite demands by the British to allow the Iraqi military in and cease all resistance.

August 1945 – Resolution by the Iraqi government to put down the revolt militarily.

August–September 1945 – Initial successes for Mullah Mustafa Barzani's peshmerga, but loss of support under British pressure.

September 1945 – Decision to withdraw from Iraq by Mullah Mustafa Barzani and 3,000 of his followers.

22nd January 1946 – Official declaration of the Republic of Mahabad.

June 1946 – Soviet withdrawal of support for Republic of Mahabad.

16th August 1946 – First PDK conference.

Late 1946 – Negotiations with Iranian forces as they refused to engage with Barzanis.

30th March 1947 – Execution of Qazi Muhammad and key followers by the Iranian regime.

19th April 1947 – The Barzanis cross from Iran back into Iraq.

1947 – Mullah Mustafa Barzani and those followers most likely to be arrested if they stay flee to the Soviet Union, specifically to Azerbaijan.

1948 – Baku Conference founding nationalist movements for Iraq and Iran.

1949 – Move from Soviet Azerbaijan to Soviet Uzbekistan.

March 1949 – Imprisonment of Mullah Mustafa Barzani. Forced labour for his followers.

1951 – Mullah Mustafa succeeds in bringing the situation to Stalin's attention. He and his followers are freed and a committee is established to investigate.

1953 – Stalin's death. Mullah Mustafa Barzani travels to Moscow to seek a meeting with Khrushchev.

The Idea of Kurdistan

1958 – Overthrow of the monarchy in Iraq. Mullah Mustafa Barzani returns to Kurdistan.

1959 – PDK fighters help to put down Ba'athists in Mosul, creating a possible starting point for longer term conflicts between them.

1960 – Mullah Mustafa Barzani journeys to the Soviet Union to seek support. Abdul Karim Quasim starts to reduce Kurdish involvement in Iraqi public life.

September 1961 – Kurdish uprising against the Iraqi government as the government sought to extend control over Kurdistan.

1963 – First Ba'ath coup in Iraq. Truce between PDK and the new Iraqi government.

July 1964 – Split between Mullah Mustafa Barzani and Jalal Talabani, resulting in the latter's removal from the PDK.

1965 – President Arif takes power in Iraq. Conflict between Baghdad and Kurdistan over the question of autonomy.

1966 – Death of President Arif. Continuation of the conflict after his brother comes to power.

1968 – Second Ba'ath coup in Iraq.

1969 – Death of Sheikh Ahmad Barzani. Escalation of the conflict between Baghdad and Kurdistan through the year. Jalal Talabani accepts a role with the new government.

1970 – Direct peace talks between Mullah Mustafa Barzani and Saddam Hussein lead to the 1970 peace accord. The regime is given until 1974 to implement its terms.

1971 – Attempt to assassinate Mullah Mustafa Barzani using explosives in a meeting with imams.

1972–74 – Preparations for potential conflict, including substantial Arabisation of Kirkuk by the Baghdad government and the nationalisation of Western oil interests in 1972.

1974 – The failure of attempted autonomy legislation sparks conflict between Kurdistan and the central government, with Iranian and US backing for the peshmerga.

1975 – Algiers accords between Iran and Iraq pave the way for

Key Dates

peace between those countries, but effectively strip Kurdistan of all support.

11th March 1975 – The Shah of Iran gives Kurds just thirty days if they wish to cross the border, before it is to be closed.

1975 – Exodus of more than 100,000 Kurds from Iraq, including Mullah Mustafa Barzani, as the revolt collapses. Mullah Mustafa Barzani travels to the USA on medical grounds, but seeks to contact officials there.

October 1975 – Mullah Mustafa Barzani is returned to Iran.

1976 – Mullah Mustafa Barzani is able to return to the USA, but is forbidden contact with journalists.

1977 – Roberta Cohen arranges a press conference for Mullah Mustafa Barzani in the USA.

1st March 1979 – Death of Mullah Mustafa Barzani.

1979 – Fatwa against Iranian Kurds.

1983 – Murder of more than 8,000 Barzani men and boys.

1988–89 – The murder of more than 182,000 people during the Anfal, as well as the displacement of many more.

2nd August 1990–28th February 1991 – First Gulf War.

1991 – Simultaneous uprisings in Kurdistan and Iraq, quickly put down in much of the country. More than 1.5 million Kurds evacuated from Iraq. Imposition of no fly zone by West.

1994 – Beginning of Civil War in Kurdistan.

1998 – End of Civil War in Kurdistan.

2002 – First meetings of the Kurdish Parliament.

2003 – Overthrow of Saddam in Iraq. Massoud Barzani becomes president of Kurdistan Regional Government, while Jalal Talabani becomes Iraqi President.

About the Author

Davan Yahya Khalil is a student of law, author, political activist and supporter of the PDK (Partîya Demokrata Kurdistan – Kurdistan Democratic Party).

This is Davan's second book on the history of Kurdistan. While the autonomous region of Iraqi Kurdistan has come to the world's attention this summer of 2014, there is still little known about it, something the author intends to change. He hopes to eventually see the region recognised as an independent state and explores the potential future by examining the past.